Madcaps, Screwballs, and Con Women

Feminist Cultural Studies, the Media, and Political Culture

Series Editors
Mary Ellen Brown
Andrea Press

A complete list of books in the series is available from the publisher.

Madcaps, Screwballs, and Con Women

The Female Trickster in American Culture

Lori Landay

PENN

University of Pennsylvania Press

Philadelphia

10 9 8 7 6 5 4 3 2 1

Published by
University of Pennsylvania Press
Philadelphia, Pennsylvania 19104

Library of Congress Cataloging-in-Publication Data
Landay, Lori.
    Madcaps, screwballs, and con women : the female trickster in American culture /
Lori Landay.
        p.   cm. — (Feminist cultural studies, the media, and political culture)
    Includes bibliographical references (p.   ) and index.
    ISBN 0-8122-3435-9 (acid-free paper). — ISBN 0-8122-1651-2 (pbk. acid-free paper)
    1. Women in popular culture—United States.   2. Women in mass media—United
States.   3. Women in literature.   4. Women—United States—Comic books, strips, etc.
5. Man-woman relationships—United States.   6. Feminist theory—United States.
I. Title.   II. Series.
HQ1426.L34   1998
305.42'0973—DC21   97-32805
                                                                                    CIP

This book is dedicated to my grandfather, Samuel Harrison, not only for his support and determined encouragement but also for his one-liners. When we slipped away from the tour of Nathaniel Hawthorne's House of Seven Gables in Salem and into one of the back rooms, the tour guide was not impressed with my assurance, "Don't worry, I'm a scholar." As we were being shown to the door, Papa said to me loudly, "Tell 'em, Lala: we've been kicked out of better joints than this."

Contents

Preface: "Whenever I Take a Notion"

In January 1930, Trixie Perry, a twenty-eight-year-old textile worker, was on trial in Elizabethton, Tennessee, for breaking the injunction against striking. The main charges against Trixie Perry and her friend known as "Texas Bill" concerned their behavior toward the National Guard on the picket line. In response to accusations that they dared the guardsmen to cross a line in the road drawn by the women, taunted the soldiers, and blocked the road to the factory, Trixie Perry mocked the government's case. When asked whether she blocked the road, Perry answered, "A little thing like me block a big road?" She further delighted the sympathetic courtroom audience by recounting her retort to the threat of a tear gas bomb: "That little old fire cracker of a thing, it won't go off."

When Trixie Perry appeared at the East Tennessee District Supreme Court to face the charges against her, she did so in a dress made from red, white, and blue bunting and a cap made from an American flag. Perry's costume prompted the following exchange, culled from the court records by historian Jacqueline Dowd Hall:

"You have a United States flag as a cap on your head?"
"Yes."
"Wear it all the time?"
"Whenever I take a notion." (quoted in Hall 373)

Trixie Perry's tricky use of costume further reinforced her participation in what Hall calls the "venerable tradition of 'disorderly women,' women who in times of political upheaval, embody tensions that are half-conscious or only dimly understood" (Hall 356). By transforming the American flag into an outfit, Perry both used and subverted traditional symbols of patriotism and femininity for her own ends. Her testimony also plays on traditional—and obviously outmoded—definitions of femininity, and ridicules the masculinity of the National Guard as ineffectual against even a group of "little" women. Especially interesting for this discussion of the female trickster, Perry's mock-explanation, "Whenever I take a notion," reverberates with cultural images of headstrong madcaps from Capitola on.

Perry's friend and co-ringleader, a woman known as "Texas Bill" because of her preference for "cowboy" clothes, also used costume to create the image of public femininity with which she took the stand. In contrast to Perry's red, white, and blue, Texas Bill chose a black coat and picture hat, and answered the prosecutor's questions with what a reporter called "an assumed ladylike dignity" (J. D. Hall 373). One of the charges against Texas Bill was that she took a National Guardsman's gun away from him, which is not surprising when we picture her in her usual "cowboy" clothes, but certainly an act in contradiction to her court costume.

Hall concludes:

What is impressive here is how Trixie Perry and Texas Bill handled the dichotomy between ladyhood and lewdness, good girls and bad. Using words that, for women in particular, were ordinarily taboo, they refused deference and signaled disrespect. Making no secret of their sexual experience, they combined flirtation with fierceness on the picket line and adopted a provocative courtroom style. And yet, with the language of dress—a cap made of an American flag, an elegant wide-brimmed hat—they claimed their rights as a citizens and their place in the female community. (J. D. Hall 375)

The story of Trixie Perry and Texas Bill's deployment of the "language of dress" in their performances in court is a story of female trickery in everyday life. Buried in Appalachian court records and brought to our attention by a historian, this story survives, unlike the doubtless myriad of others that were never recorded or researched. Moments like the ones Hall recovered show us the energy and determination expressed by being disorderly, despite the mainstream cultural discourses that condemn such behavior. Trixie played the madcap in her homemade outfit and Texas Bill the con woman in her cross-class impersonation, and both parodied the middle-class conventions of gender they transgressed on the picket line, in the courtroom, and in their everyday lives.

Texas Bill—the name itself is richly suggestive of this woman's unconventionality and independent spirit. Along with being a masculine name, it is also reminiscent of Texas Guinan, the Jazz Age speakeasy owner and burlesque performer famous for her shocking performances that ended with the tag line, "So long, suckers!" Moreover, the description of Texas Bill's appearance and demeanor in the courtroom reminds me of Mae West's highly publicized, flamboyant, and crowd-pleasing courtroom appearances on indecency charges in 1927 and 1930. Perhaps Texas Bill, with her big picture hat, fancy dress, and self-conscious performance, anticipated West's dramatization of those courtroom experiences in her film *I'm No Angel* (1933). Surely Texas Bill would have enjoyed West's punch line in the courtroom scene of *My Little Chickadee* (1940):

JUDGE: Are you showing contempt for this court?
FLOWER BELLE LEE: No, I'm doing my best to hide it.

To be sure, the connections between Texas Bill and Mae West are tenuous and intuitive rather than traceable and logical; much of this book stems from such an unmethodological methodology. Exploring the transformations of one facet of culture through history and across media necessitates a *bricolage* of print and audiovisual images. And the trickster, slippery figure that she is, mocks conventional scholarly discourse.

My speculation that Texas Bill drew on West's infamous courtroom behavior cannot be proven, but it does suggest a connection between how popular figures inflect people's everyday lives—and how ideas, mannerisms, and styles spread throughout a culture. Heroines in books, films, and television shows, images in advertisements, stars in the popular media, and stories in popular journalism: these provide examples of behavior, whether they are framed as ideal or reprehensible, successful or self-defeating. The madcaps, screwballs, and con women who emerge in the culture industry's mass-reproduced, mass-marketed, mass-consumed texts stem from figures from folklore, who were constantly made new and relevant through storytelling. In mass consumer culture, fictional characters and celebrity personas are created by individuals and groups who reflect, critique, endorse, recast, and reject their personal experiences of the society they live in. The resulting constructs are fantasy figures who do what we cannot or dare not, and they call our attention to where we draw the lines that separate what is appropriate and shocking, possible and impossible. And imagining the impossible, finding an escape from what seems inescapable, creating room where others find only restriction: this is what the female tricksters discussed here do, a powerful act of imagination that can produce real-life possibilities.

Introduction

Imagine that you are Scheherazade. For three years, King Shahryar has married a woman every evening and had her executed the next morning; this was his response to his first wife's infidelity. You have been protected from King Shahryar's lethal marriage because your father holds an important position in the court, but you know your turn is coming. And even more worrisome than your own fate is that of your beloved younger sister, who will be next in the trip from altar to marriage bed to grave. How will you survive and protect your sister? What options can you see or create? What resources are at your disposal?

When you put yourself in the mythic Scheherazade's situation, you enter the terrain of the female trickster. Despite the failures of three years' worth of women, Scheherazade survived because, as the narrator of the Tales of the Arabian Nights, she drew on her imagination and created a position for herself as a clever storyteller. The story goes that on her wedding night she begged the king to send for her sister, who asked her to tell a story. She began, and told tales the whole night through. But as she saw that the dawn was approaching, she cleverly grew silent. Shahryar, unwilling to have the story left unfinished, did not send for the executioner. And each night, for a thousand and one nights, she entertained and enlightened the king with her tales. And each morning, as she saw that the dawn was approaching, she stopped telling the tale. By suspending the narrative before the end, she saved her life again and again.

By serializing her tales, Scheherazade manipulates folk culture into a tricky scheme that subverts the king's power over her and transforms him into a dependent listener who is kept hanging, just as Scheherazade's life is extended, hanging fire day after day. By tricking Shahryar to capture his interest, Scheherazade is a tightrope walker, poised ironically in the liminal space "betwixt and between" night and day, life and death, victim and survivor, concubine and wife.[1] She transforms her position as rape and murder victim into that of an enchantress who keeps

Shahryar interested, indeed fascinated, by her stories (and her sexual and procreative skills, bearing him three children over the course of the thousand and one nights). All the while she instructs him on a way of behaving that is more appropriate than the nightly violation and daily murder of women.

Scheherazade is the prototype of the specific female trickster figure that is the focus of my project. The term "trickster" originates in Daniel Brinton's 1868 study of the contradictory figure of Native American tales and myth who is both fooler and fooled, heroic and base. By the end of the nineteenth century, the term was widely used in anthropology and folklore scholarship (Pelton 7).[2] In general, trickster figures are representations of liminality, duality, subversion, and irony. Tricksters illustrate theorist Michel de Certeau's maxim, "People make do with what they have" (18); they use impersonation, disguise, theft, and deceit to expose hypocrisy and inequality, to subvert existing social systems, and to widen their sphere of power.

Although anthropologists and folklorists acknowledge that tricksters often switch gender from masculine to femine and back again, they implicitly include the criterion of masculinity and the privilege of autonomy and mobility with which masculinity is synonymous.[3] That emphasis is pervasive, from Paul Radin's classic account of the Winnebago Native American trickster cycle, to Jung's archetypal theory, to anthropologist Robert Pelton's study of African tricksters, to Karen Ruth King Keim's exploration of trickster figures in precolonial and postcolonial Cameroon, and to the analyses of American humor by critics such as Constance Rourke and Walter Blair. An example is the assumption of masculinity in anthropologist Mary Douglas's discussion of Radin's work on the trickster cycle: "The trickster starts as an unselfconscious, amorphous being. As the study unfolds he gradually discovers his own identity, gradually recognizes and controls his own anatomical parts; he oscillates between female and male, but eventually fixes on his own male sexual role, and finally learns to assess his environment for what it is" (79).

In a sexist society, the male trickster clearly has the advantages of masculinity: mobility, autonomy, power, safety. He is able to be a liminal figure who can move between the margins and centers of society as he deconstructs the power systems with his humor and trickery. In fact, his experiences in female form are often a period of stability which he leaves behind to continue on his adventures. He performs his tactical ridicule in the public sphere, mocking and subverting the existing political, social, and economic structures. Obviously, women have not had the same opportunities for such a high degree of mobility (physical as well as psychological, social, economic, artistic, and political). Thus when scholars have looked for trickster figures using definitions based on the assumption of the trickster's masculinity, they haven't found female figures who fit. In order to identify female tricksters in American (or any) culture, therefore, we must turn from the margins of dominant society to the centers of women's space—the parlors, kitchens, and bedrooms of domesticity.

So we find Scheherazade telling her fabulous myriad of tales while physically captive in Shahryar's bedroom but linguistically and narratively capitalizing on the exploits of the heroes of her tales. From her position in the private sphere of domesticity (the sphere to which women are relegated), Scheherazade enacts a covert strategy of *influence* over the king and husband who decides whether she lives or dies. Scheherazade does not attempt to escape by fleeing or plot to murder Shahryar in his sleep; instead, she transforms the place of her victimization into a base from which to seduce, charm, interest, and most importantly, *change* him. At the end of the thousand and one nights, not only has Scheherazade saved herself, her sister, and countless other women, but she has created an ideal man to be her husband and partner. By the end of the thousand and one nights, Shahryar has internalized Scheherazade's lessons, and Scheherazade has liberated herself from the position of captive and slave.

The covert strategy Scheherazade exemplifies is based in the private sphere and does not challenge the division between what is culturally defined as public (male) and private (female).[4] Scheherazade does not challenge Shahryar's power as king, but modifies him into a "kinder, gentler" ruler who does not have to murder all the women in the land to avenge his wife's infidelity. Despite her obvious cleverness and creativity, Scheherazade does not expect to govern, but only to be granted her life and chosen as a wife.

In sharp contrast to the covert exercise of female power exemplified by Scheherazade is the character of Catwoman in the movie *Batman Returns* (1992), who embodies the overt strategy of *action*. Catwoman rejects the covert model in favor of physical mobility and prowess, self-transformation rather than transformation of the master, tactics of revenge and justice instead of seduction and the sentimental notion of "love," and an insistence on self-reliance rather than dependence. Further, Catwoman also draws on supernatural and superhuman forces, especially her use of the cat as a totem animal, which aligns her with animal tricksters such as the Native American Coyote and the African-American Signifying Monkey.

Moving from Scheherazade to Catwoman telescopes thousands of years of human history, disparate cultures, and radically different media. This jump suggests the scope of the female trickster—from antiquity to the present—and points to both the universality of the trickster figure in human cultures and the specificity of how that figure is represented at different historical moments. Scheherazade and Catwoman are our metaphoric bookends, bracing between them the full range of influence and action strategies.

To summarize the Catwoman subplot briefly: Lonely secretary Selina Kyle is murdered by her villainous boss, Max Shreck, general ill-doer and owner of the Macy's-like Shreck's department store. But Selina is revived and resurrected by a swarm of cats. She staggers home and, in a fit of rage, trashes her apartment; amid the rubble of chopped-up stuffed animals and other feminine accoutrements, Selina outfits herself as Catwoman with a bricolage of household items. She transforms herself from a mousy secretary who could not stand up to her condescending boss (Fig. I.1a) to a creature who does handsprings down the crime-ridden streets of Gotham City at night, beating up would-be rapists, causing explosions in Shreck's store, and holding her own in fights with Batman, whom she deems her nemesis (Fig. I.1b).

The Catwoman narrative is a feminist-influenced tale of transformation from passivity to action. It uses the cultural equation of feline and feminine to revise one of the central myths of the female American dream: the working girl marries the boss and never has to "work" again (which is what happens at the end of the 1927 silent film *It*, discussed in Chapter 2). Instead, Catwoman kills the boss who tried to kill her. Instead of Selina the helpless victim saved by Batman, she is the Catwoman, hurling antipatriarchal wisecracks and actively engaging in the world around her. When Shreck kills Selina, he kills off the wage-earning, sexually inactive single woman whose only company is her cat; what emerges from the physical and psychic trauma is an antiauthoritarian, sexually alluring, and empowered superheroine. Her rejection of Batman at the end of the film is a further surprise that subverts the conventional equation of heterosexual romantic union with narrative closure; Catwoman remains independent and autonomous. In opposition to the influence strategy of female tricksterism represented by Scheherazade, Catwoman has direct agency, freedom of movement, and the kind of physical strength and fighting technique that would be enough to make any woman skip down the city streets. Her transformation is from fearful victim to anarchic female trickster; in one fell swoop, male violence (economic and psychological as well as physical) against women results in a vengeful, competent fantasy figure of women's rejection of victimhood, sentimentalism, passionlessness, physical weakness, domesticity, and secretarial drudgery.

Both Scheherazade and Catwoman demonstrate the ability to survive in situations that are specifically hostile to them as women; the impor-

a

b

Figure I.1. Michelle Pfeiffer dramatizes the transformation of her character from *a*. Mousy Selina to *b*. Catwoman. Frame enlargements from *Batman Returns* (1992).

tant difference is how—by influence from within the system or action from outside it. Both create roles for themselves, one in the warped representation of the domestic realm of Shahryar's bedroom, and the other in the hostile and villainous city, formerly the province of men.

Scheherazade and Catwoman illustrate the difference between what animal behaviorists have termed "agonic" and "hedonic" modes of power. Agonic power is based on actual or threatened force. For humans, weapons, education, expertise, strength, and money are the sources of agonic power. Hedonic power is achieved through adornment, display, and indirect methods of control like charisma, withholding of affection or sex, and dependency. Psychologist Rita Freedman explains how the assignment of the agonic mode to men and hedonic to women reinforces the importance of women's appearance: "As women learn to channel energy into being seen rather than into being strong, attracting becomes a substitute for acting" (72).

This dualistic structure of modes of power is replicated in mass consumer society as, concurrently, women enter the public sphere and the public sphere is redefined as increasingly economic rather than political.[5] Hedonic power became conflated with commodification as the use of cosmetics was deemed acceptable and then necessary to fulfill dictates of female beauty. The change from nineteenth-century representations of makeup as "paint" used only by immoral and insincere women (prostitutes, actresses, con women) to twentieth-century advertisements of commodities, which, if used skillfully, would be indispensable to attracting men, exemplifies the shift in cultural values from Victorian-sentimental to consumer-hedonist.[6] Moreover, the increased focus on women's appearance, the most readily commodified aspect of the social roles modern American culture encouraged women to play, subsumed other measures of women's value (measured externally and internalized) such as intelligence, creativity, social and political participation, and productivity. Women's ability to embody ideals of female beauty, like men's economic success, was the most important aspect of dominant definitions of gender roles.

Cultural standards of feminine appearance, bodily comportment, and behavior inscribe a set of social practices that comprise socially sanctioned femininity. The ideological implication is that if women create themselves to better fit the always changing ideals of "good" femininity —being a lady, a moral mother, a "little woman," Mrs. Consumer, a war worker, a companionate wife, a happy housewife, a superwoman who "has it all"—they will not only be rewarded, but be safe from danger and punishments. The mythos of the "love economy" (Johnston ix) promises that by playing the appropriate role—knowing her "place" and channeling her "power" into maintaining that place—a woman can achieve the good life of the American dream.

Mainstream American culture has portrayed women's access to the good life as dependent on their ability to attract, lure, marry, and keep a husband who will provide them with the economic means with which to participate in mass consumer society and satisfy their desires. A 1953 swimsuit advertisement (Fig. I.2) articulates the importance of women's appearance with its description of "the practical advantage of 'curval-lure'" that "affects the rest of the world"; the picture of a woman, stand-ing still and offering herself as an object of men's gaze (eyes closed, she does not return the look), illustrates the headline "woman at work."

The idea that being seen and judged to be pleasing is women's "work" has implications not only for appearance and costume but also for women's behavior and bodily comportment. In her essay "Throwing Like a Girl: A Phenomenology of Feminine Body Comportment, Mo-tility, and Spatiality," social philosopher Iris Young explains the link between being feminine and experiences of physical restriction in con-temporary society: "The more a girl assumes her status as feminine, the more she takes herself to be fragile and immobile and the more she actively enacts her own body inhibition" (154). The cultural objectifica-tion of women is one source of feminine bodily practices internalized by women; thus an image like the unseeing and inactive "woman at work" in the swimsuit ad does not appear contradictory but merely an explicit articulation of a cultural assumption.

Young's assertions about the sources and implications of feminine bodily modalities suggest a meaning of "woman's place" that goes be-yond "woman's sphere" of the home. Ultimately, a woman's place is in a feminine body: immobile, fragile, objectified, commodified, and—in-adequate on its own—enhanced by makeup and beauty products. The feminine body is truly a "docile body," to use Foucault's term, judged by "a panoptical male connoisseur [who] resides within the consciousness of most women" (Bartky 72). Advertisements demonstrate and reinforce the idea that women must imagine how they appear to men in order to construct themselves for the desired effect of pleasing men.

Another strain of representation in popular American culture is the New Woman, who is physically strong, active, self-assured, self-reliant. She relies not only on the influence of a feminine body, but on its active power as well. A 1932 Jantzen swimsuit advertisement depicts an image very different from the 1953 ad. The drawing shows a woman looking straight ahead, arms folded definitively, her feet planted firmly on the ground (Fig. I.3). The drawing of the woman is foregrounded so that the frame of the ad does not contain her completely. The copy in this ad,

Figure I.2. An image of a working woman? This advertisement plays on contradictions in postwar definitions of women's place and female power. *Look*, June 1953. Advertising reproduction courtesy of Jantzen, Inc.

Figure I.3. Boldness in the foreground, coyness in the back. The triangular lines in this advertisement imply relationships between the confident New Woman, the smaller, more traditionally feminine figure in the background, and the consumer/viewer. *Cosmopolitan*, June 1932. Advertising reproduction courtesy of Jantzen, Inc.

"Fashion swims in perfect-fitting Jantzen," stresses the style and "complete swimming freedom" of the suit, as opposed to the 1953 ad's reference to the hedonic power of "curvallure."

There is another drawing of a woman, smaller, and in the background, that raises an issue that will emerge as central to this discussion of the female trickster in American culture: the double. The second drawing depicts the same "model" in another bathing suit, this time from a rear view. In contrast to the larger image, the smaller woman looks coyly over her shoulder in a pose that anticipates the pinup pose of the early 1940s. Of course, the advertiser is showing two different suits, one from the front and the other from the back view. But these two images are also an example of doubling, a mimetic representational strategy that defines two figures in terms of the other. Doubles in cultural texts often show two sides of the same coin—the dualities that the imagination conceives of as opposite and irreconcilable. Because the public discourses about femininity are riddled with contradictions, most revolving around polarized notions of "good" and "bad" women, the creation of the double is one way to achieve complexity in representations. Further, in art and advertising there is also the tradition of depicting women looking into mirrors as a way of dramatizing—and in advertising, reinforcing—the split in feminine consciousness that John Berger describes in *Ways of Seeing* as the "surveyor"and "surveyed":

To be born a woman has been to be born, within an allotted and confined space, into the keeping of men. The social presence of women [closely linked with appearance and behavior] has developed as a result of their ingenuity in living under such tutelage within such a limited space. But this has been at the cost of a woman's self being split into two. A woman must continually watch herself. She is almost always continually accompanied by her own image of herself. (46)

Berger's ideas about the "cost" of the "ingenuity" of the public self are central to my ideas that the female trickster embodies the fantasy of escaping that cost and, often, making the system pay.

When advertisements play on women's desires to create the best, most useful social presence—and in fact try to cast those desires in terms of needs and duties—they often do so with doubling, as in the 1932 Jantzen ad. Where the larger figure looks straight ahead at the viewer, the smaller figure is like a coyer, more submissive "shadow" of the bold, active woman. Both figures watch themselves being surveyed, and the more deferential body position of the smaller offers a muted alternative that is not as defiant as the main figure. Visually, the ad creates triangular shapes in the posture of the main figure, with the towel in the "shadow" figure, and with the horizontally placed trademark of the

Red Diving Girl, who embodies the combination of style and function achieved by Jantzen swimwear.

We can see that this ad, like the 1953 ad and the many others that are reproduced and analyzed in this book, exemplifies how popular culture hinges on women looking at images of women (and images of women looking at each other)—on the "gaze," as it has been called in feminist film criticism.[7] Whether the gaze is that of an onlooking woman or man, or an imagined perception of what someone else would see, the female figures in the ads and the female consumers at whom they are aimed are encouraged to be self-conscious of themselves as objects and to recast their own individualistic, subjective perspectives in terms of how others will judge them according to external norms and ideals.

The trickster, a mythical figure associated with duality,[8] is often a symbol of doubleness. For the female trickster, that doubleness is inflected with the split in feminine consciousness described by Berger and others. When female tricksters save their sentimental counterparts, as in nineteenth-century fiction, the more dominant trickster is shown to need the shadow in order to survive. Similarly, when modern female tricksters impersonate other "types" of women in order to take advantage of people's belief in social hierarchy, as they do in twentieth-century representations up to World War II, they create their own doubles—either the "cover" of the sentimental heroine or the disruption of the showgirl/criminal. In the late thirties and into the mid-forties, the female trickster splits herself into "good" and "shadow" doubles whom others perceive to be separate women, and thus becomes her own rival. After the war, postmodern female tricksters present a myriad of public personas, fluidly shifting between different impersonations as the situation dictates or destroying the old self to become a super-self.

The trickery practiced by characters in print and visual media manifests in the distorted mirror of advertisements for the beauty industry. The hedonic power promised in the ads takes the form of the social practice of female trickery in everyday life. Women, encouraged to manipulate their appearance and sublimate assertive impulses behind a mask of feminine behavior, are necessarily involved in everyday duplicitous practices. The emotional, sexual, and social machinations of the dating and marriage market, the self-objectification that presents an appealing facade: these are achieved by employing the trickster tactics of deception, impersonation, disguise, duplicity, and subversion. Because the social practice of femininity is a form of trickery, tricksters in cultural texts resonate with and expose a fundamental tenet of the social relations of the sexes in American culture: The only way for women to survive, given their subordinate position and limited opportunities for exercising overt power, is to use the covert power of female trickery.

On the other hand, female tricksters transgress cultural definitions as "bad girls" who behave in ways that are antithetical to good womanhood. Often, female tricksters behave as shadow figures who break the rules and call attention to possibilities outside gender roles and ideals, but just as often they are simply transgressive in the gluttonous, scatological, overly individualistic manner of tricksters in general. Such transgression, however, has specific meanings in the contexts of cultural definitions of femininity.

Before we continue with the development of the female trickster in American culture, a survey of the scholarship on the trickster in American culture is in order. Although, as anthropologist Michael Jackson argues in his study of Kuranko narratives, "we should never assume that [the trickster] will have identical attributes in every society" (*Allegories* 94), it is important to place American female tricksters in the wider context of the kinds of cultural work that other trickster figures have performed, and we must recognize that the trickster is a scholarly conceit. The trickster has figured prominently in three areas of American cultural study: as a mythic figure in Native American oral and written narrative traditions; as an articulation of racial "double consciousness" and survival skills in African-American folklore and literature; and as the nineteenth-century confidence man, who represents the shifting border between wilderness and civilization, gentlemanly and vernacular language, and class-based and fluid ideologies.

Native American Tricksters

The study of the trickster in an American context begins with anthropological and folkloric studies of Native American trickster figures such as Trickster in the tale cycles of the Winnebago Indians, Raven in the myth systems of the Northwest and Arctic regional cultures, Hare in the East, Wolverine or Canada Jay in the North Woods, Spider or Old Man on the Plains, and Coyote in the Far West (Wiget 16–21). American Indian trickster tales can be categorized in three types: those that focus on bodily functions (food, sex, excrement) and "undermine [hu]man's belief in his own ability to govern himself" (Wiget 16); those that use the burlesque to satirize religious and/or social conventions; and those that embody "an undisguised attack on the dangers of institutional power in a social setting" (17). In these tales, Trickster is a "culture hero": a "Trickster-Transformer" who appears as a Heroic Transformer and attains power through heroic action; a Cunning Transformer who gains power by outsmarting opponents in games or by shape-shifting (human/animal, dis-

guise, sex change, inanimate object); and an Overreacher who is humili-
ated or hurt by trying to achieve more than possible.[9]

Interpretations of Native American tricksters can be categorized as
Jungian, Promethean, and liminal. Jungian interpretations advanced by
Paul Radin, Jung, and Franz Boas define Trickster as, in Radin's words, at
"the same time creator and destroyer, giver and negator, he who dupes
others and is always duped himself. . . . He knows neither good nor evil
yet he is responsible for both. He possesses no values, moral or social,
is at the mercy of his passions and appetites, yet through his actions all
values come into being. . . . He is primarily an inchoate being" who is
protohuman (165). The Promethean function of the trickster is exemplified by M. L. Ricketts's interpretation of "the Trickster-transformer-
culture hero" who parodies what ritual reveres and whose crucial function is a parody of shamanism and uncritical acceptance of religious
ritual and institutions. The third perspective sees the trickster as "paradox personified," a liminal figure whose "creative cleverness amazes us
and keeps alive the possibility of transcending the social restrictions we
regularly encounter" (Babcock-Abrahams 147–48), a liberatory figure
whose dualism is a major trait.[10]

Drawing on and revising previous work on the trickster by Jung,
Radin, Brinton, Ricketts, and Turner, Barbara Babcock-Abrahams summarizes the centrality of binary oppositions in the trickster:

The most important characteristics of these related dualisms [order/disorder,
life/death, creative/destructive], however, is their expression of ambiguity and
paradox, of a confusion of all customary categories. The clown or trickster epito-
mizes the paradox of the human condition and exploits the incongruity that we
are creatures of the earth and yet not wholly creatures of the earth in that we
have need of clothing and spiritual ideals to clothe our nakedness, of money,
and of language — of human institutions. Further, he embodies the fundamental
contradiction between the individual and society, between freedom and constraint. (160–61)

Recent scholarship on tricksters in Native American cultures has, to
some extent, encompassed the idea of female tricksters.[11] In their entry
"The Native American Trickster" in the *Dictionary of Native American
Literature*, Barbara Babcock and Jay Cox summarize: "That trickster is
generically male and characterized by exaggerated phallicism may be
the result of male bias in the collection and interpretation of trickster
tales compounded by the Anglo bias of identifying Indian women with
stability" (100). This would explain why until recently, little attention
has been given to the Keresan Coyote Girl and Kochininako (Yellow
Woman) stories Franz Boas included in *Keresan Texts* (1928), or why it
is only recently that Hopi stories about female Coyotes such as "Coyote
and the Witches" and "Coyote and the Bird Girls" were translated.[12]

Although they may have been marginalized in Anglo accounts of trickster tales, female tricksters have emerged in contemporary literature by Native American writers including Leslie Marmon Silko, Gerald Vizenor, Louise Erdrich, Joy Harjo, Nia Francisco, and Nora Naranjo-Morse. Novelist and critic/theorist Gerald Vizenor's representations of trickster include both male and female characters. In an interview, he describes how he plays on his reader's assumptions about gender in the beginning of his novel *The Trickster of Liberty*:

What I've created in fiction is a whole family of trickster storytellers. And each of the characters gets a couple of stories each. [Chuckles.] But it opens with a character named "Alex" talking to an anthropologist. And the anthropologist is asking critical questions as a social scientist, about things. Alex, the Native American character, is confronting, contradicting, tricking. Well, it turns out that the reader is also tricked. Because most readers would assume that the name Alex is masculine. But a few pages in, I think when the reader has already accepted this character as being male and talking to a male anthropologist, right, it turns out that Alex is female, Alexine? And this is a nickname. (Miller 93)

As his comments illustrate, Vizenor crosses the boundaries between fiction and literary theory in his novel as a mode of "postmodern" trickery and self-reflexivity. In his critical essay "Trickster Discourse," he explains:

Freedom is a sign, and the trickster is chance and freedom in a comic sign; comic freedom is a "doing," not an essence, not a museum being, or an aesthetic presence. The trickster, as a semiotic sign, is imagined in narrative voices, a communal rein to the unconscious, which is comic liberation; however, the trickster is outside comic structure. . . . The trickster is agonistic imagination and aggressive liberation, a "doing" in narrative points of view, and outside the imposed structures. (285)

Female characters who express the "doing" in narratives have come to light in critical considerations of writing by Native American women. In her essay " 'This Woman Can Cross Any Line': Feminist Tricksters in the Works of Nora Naranjo-Morse and Joy Harjo," Kristine Holmes argues that Pearlene in Pueblo artist Naranjo-Morse's poetry and clay figures and Noni Daylight in Harjo's poetry are " 'hell-raising' alter egos who symbolize, like Coyote, survival and continuance, [and] the poets portray them in a female-inflected way, setting forth a feminist revision of tricksterism" (46).

The rich and complex interconnections among the trickster, storytelling, and gender in Native American culture are at the center of Leslie Marmon Silko's remarkable book *Storyteller* (1978). The story "Yellow Woman" is one of several retellings of the Keresan tales of Kochininako,

or Yellow Woman, a mythic figure who wanders away from her pueblo
and goes off with a ka'tsina mountain spirit. In an interview, Silko explains:

She's a . . . what do you call it in anthropology or sociology, one who shatters the
cultural paradigms or steps through or steps out. She does that because there's
a real overpowering sexual attraction that's felt. The attraction is symbolized by
or typified by the kind of sexual power that draws her to the buffalo man, but
the link, the animal and the human world, those two being drawn together. It's
that power that's really operating, and the sexual nature of it is just a metaphor
for that power. (Barnes 57)

What Silko describes but does not name is, I believe, a female trickster—when the overstepping is represented in a comic way that ends,
the way the Yellow Woman stories do, with the character as a part of the
community.

The narrator of "Yellow Woman" is a contemporary Laguna Pueblo
woman with a husband and a family who meets up with Silva, a stranger,
in the liminal landscape of the riverbank. As I interpret the story, the
narrator first casts herself as Yellow Woman and Silva as the ka'tsina
spirit so she can allow herself to be carried away emotionally and participate in the sexual adventurousness and mobility articulated by the
mythic Yellow Woman. Her impersonation of Yellow Woman is a temporary tactic. The next day, she becomes confused—surely, she is not
really Yellow Woman, as Silva calls her, but herself. And yet maybe she
is Yellow Woman—or rather, Yellow Woman is her: "I was wondering if
Yellow Woman had known who she was—if she knew that she would become part of the stories. Maybe she'd had another name that her husband and relatives called her so that only the ka'tsina from the north
and the storytellers would know her as Yellow Woman" (33). In creating
these intersections between everyday life and myth, between a self that
is ordinary and one that is timeless and outside the boundaries of convention, Silko weaves a metaphor of the trickster figure as part of everyday life. The power of Silko's story is that it calls attention to the power
of stories—as part of the present, not just the past, as self-definition,
as deliberate constructions to keep us in or out of trouble. For a time,
the narrator is Yellow Woman, and the narrator's suggestion that Yellow Woman is made up of ordinary women who temporarily become or
merge with the spirit/identity/plot of Yellow Woman shows the living
connections between the traditional tales and contemporary life and
suggests that the female trickster's identity is a temporary one.

That Yellow Woman returns to her community, in both the traditional
stories (ten months later, with twin sons) and in Silko's story (two days
later, to her family) yields an important insight into the Native Ameri-

can trickster. The trickster is part of the community who may venture outside, but who always starts and ends within. As scholar Franchot Ballinger explains, the trickster's behavior is asocial, and the consequences of the trickery often have negative consequences for the community, but "rather than seeing him [or her] as a marauding outsider or as a fringe on the social fabric as our critical metaphors would have it, it may be possible that Native American storytellers and audiences traditionally perceive Trickster as an *insider* gone awry. An apt image for his relationship to society may be to say that he lives sideways; he moves at a diagonal to the rest of society's parallels" (21). This image may help us understand how being Yellow Woman for a while enables the narrator to live "sideways" individualistically, to move diagonally toward possibility, and to participate in the liminal landscape of myth.

African-American Tricksters

In the field of African-American studies, the trickster emerges as one of the most resonant tropes for the African-American experience of resistance to enslavement. The scholarship of literary critic Henry Louis Gates Jr. and folklorists Lawrence Levine and John W. Roberts is grounded in the connections between African trickster figures and the African-American trickster figures who recur in folk culture from the slavery and postemancipation eras. Their explorations of African-American tricksters provide models for understanding how tricksters emerge from specific social and cultural contexts, how those figures change as the contexts change, and how the trickster articulates resistance to oppression.

In *The Signifying Monkey: A Theory of Afro-American Literary Criticism,* Gates connects the vernacular African-American Signifying Monkey to the Pan-African trickster Esu-Elegbara; in his eloquent words, "If the Dixie Highway leads straight to New Guinea, then Esu-Elegbara presides over its liminal crossroads, a sensory threshold barely perceptible without access to the vernacular" (6). By suggesting the connection between Esu and the Signifying Monkey, Gates presents a model of a premodern figure that emerges as a "hero of black myth, a sign of the triumph of wit and reason, his language of Signifyin(g) standing as the linguistic sign of the ultimate triumph of self-consciously formal language use" (77). In Gates's project "to define an indigenous black metaphor for intertextuality as configured in African-American formal literary discourse" (59), he ultimately uses the trickster figure of the Signifying Monkey as emblematic of the intertextuality and doubleness of an African-American literary tradition.

Levine's work *Black Culture and Black Consciousness: Afro-American Folk Thought from Slavery to Freedom* is a social and cultural history that divides trickster tales into two groups: those with animal trickster figures and those with human tricksters. The crucial difference between the two groups is the level of realism in the tales: "human trickster stories were more restricted by the realities of the slaves' situation. It was in their animal trickster tales that slaves expressed their wildest hopes and fears." (132)

Levine explains that in the human trickster tales, slaves expressed "patterns of behavior which more often than not could with some modification be incorporated into the slaves' own life . . . and more than any other form of African-American expressive culture [the tales] clearly depicted the possibilities and the limits of slave existence" (132).[13] The example of Slave John provides a model for interpreting the way that tricksters express and inform subordinate peoples' experiences of power structures in American culture.

In John, slaves created a figure who epitomized the rewards, the limits, and the hazards of the trickster. He could improve his situation through careful deception, but at no time was he really in complete control; the rewards he could win were limited by the realities of the system within which he existed, and the dangers he faced were great. Time and again the more elaborate schemes of the slave trickster failed, and he saved himself only by last minute verbal facility and role playing—two qualities which these stories emphasized were crucial for all slaves to cultivate. (Levine 128)

Levine's description of Slave John serves as a paradigm of how the trickster is a specific articulation of tactics of survival in a society that systematically victimizes and marginalizes people; he uses trickery, parody, and disguise to expose hypocrisy and inequality, to subvert existing social systems, and to gain power.[14]

In *From Trickster to Badman: The Black Folk Hero in Slavery and Freedom*, Roberts revises and extends Levine's discussions of trickster tales, taking an Afrocentric perspective that sheds new light on black folk heroic creation and on how heroes are constructed culturally. He asserts that "we must recognize that culture-building is a recursive, rather than linear, process of endlessly devising solutions to both old and new problems of how to live under ever-changing social, political, and economic conditions. While culture is dynamic and creative as it adapts to social needs and goals, it is also enduring in that it changes by building upon previous manifestations of itself" (11). Roberts's discussion of the connections between the trickster and the "badman" outlaw hero is particularly useful as a model for understanding a continuum of trickster figures as they change in response to historical and cultural conditions.[15] He explains, "In essence, as the law emerged as the institutional framework within which whites defined and dealt with African Americans in the society, it had a dramatic impact on their ability to accept behaviors embodied in trickster tales as adaptable to real-life situations" (186). This concept has implications for discussions of the con woman: the way Roberts treats the law in the transition from slavery to emancipation can serve as a model for exploring the transition from feme covert status to the postsuffrage redefinition of woman as a public as well as a private being.

The different yet complementary perspectives that inform the treatments of trickster figures by Gates, Levine, and Roberts provide models for understanding the cultural work of trickster figures in modern cultures, specifically how trickster figures articulate the contradictions of race in American society. Gates's scholarship highlights the linguistic practice of "Signifyin(g)" as a black vernacular rhetoric in which he locates an African-American literary tradition. Analogously, we can explore how female tricksters use linguistic trickery and ironic layering of resistance and dominant meanings. Roberts's contextual approach to the development of the African-American trickster hero can also be used as a touchstone for exploring both the antecedents of the twentieth-century female trickster and the links between the kinds of female tricksters I have identified as madcap, screwball, and con woman. His emphasis on value systems as a key to understanding what tricksters signify is an important contribution to appreciating how the female trickster articulates and subverts dominant models of femininity.

That these scholars do not address even the idea of female trickster figures illustrates a gap in trickster scholarship which my study begins to fill. It is possible that there are no examples of female tricksters in African-American culture because the folktales that were recorded were done so by men, and, analogous to the argument made about Native American trickster tales, there may be unrecovered trickster stories that were part of traditional African women's subcultures. Perhaps the tellers or recorders of folktales were unwilling to represent female trickery because it goes against dominant definitions of femininity. However, the woman of Charles Chestnutt's *The Conjure Woman* is curiously absent in discussions of Chestnutt's representations of the trickery of conjure, although his male characters are discussed by Roberts. More likely, it is the overwhelming assumption that the trickster is male that has influenced these scholars.

Although female tricksters may be represented in African-American literature in the late twentieth century, they are curiously absent in representations in the period under consideration here, roughly 1850 to 1955. This suggests that during this time the female trickster was a white phenomenon. The heroines of the "passing" novels are liminal characters who move "betwixt and between" racial social spaces, but they are not figures who articulate the laughter, delight, and subversion that is central to the cultural work of the trickster. To be sure, there are characters, such as Aurelia and Venus in Pauline Hopkins's serialized novel *Hagar's Daughter* (*Colored American Magazine*, 1901–2) who use disguise and female trickery to attain their desires, but overall the deceptions practiced by women characters in nineteenth- and early-twentieth-century African-American literature are confessed or represented within the moral context of the "fallen woman."

Take Harriet Jacobs's slave narrative *Incidents in the Life of a Slave Girl* (1861). Jacobs wrote her autobiography to convey the horrors of chattel slavery for a woman to her white, Northern, woman-identified readers. She wanted to make her case against "the southern patriarchy for its sexual tyranny over black women herself, yet she could not do so without confessing with 'sorrow' and 'shame' to her willing participation in a miscegenetic liaison that produced two illegitimate children" (W. L. Andrews 240). The narrator tricks the slave owner into thinking she has escaped to the North, but in reality she is hiding in the garret of her grandmother's house. The narrative is a heartbreaking tale, especially in Jacobs's descriptions of watching her children through a crack in the wall but being unable to interact with them or let them know she is there. It succeeds in its rhetorical mission of appealing to the implied white reader's emotions. Certainly Harriet uses trickery, but the trick she plays renders her invisible and absent. In contrast to the increased mobility and social flexibility exemplified by the trickster, Harriet is immobile. Immobile, silent, invisible. Nevertheless, she creates the impression that she is free at the same time that she retreats into an interior space that is, within its restrictions, free. Jacobs's narrative shows how the genre stressed that chattel slavery bars women from living as true women.[16] It also reveals the secrets and silences that may have prevented stories of female tricksters from being told to folklorists.

In the genre of the "passing" novel, liminal mixed-race women characters use the trickster tactics of deception, boundary crossing, and what can be seen as "shape-shifting," but their experiences while passing as white tend to be tragic ones. Unlike women in slave narratives who pass in order to survive, escape chattel slavery, and create a free identity, women in the passing novels are motivated by selfish, material greed, which is antithetical to the progress of "the race." They attain privileges and luxuries because they are visibly white and invisible as black women.

Angela in Jessie Redmon Fauset's *Plum Bun* (1928) and Clare in Nella Larsen's *Passing* (1929) both use the social practices of female trickery in everyday life, but these characters have more in common with the femmes fatales of forties' film noir than with contemporaneous white characters. Although a Jazz Age trickster like Lorelei Lee in *Gentlemen Prefer Blondes* (1925) is a gold digger who is motivated by gem lust, her trickery leads to endless possibility and strengthens the economy and society. For Angela, the trickery of passing is a dead end, and the happy ending of *Plum Bun* hinges on her coming out as a Negro and returning to the sister and community she had wrongly judged as inferior. For Clare, passing back and forth between Negro and white social spaces leads to her death by her double who lives as a Negro and passes only now and then to participate in white privilege. The men with whom Clare and Angela get involved while passing as white are vocal in their racism and incapable of providing anything other than a level of material comfort that is only slightly better than that of the women characters who are part of the Negro community. Although neither of these novels were read widely, Fannie Hurst's best-selling novel *Imitation of Life* (1933)—and the popular 1934 and 1959 film versions—also discouraged passing by representing it as the denial of the mother (very bad in maternal melodrama) and a poor strategy for happiness. In each of these examples, passing is treacherous to the race and the individual and, as critic Valerie Smith argues, the representation of "passing as betrayal, blackness as self-denial, whiteness as comfort—has the effect of advocating black accommodationism, since the texts repeatedly punish at least this particular form of upward mobility. These texts thus become sites where antiracist and white supremacist ideologies converge, encouraging their black readers to stay in their places" (44).

The trickster always refuses to stay in place; even Harriet Jacobs created the ruse that she was living freely in the North. The class-based New Negro ideology that informs *Passing* and *Plum Bun* hinged on presenting the "image of the Negro as exemplary within the context of conventional morality" (Huggins 148). Therefore, although a discussion of representations of passing as female trickery would make an interesting contribution to the considerable critical attention given to passing narratives in general and Larsen's fascinating, maddening *Passing* in particular, I cannot argue here that Clare, Irene, Angela, and Peola are trickster figures. Because the mixed-race heroines are never invested with the spirit of the adventuress but are essentially sentimental, melodramatic characters, the genre of passing narratives casts liminality, masquerade, and deception as wrong, dangerous, and unacceptable—as tragic—instead of comically as playful, subversive, and joyous.

Moreover, the only character in *Plum Bun* who practices female trickery successfully is white. Angela is impressed by but cannot emulate the unconventional, sexually active white adventuress Paulette, who declares, "I've learned that a woman is a fool who lets her femininity stand in the way of what she wants. I've made a philosophy of it. I see what I want; I use my wiles as a woman to get it, and I employ the qualities of men, tenacity and ruthlessness, to keep it. And when I'm through with it, I throw it away just as they do" (105). But neither the novel nor the genre allows for the substitution of "race" for "femininity" in Paulette's statement, and so, in African-American as well as white literary traditions, female tricksters tend to be white.

Despite the numerous depictions of men as tricksters in the folklore of the early twentieth century and in literature of the Harlem Renaissance, especially in the comic novels of the period, the only female trickster appears in Wallace Thurman's satire *Infants of the Spring*.[17] Sweetie May, a vicious and barely disguised portrait of Zora Neale Hurston, plays up to white ideas of "darkies" because, as she says,

I have to eat. I also wish to finish my education. Being a Negro these days is a racket and I'm going to make the most of it while it lasts. Sure I cut the fool. But I enjoy it, too. My ultimate ambition . . . is to be a gynecologist [Anthropologist]. And the only way I can live easily until I have the requisite training is to pose as a writer of potential ability. *Voila!* I get my tuition paid at Columbia. I rent an apartment and have all the furniture contributed by kind hearted o'fays. . . . About twice a year I manage to sell a story. It is acclaimed. I am a genius in the making. Thank God for this Negro literary renaissance. Long may it flourish! (quoted in Huggins 129)

The embodiment of Thurman's bleak interpretation of the Harlem Renaissance as a sham and a scam, Sweetie May is the con artist in the "new country" of the interracial city—what Ann Douglas calls mongrel Manhattan. The strategy she articulates, the radical individualism she enacts are not significantly different from those of Jazz Age trickster Lorelei Lee in Anita Loos's *Gentlemen Prefer Blondes* (1925), although her understanding of the hand she has been dealt and her ability to articulate it are. The systems they exploit—the artistic/racial economy for Sweetie May and the sex/love economy for Lorelei—vary only in the details. Money and self-advancement are the goals, and they exploit the economy in which their physical appearances make them valuable.

The bleak tone of a novel written, Nathan Huggins argues, "to bury the [Harlem] renaissance once and for all" (241) complicates Sweetie May as a comic character, but her individualism, her willingness to play the part she has been assigned by a racist culture for her own benefit, and her pleasure in her performance and trickery makes her a survivor. Although Thurman doesn't address the idea of the female trickster explicitly, his characterization of Sweetie May raises interesting questions. What is unclear is Sweetie May's relationship to the race: Is she an accommodationist who cares only for her self-advancement? Does this align her more closely with white female tricksters of the Jazz Age than with the ultimately community-oriented African-American trickster figures? Or is there a shift in the relationship between the trickster and his or her community after chattel slavery ends? Perhaps Sweetie May will become the anthropologist who will pay attention to the stories of female tricksters. Or will her career as a social scientist be an extension of her con game? [18]

The invisibility of Harriet Jacobs hidden in her garret, the passing heroines who cultivate the appearance of whiteness, and Sweetie May's playing the fool can be seen as a metaphor of African-American women's representation in mainstream American culture. More recently, black women writers like Toni Morrison, black actresses like Whoopi Goldberg (to whom we'll return in the last chapter), and black filmmakers like Julie Dash (whose film *Illusions* [1982] concerns a woman who passes in 1940s Hollywood in order to increase opportunities for black women) have made the trope of invisibility and visibility central to their work.

Confidence Men

There are two manifestations of the trickster as confidence man in antebellum nineteenth-century American culture: urban villain and frontier hero. Cultural historian Karen Halttunen locates the confidence man as villain in advice literature that delineated the ideology of sentimental middle-class American culture. She defines the confidence man as "a master of human psychology" (5), an evil manifestation of "influence," who seduces an unsuspecting young man, new to the city, into a corrupting life of vice (drinking, sex with prostitutes, carousing, gambling, and other libertine behaviors) with the goal of reducing the young man to a slave. She categorizes three types of con men found in advice literature and fiction: the urban companion of the youth, the demagogue, and the gambler. Drawing on anthropologist Mary Douglas's work, Halttunen summarizes:

The confidence man of antebellum advice literature, who invariably approached his victim with an offer of friendship that proved to be part of a confidence trick, was a modern industrial version of the trickster. . . . Within Douglas's theory, the confidence man's powers to pollute young men resided in the threat he presented to the legitimate leaders of the American republic. The villains of antebellum advice literature were all presented as tricksters because they threatened to usurp the traditional authority exercised by the legitimate leaders of preindustrial America. Here lay the ultimate danger of the new horizontal society: by leveling the traditional, vertical social structures, it made authority a function not of fixed social status but of fluid self-aggrandizement. In the horizontal society, any man could seize authority over others: the licentious youth who rose from nowhere to become a leader among his youthful peers, the unprincipled demagogue who rose from nowhere to manipulate the passions of the mob, the avaricious gambler/speculator who rose from nowhere to seize control of the economic lives of those foolish enough the play his game. (24–25)

Another characterization of the confidence man during the same period (one read by the same class of urban gentlemen) emerges from the body of sketches and stories known as the humor of the Old Southwest. In these stories, the confidence man, although just as morally suspect as in the advice literature, is portrayed more as a hero, a vernacular trickster who personifies the newness of the ever-expanding, fluid America of the "flush times" when little was codified and opportunity was there for the taking, or the tricking. In the words of the motto of Johnson Jones Hooper's rapscallion-hero Simon Suggs: "IT IS GOOD TO BE SHIFTY IN A NEW COUNTRY" ("Simon Plays the 'Snatch' Game," repr. in Cohen and Dillingham 207).

Unlike the urban villain, who represents what is poisonous and to be avoided, the confidence man as Southwest hero embodies the changing definitions of masculinity from genteel and aristocratic to vernacular and democratic. As William E. Lenz argues, the confidence man is "a distinctly American version of the archetypal trickster" who "emerges as a local rather than mythic figure; he relies not on supernatural powers or charms or courts but on the fluid nature of society in the New World with its unique opportunities for self-government, self-posturing, and self-creation" (1).[19] The tensions between the constrictions of civilization and the freedom and fluidity of the frontier receive their fullest expression in Mark Twain's masterpiece *Huckleberry Finn*, which draws heavily on the tradition of humor of the Old Southwest.[20]

Of course, the "self-government, self-posturing, and self-creation" that Lenz finds definitive of the confidence man's story are particularly vexed for nineteenth-century women. As Nathan Huggins observes in *Harlem Renaissance*, "It is easier to image men as roustabouts, vagabonds, and heroes, harder to draw sympathetic females whose whole existence is their bodies and instincts" (188).[21] However, despite the antithetical relationship between tricksterism and cultural constructs of femininity, representations of female tricksters not only exist but have been prevalent in the newest forms of popular culture. From the serialized fiction of the nineteenth and early twentieth centuries, to the silent films of the twenties, radio comedies and "talkies" of the thirties, and the early television series of the fifties, female tricksters have been pioneers in the "new country" of the frontier of mass consumer culture.

Comedy and the Trickster

The forms of popular culture in which female tricksters recur have tended to be in the genre of comedy. My working definition of comedy comes from Arthur Koestler's theory of the bisociation of two operative fields or associative contexts. Koestler explains in his entry on "Humor and Wit" in *The Encyclopedia Britannica*:

> It is the sudden clash between these two mutually exclusive codes of rules—or associative contexts—that produces the comic effect. It compels the listener to perceive the situation in two self-consistent but incompatible frames of reference at the same time; his [or her] mind has to operate simultaneously on two different wavelengths. While this unusual condition lasts, the event is not only, as is normally the case, associated with a single frame of reference, but "bisociated" with two. The term bisociation was coined by the present writer to make a distinction between the routines of disciplined thinking within a single universe of discourse—on a single plane, as it were—and the creative types of mental activity that always operate on more than one plane. In humor, both the *creation* of a subtle joke and the *re-creative* act of perceiving the joke involve the delightful mental jolt of a sudden leap from one plane or associative context to another. (5–6)

I am drawn to Koestler's definition because it is broad enough to include specific kinds of bisociation—the clash between the human and the mechanical in Henri Bergson's theory, the reversal of George Santayana's carnival and Mikhail Bakhtin's carnivalesque, Northrop Frye's juxtaposition of the "green world" of possibility and the ordinary, rational world, Freud's repression and release, Turner's liminal figure who is "betwixt and between"—and because of the way it explains both what a joke is and how a person perceives it. Koestler's concept of comedy as the bisociation of incompatible operative fields defines comedy in terms that connect it to the trickster, who is "paradox personified" and dualistic.

Theories of comedy often contrast the genres of comedy and tragedy. Koestler argues that when aggression, which is necessary in comedy, is replaced with sympathy, a situation shifts from comic to tragic and will result in pity and not laughter. Scholar Harry Levin explains the difference in terms of the antagonist in *Playboys and Killjoys: An Essay on the Theory and Practice of Comedy*: "When an actual villain rather than a trickster—killjoy rather than playboy—spins the plot, comedy moves perilously close to melodrama" (75). Sociologist Murray S. Davis takes yet another tact: "Tragedy paints the self's slow evolution whereas comedy sketches its sudden conversion" (282).

Literary critic Northrop Frye, who has made compelling and influential arguments for why comedy should be treated seriously, draws several distinctions between tragedy and comedy, including the different endings: "Happy endings do not impress us as true, but as desirable, and they are brought about by manipulation. The watcher of death and tragedy has nothing to do but sit and wait for the inevitable end; but something gets born at the end of comedy, and the watcher of birth is a member of a busy society" ("The Mythos of Spring: Comedy" 148). The insight that the happy ending of comedy is "desirable," not inevitable or true, points us toward comedy's utopian function. Comedy presents a fantasy world in which the illusions, misunderstandings, and misrecognitions that set the comedy in motion are unmasked and untied with the twist or *anagnorisis* that provides a desirable resolution. As Susan repeatedly says during the many moments of chaos and confusion in the screwball comedy *Bringing Up Baby* (1938), "Everything's gonna be all right."

Comedy and the trickster have much in common, and we can understand their convergences through the idea of "play." Harry Levin makes connections among play, the trickster, and comedy by putting trickery at the center of the comic plot:

Play can have both an intransitive and a transitive purport. Children can go out to play, or else play a game. Prodigals can play around, or can play a trick upon somebody else. Thus we arrive at a cast of characters: the player and the one that is played upon, the trickster and he who gets tricked, the cheater and the cheated. Already we discern the outline of a comic plot. For what is a plot if not a prank, a series of tricks or transactions in trickery eliciting counterplots, whether they be tragically conspiratorial or comically intriguing? (149–50)

Taking a different tact, anthropologist Victor Turner explains play as expressing the "subjunctive mood" of verbs: if I could, if I were, if things were as I desire, were I able. The trickster enacts the subjunctive mood and represents the realms of supposition, hypothesis, desire, and possibilities, the terrain of liminality.[22] In his classic study *Homo Ludens,* Johan Huizinga stressed that play stands outside of "ordinary life" because it is not serious, but it is serious in that it absorbs the player completely (13). In his scholarship, Roger Callois further develops the theory of play by differentiating between two poles: *paidia,* from the Greek word for child, which is "an almost indivisible principle, common to diversion, turbulence, free improvisation, and carefree gaiety" and *ludus,* from the Latin word for a game or a play, which counters the childlike fantasy with rules and conventions (Turner, *Anthropology of Performance,* 125). The trickster presides over both poles of play: the childlike fantasy of the subjunctive mood and the game rules and genre conventions in which play is experienced. The oscillation between the two poles characterizes the trickster, who is rule-breaker and yet exploiter of the rules of the game.

Play, comedy, the trickster: these three concepts form a bridge between unindustrialized premodern culture and mass consumer culture.

As rituals have declined in industrializing and industrialized societies, play and the genre of comedy have taken up some of the moral self-reflexivity that used to be in the ritual/religious sphere: "The play frame, where events are scrutinized in the leisure time of the social process, has to some extent inherited the function of the ritual frame. The messages it delivers are often serious beneath the outward trappings of absurdity, fantasy, and ribaldry, as contemporary stage plays, some movies and some TV shows illustrate" (Turner, *Anthropology of Performance*, 124). The interplay between the comic narrative and the serious messages it often contains is at the center of my study, which focuses on the cultural work that some specific comic texts perform in representing possibility, hope, and, for at least a time, triumph over structure. In Chapter 1, I discuss feminist perspectives on women's uses of comedy. Subsequent chapters explore comedy in different media and historical periods.

Defining the Female Trickster

This inquiry as a whole will document the incidence and popularity of female tricksters in American culture. Suffice it to say here that female tricksters articulate the paradox of femininity and autonomy, of representations of women who draw from the spectrum of human attributes and behaviors regardless of the constraints of cultural definitions of gender. By transgressing the cultural delimiters of "woman's sphere," domesticity, sentimentalism, repression of the body, and suppression of the mind, female tricksters violate the boundaries between men's and women's spheres and enter into the "new country" of the public sphere, participating in an antidomestic and antisentimental tradition in American women's culture.

Although the specific form of the trickster differs from the irrepressible comic nature of the madcap and screwball to the controlled calculation of the confidence woman, female tricksters are cultural archetypes (to use a Jungian concept) and "transfer points" (to use a Foucauldian one) where conflicting symbol systems are represented in a paradoxical figure.[23] Representations of female tricksters offer us a chance to understand the gender system through imagining what tactics are necessary to escape the system as well as what factors prevent that escape. In short, female tricksters are fantasy figures, much like Slave John, who present tactics of resistance, self-preservation, and self-definition that could be used in everyday life.

Scholars of folklore, anthropology, and religious studies have debated the definition of the trickster. Their debates center on two main issues: whether there is a category of mythic figures that, despite particular appearances in specific cultures, can be defined as tricksters, and what the common characteristics might be. The scholars who participate in discourses of "trickster studies" are obviously hinging their work on the theoretical assumption that "tricksters" is a useful category of cultural figures. In a collection of essays from the Trickster Myth Group within the American Academy of Religion, William J. Hynes presents a synthesis of the characteristics through which scholars have defined the trickster:

> At the heart of this cluster of manifest trickster traits is (1) the fundamentally ambiguous and anomalous personality of the trickster. Flowing from this are other such features as (2) deceiver/trick-player, (3) shape-shifter, (4) situation-invertor, (5) messenger/imitator of the gods, and (6) sacred/lewd bricoleur. . . . Several scholars . . . have suggested that one could use such shared characteristics as a matrix by which to survey all known examples of tricksters and to judge their degree of "tricksterness." This might be a very useful way of testing the degree of commonality of such characteristics, but one should be cautious about the imposition of communality from without. (in Hynes and Doty 34)

Indeed, the "imposition of communality from without" is what has defined the trickster as male. Although William G. Doty and other contemporary scholars play down the masculinity of the trickster by using gender-neutral language (in contrast to the gendered terminology of earlier writers such as Radin), they nevertheless perpetuate a theoretical quagmire of definition that continually recreates the intellectual, scholarly concept of "trickster."

A study of trickery as social practice inflected by gender is in accord with the goals Hynes and Doty set for trickster studies: "We look for models that enable the interpreter to hone the interpretive tools, and defensible generic or archetypal analysis does precisely that: it sets up patterns of anticipation for particular works, given the accumulated details of a more or less cohesive pattern found in similar situations. The interpreter seeks not law-like results, but the most plausible interpretations for the situations. . . . [S]uch a project, by forcing comparisons, can reveal some aspects of being human that might otherwise not surface at all" (27). If explorations of the trickster yield a greater understanding of what it means to be human, then my discussion of female tricksters contributes to the ongoing fight for female inclusion in discourses of what it means to be human.

This project participates in three scholarly discussions: so-called trickster studies, studies of the development of mass consumer culture in America, and feminist scholarship on the ideology of gender and feminist consciousness in America. Gender is a previously neglected yet important aspect of trickster figures, especially in advanced industrialized societies, and I interrogate assumptions that can obscure understanding about what a trickster might be. By shifting the focus from the character-istics of the trickster to the social practice of trickery and investigating the cultural work a trickster figure performs, my study bridges the gap between scholarship that has tended to focus on pre- and early modern societies and the particular complexities and contradictions of modern industrial culture.

My focus on a recurring figure, the female trickster, in the devel-oping mass consumer culture of modern America serves as a way of adding gender to current discussions about consumption. As histori-ans Richard Wrightman Fox and T. J. Jackson Lears argue, "to discover how consumption became a cultural ideal, a hegemonic 'way of seeing' in twentieth-century America, requires looking at powerful individuals and institutions who conceived, formulated, and preached that ideal or way of seeing" (*Culture of Consumption* x). My corollary to Fox and Lears's stance is that the "powerful individuals and institutions" that created the ideology of femininity in mass consumer society include not only the "professional-managerial stratum" pinpointed by Fox and Lears and similar-minded cultural historians but public women such as authors Anita Loos and Elinor Glyn and performers Clara Bow, Mae West, and Lucille Ball—women who had specific individual agendas that were sup-ported or resisted to different degrees by the culture at large. The stories of how they attempted to do cultural work and what representations emerged from the collaborative creative processes of mass consumer culture are interesting side notes about how a "way of seeing" is crystal-lized and disseminated. The stories show the intersections of individual careers and wider cultural trends: Loos's inability to inflect the popular reception of her "dumb blonde" Lorelei Lee with her satirical perspec-tive, Glyn's capitulation to emerging ideals of modern femininity em-bodied by the flapper which were in opposition to her elitist ideals of ladylike "repose," the censorship and blacklisting Mae West faced when she tried to put representations of sex into mainstream public discourse, and Lucille Ball's apparent success at combining career, marriage, and family by paralleling her "real life" with the "fiction" of the television series *I Love Lucy*, a popular facade that obscured a less attractive reality. My project speaks to a gap between the work of historians of the culture of consumption, historians of women's experience in America, popular culture critics, and feminist cultural critics.

Finally, the interdisciplinary nature of this inquiry attempts to bridge different concerns, lexicons, and methods of the humanities and social sciences so as to contribute to a fuller understanding of how gender, culture, ideology, and society form a complex and changing whole. Through the mythic terrain of American literature, film, television, ad-vertising, and other popular discourses, I explore the relationships be-

tween representations in cultural texts and the development of the hegemonic ideology of gender.

Now, to narrow my focus to a relatively small portion of human history: American culture from 1850 to the present, and the cultural work
performed by representations of female characters who practice trickery. I chose the texts I will analyze because their popularity suggests
that they resonated through American popular culture. When these examples of tricky women characters are seen on a continuum, they tell
a story about woman's place and women's power during the sexual de-
segregation of American society. They also tell a story about the social
relations of the sexes, about the ways in which women's exertions of
covert and overt power in the sociosexual marketplace have been represented as both instructive models and cautionary tales. These texts articulate contradictory views of female trickery, which parallel the issues
raised by the deceitful, duplicitous, subversive trickster figure, but they
are also inflected by issues of gender. For example, the tension between individual freedom and social responsibility is problematized by
trickster figures as diverse as the Cameroon Kulu the tortoise and Old
Southwest humorist Augustus Baldwin Longstreet's vernacular character Ned Brace (who drinks the buckets of water passed to him in the fire
line while the house burns down). For female tricksters, however, there
is the added dimension of women's struggle for autonomy from men,
which conflicts with their responsibilities to family and society. Female
tricksters represent a threat to social stability with their individualistic
pursuit of satisfaction and autonomy.

Female trickery highlights the issue of women's exercise of covert
power, which necessitates that practitioners maintain positions of submission. Covert manipulations may not increase self-esteem or self-
worth and certainly do not challenge sexist ideology; instead, as historian Carolyn Johnston puts it, "Covert power without public power led
to a loss of self-esteem and to physical and economic vulnerability" and
perpetuates women's private, feme covert status (243).

An issue that arises from representations of female trickery is cultural
ambivalence about acknowledging the "secrets" of trickster tactics. Exposing covert power deflates images of women as angels and reifies ideas
of female power as sneaky—"feline" as so many of these texts term it—
rather than overt. Of course, a preference for more honest, overt power
stems from the bourgeois standards of morality and sincerity that the
trickster so often mocks. The point here is that the texts are riddled with
uncertainties about the loss of women's covert power base without the
means for overt power to replace it.

The characters discussed here are mainstream representations. Their
predominantly white race, heterosexual orientation, assumed Christian-

ity, and middle-class (sometimes working-class) values reflect decisions made in the culture industries about what and who would be included and excluded in popular culture.

Because the issues surrounding depictions of female trickery change in response to shifts in the cultural definitions of woman's place and female power, the chapters that follow are organized chronologically by historical era. Each chapter discusses several female tricksters in the contexts of the increasingly permeable boundaries between the public and private spheres and the ideals of femininity against which female tricksters rebel. Each chapter also explores the connections between representations of female trickery in cultural discourses (such as magazines and advertisements) and the popular heroines whose social practice of female trickery calls attention to the tensions between women's ambition and the limitations of femininity. In their pursuit of autonomy and active participation in the world around them, the characters deploy trickster tactics such as deception, disguise, duplicity, subversion, feigned submission, parody, and impersonation in concert with specifically female practices such as the uses of makeup, sex appeal, emotional manipulation, and exploitation of the inconsistencies of the sex-gender system.

The first chapter, "Running Mad, Taking Cover: Female Tricksters in Nineteenth-Century Fiction by American Women," describes a group of antisentimental heroines who use trickster tactics to move beyond the confines of Victorian-sentimental ideology. The chapter focuses on Capitola in E. D. E. N. Southworth's novel *The Hidden Hand, or Capitola the Madcap* (1859), Jean Muir in Louisa May Alcott's thriller *Behind a Mask* (1866), and the narrator of Mary Wilkins Freeman's chapter in *The Whole Family: A Novel by Twelve Authors* (1908). Chapter 2, "Economics and Erotics: The Female Trickster in the Jazz Age," moves between print and film; in my discussion of twenties' advertising, Anita Loos's novel *Gentlemen Prefer Blondes* (1925), the silent movie *It* (1927), and Nella Larsen's novel *Passing* (1929), I show how female trickery is central to definitions of femininity emerging from and shaping mass consumer culture. Chapter 3, "Out of the Garden and into the War: Female Tricksters in the Depression and War Years," explains how radio and film comedy portrayed female trickery as a successful and necessary mode of interaction in a rapidly changing, illogical society. It moves from a discussion of how Mae West functioned as a female trickster in American culture to contextualized critical readings of the films *The Awful Truth* (1937), *Bringing Up Baby* (1938), and *The Lady Eve* (1941); the chapter ends with a section on the fantasy figures of the war years, the screwball heroines of comedy, and the femmes fatales of film noir. Chapter 4, "Liminal Lucy: Covert Power, Television, and Postwar Domestic Ideology," begins with a section on the fifties' ideals of femininity and female trickery as represented by Marilyn Monroe's portrayal of Lorelei Lee in Howard Hawks's film *Gentlemen Prefer Blondes* (1953) and then delves into the cultural, institutional, and production contexts surrounding the television series *I Love Lucy*. The book concludes with "You Can't Go Home Again: Feminism and the Female Trickster in Contemporary American Culture," which places contemporary representations of female trickery in the contexts of second wave feminism, backlash culture, and fin de siècle ideology. The chapter focuses on television since 1960 and on films such as *Thelma and Louise* (1991), *Desperately Seeking Susan* (1985), *House of Games* (1987), *Batman Returns* (1992), and *Sister Act* (1992).

What follows traces one of the myriad of stories in American culture, only one out of an infinite number of threads in the tapestry, strands in the web. Several subplots develop within the story of how the female trickster has been central to American popular culture: the implications of the trickster's characteristic duality for women characters, the trope of the catwoman, the ideals created and violated by star personas, the representational strategies that advertisers thought would work on women throughout history, ideas about courtship and marriage, what can be represented and what must remain invisible and silent, and the story of the level of feminist consciousness represented in mainstream American culture. Starting with turn-of-the-nineteenth-century novels and ending on the precipice of the twenty-first century, here are some of the manifestations of the female trickster.

Chapter 1
Running Mad, Taking Cover
Female Tricksters in Nineteenth-Century Fiction
by American Women

"My beloved Laura (said she to me a few Hours before she died) take warning from my unhappy End & avoid the imprudent conduct which has occasioned it . . beware of fainting-fits . . Though at the time they may be refreshing & Agreable [*sic*] yet beleive [*sic*] me they will in the end, if too often repeated & at improper seasons, prove destructive to your Constitution. . . . Beware of swoons Dear Laura . . . A frenzy fit is not one quarter so pernicious; it is an exercise to both the Body & if not too violent, is I dare say conducive to Health in its consequences—Run mad as often as you chuse; but do not faint."

—Jane Austen, *Love and Freindship* [*sic*] (1790)

This deathbed wisdom about the choice between two alternative "feminine" responses of running mad and fainting articulates the comic perspective from which characterizations of the madcap emerge. Reject the sentimental behavior of fainting, the dying Sophia insists, in favor of the "exercise" of temporary madness. The insight here—embedded in the joke of one friend giving tactical advice about appropriately "sensible" responses to life's surprises—is typical of Austen's recognition of the limitations that constructs of femininity impose on women's choices.

In America at roughly the same time, in Tabitha Gilman Tenney's novel *Female Quixotism* (1801), heroine Dorcasina Sheldon is under the sway of the English romantic novels she reads. By basing her self-definition in fiction, she makes a series of foolish choices about suitors that leave her old and alone at the end of the novel. Although Capitola's desire for adventure and heroism smacks of "female quixotism," she has more in common with Dorcas's antiromantic friend Harriot, who impersonates a male suitor to prevent Dorcas from marrying her servant, who in her romantic delusion is really a nobleman in disguise. The anti-sentimental heroine Capitola rescuing the sentimental Clara is parallel to the antiromantic Harriot's rescue of the deluded Dorcas.

That Austen's version of female madness is a temporary tactic rather than a permanent condition—that madness expresses itself in the bodily exercise of running mad rather than in the captivity and repressed rage of later representations such as Bertha Rochester, the paradigmatic figure that literary critics Sandra M. Gilbert and Susan Gubar term "the madwoman in the attic"—suggests two important points. First, there are survival strategies women can employ that are less self-destructive than the parodically sentimental option of "lying totally inactive on the Ground" (Austen 226). Second, the escape route of temporarily running mad is imaginable only from a comic perspective that ridicules the prevailing ideology, which in Austen's case was the cult of "sensibility" in fashion in the late eighteenth century.

Austen's comic articulation of running mad as an alternative to the deadly practices of sentimentalism can be read as a paradigm of comic representations of the madcap as a female trickster in nineteenth-century fiction by American women.[1] In contrast to the sentimental heroines who strive to fulfill Victorian dictates of femininity, a group of antisentimental heroines rejects dominant demarcations of gender that limit woman's sphere to domesticity and female power to sentimentalism.[2] Some, such as the slave Cassy in Harriet Beecher Stowe's novel *Uncle Tom's Cabin*, appear as minor figures within a sea of sentimental models. Cassy escapes from and wreaks revenge upon the evil slaveholder Simon Legree by impersonating the ghost of her predecessor as Legree's sexual chattel. Cassy's machinations from her hiding place in the attic play on Legree's superstitions; her "fearful, unearthly screams" guarantee that Legree will not go into the attic (Stowe 206). Although a figure such as Cassy provides an interesting counterpoint to the domestic and sentimental ideology Stowe's book perpetuates, more striking still are those antisentimental heroines who, as central figures in novels and stories, embody their authors' critique of dominant ideals of femininity and the relegation of women to the private sphere of domesticity.

To be sure, subversion, antisentimentalism, and the limitations of domesticity have become central tenets in discussions of nineteenth-century women's literature.[3] This scholarship provides a context within which to examine three examples of female tricksters in nineteenth- and early-twentieth-century American women's fiction: Capitola in E. D. E. N. Southworth's novel *The Hidden Hand, or Capitola the Madcap* (1859), Jean Muir in Louisa May Alcott's thriller *Behind a Mask, or A Woman's Power* (1866),[4] and Aunt Elizabeth in Mary Wilkins Freeman's contribution to the multiauthored serialized novel *The Whole Family* (1908). Exemplary of the madcap, con woman, and screwball heroine, respectively, these characters employ the trickster tactics of deception, impersonation, theft, duplicity, and subversion in their attempts to secure autonomy and to rebel against the cultural dictates that limit woman's place to the home and women's power to influencing others. In doing so, these female tricksters exaggerate the nineteenth-century heroine's movement between socially sanctioned feminine traits and behavior and masculine ones, a transgression of the social boundaries of separate spheres that calls attention to the sex-gender system as artificial rather than natural.

Not surprisingly, many female tricksters are comic heroines or heroines who appear in comic texts. As scholarship on women and comedy by critics such as Judith Wilt, Emily Toth, Nancy Walker, Regina Barreca, June Sochen, Zita Dresner, and Linda Morris has shown, women have used humor to express their recognition and rejection of the conventions of femininity. Some of these critics (especially Walker and Morris) have directed their attention to rediscovering and understanding a "lost" tradition of women's literary humor in America; their scholarship combats the sexist notion that women's comedy does not exist. The title of one anthology, *Redressing the Balance: American Women's Literary Humor from Colonial Times to the 1890s* (1988), suggests the asymmetry that editors Walker and Dresner aim to correct. From early writers Anne Bradstreet and Sarah Kemble Knight to nineteenth-century humorists including Tabitha Gilman Tenney, Mrs. Mary Clavers (Caroline Kirkland), Fanny Fern (Sara Willis Parton), Anna Cora Mowatt, Ann Stephens, Frances Whitcher, and Marietta Holley, women have used humor to address "a concern with the incongruities between the realities of women's lives and the sentimental or idealized images fostered by the culture" (Walker and Dresner xxvii).

In her book *A Very Serious Thing: Women's Humor and American Culture* (1988), Walker further explains that female humorists adopt a role that necessitates their "break[ing] out of the passive, subordinate position mandated for them by centuries of patriarchal tradition. . . . To be a woman and a humorist is to confront and subvert the very power that keeps women powerless, and at the same time to risk alienating those upon whom women are dependent for economic survival" (9). According to Walker and Dresner, a woman humorist is by definition a rebellious, subversive figure whose ridicule of the dominant ideology of gender has "encouraged an enlargement of woman's sphere and protested the restrictions that, in barring women from utilizing their talents and abilities in the public arena, have countenanced their dissipating their energies in the pursuit of husbands, social status, fashion, spotless floors, perfect bodies, and super momism" (xxvii). Walker and Dresner here demonstrate the critics' tendency to equate women's use of humor with feminist protest. To be sure, women's comedy often suggests a critique that can be termed antisexist if not feminist, but not necessarily; for example, Phyllis McGinley used wit and comedy to rebut Betty Friedan's *The Feminine Mystique*.[5] In a significant portion of the scholarship on women's humor, the critics are more concerned with claiming women's comedy as feminist expression than in exploring the complex and often irreconcilable insights communicated by comedy.[6]

My discussion of the prevalence and meanings of the female trickster figure stems from a set of concerns different from those of the critics engaged in revising the canon of American humor or defining a uniquely female tradition of humor.[7] Although most of the characters and texts under consideration are comic, this is not a study of women's uses of humor per se. It is an inquiry into cultural representations of women's uses of trickery; because the comic treatment of the social practice of female trickery prevails and resonates in American culture, I often focus on gender and comedy.

The discontent expressed by female tricksters in the nineteenth century centers on sentimental and domestic ideals of women's appearance, character, behavior, and comportment. In middle-class Victorian ideology, femininity was defined in terms of mutually informing divisions between public and private and masculine and feminine.[8] As family historian Daniel Scott Smith contends, "The distinction between public and private and the corresponding allocation of men to the former and women to the latter is a central (if not *the* central) theme in the history of gender" (239–40). Or, as Nancy Cott puts it, "The central convention of domesticity was the contrast between the home and the world" (*Bonds* 64).

Sentimental heroines, best exemplified by Ellen Montgomery, the heroine of Susan Warner's best-seller *The Wide, Wide World* (1850), focus the readers' attention on the minutiae of everyday life in the home, an ideological reinforcement of women's place in domesticity that reifies the separation of the home and the world.[9] As critics from Ann Douglas and Henry Nash Smith to Jane Tompkins and Joanne Dobson have noted, Ellen's desire for self-abnegation and submission to the patriarchal authority of God and men is the driving force of a novel that is relentless in its increasingly narrow representation of woman's place and female power. In the novel's dramatization of feminine ideals, domesticity is the only imaginable sphere; female power comes only from influence through prayer, sweet entreaty, and emotional and psychic manipulation. The ultimate manifestation of the power of sentimentalism (an ideological construct that privileges feeling over thought, action, and material concerns) is, in Stowe's phrase, "feeling right," the belief that by being emotionally correct—pure and passive—women could influence material realities such as the injustices of slavery or poverty.[10] In order to open herself to "feeling right," a woman must make herself an empty vessel through which God's will can flow, an achievement necessitating the sacrifice of the individual will.

Like other attempts to redefine the dominant ideology of gender to make the confines of femininity seem liberating (akin to focusing on the immediate surroundings to the exclusion of the surrounding prison bars), the self-effacing state of "feeling right" served to obscure power inequalities in American society. A similarly paradoxical ideological construct is "passionlessness," which perpetuated the notion that women innately lack sexual desire and bodily subjectivity. As historian Nancy Cott explains, "The positive contribution of passionlessness was to replace that sexual/carnal characterization of women [prevalent through the end of the eighteenth century] with a moral/spiritual one, allowing women to develop their human faculties and their self-esteem" ("Passionlessness" 173). By downplaying sexuality, women did gain some control over reproduction, but, as Cott concludes, passionlessness, "conceived as self-preservation and social advancement for women, created its own contradictions: on the one hand, by exaggerating sexual propriety so far as to immobilize women and, on the other, by allowing claims of women's moral influence to obfuscate the need for other sources of power" (175).

The trickster characters on whom I will focus here reject definitions of femininity based on "feeling right" and "passionlessness." Fantasy figures of women's mobility (in contrast to contented stasis in domesticity) and female empowerment (which is not based on woman's moral superiority), they cross the increasingly permeable boundaries between public and private, masculine and feminine, as individual pioneers and explorers going mapless and with limited resources into the unknown and often hostile wilderness of man's sphere. Like the Southwest confidence man Simon Suggs, female tricksters often found that "IT IS GOOD TO BE SHIFTY IN A NEW COUNTRY," the new country of the public sphere. The female tricksters are "shifty" not only because they can profit from exploiting the contradictions of society, but also because covert manipulations are often the only options available for women's survival within the constraints of femininity and domesticity.

Madcap Trickery

Capitola, the heroine of E. D. E. N. Southworth's popular novel *The Hidden Hand, or Capitola the Madcap*, uses femininity as a veil she can wear and remove strategically. As the subtitle informs us, Capitola is a "madcap," a delightfully unconventional figure who interprets and participates in the world around her not according to the dominant ideology but according to her own eccentric individualism. Unlike a madwoman, who, denied her point of view by society, erupts in destructive rage, a madcap is a functional member of society despite her idiosyncratic expression of her individualism. Capitola is neither victim nor passive bystander in the melodramatic action of *The Hidden Hand,* but a fantasy figure who acts in a manner usually available only to male characters. By refusing to acknowledge that the limitations of Victorian femininity apply to her, she rejects sentimentalism and domesticity in favor of asserting her individual will. Rather than learning domestic skills and leaving the world outside the home to men, Capitola playfully roams the countryside, thinking of herself as a "damsel-errant in quest of adventure" (270), a self-definition that calls to mind the "female quixote" popular in early American fiction.

Unlike the ineffectual and foolish romanticism of a female quixote, however, Capitola's desire for heroism and adventure is balanced by the survival skills of a female trickster. As an abandoned orphan in the city, Cap donned boys' clothes so she could survive on the streets, a deception that ended as she matured into womanhood and "forgot" to cut her hair. Because she has been socialized outside the conventions of femininity that teach little girls to be little women, Cap's immediate responses have more in common with those of a wily urban newsboy than a properly feminine young woman. For example, when Capitola's guardian "Old Hurricane" forbids her to go to the fair, she replies "gaily," "sorry it's against your will, but can't help it! not used to being ordered about and don't know how to submit, and so I'm going!" (187). The dismissal of patriarchal authority evident in her response characterizes her behavior as she pursues adventure and circumvents the limitations of femininity with female trickery.

If Ellen Montgomery's achievement of "feeling right" and "passionlessness" serves as a model of Victorian femininity, then Capitola's refusal to submit provides a counterexample of self-development and active participation in the world. My reading of the novel focuses on two tricks that Capitola plays to ensure her own and her friend's survival, scenes that have not received adequate critical attention despite the fact that they are the dramatic highpoints of the novel as well as of the stage version of the novel popular into the twentieth century.[11] In these episodes, Southworth critiques sentimentalism and portrays Cap's trickery as a nondomestic, antisentimental mode of female empowerment. By rejecting the influence strategy of women's power in favor of a fantasy of action that nevertheless depends on the covert tactics of female trickery, Southworth exposes the sex-gender system as a social construction that serves to imprison women.

Capitola employs the first trick to free her sentimental friend Clara from the clutches of the villainous Le Noirs. When Capitola realizes that Clara is a prisoner in the Hidden House awaiting a forced marriage to Craven Le Noir, she invents a plan to get her friend to safety, a scheme that calls for the two women to trade clothes and roles. Dressed as the "madcap," Clara will have safe passage out of the Hidden House; dressed as the sentimental heroine, Capitola will satisfy her yearning for excitement and foil the plans of the nefarious Le Noirs.

Southworth's treatment of this exchange of female identity highlights the difference between the madcap and the conventional heroine. To be a convincing madcap, Clara must not only look but act like her heroic friend. Cap instructs Clara, "Gather your veil down close; draw up your figure, throw back your head; walk with a little springy sway and swagger, as if you didn't care a damson for anybody" (307). Cap's awareness that her comportment signals disdain for "anybody" but herself reinforces the madcap's rejection of the dictates of Victorian femininity—self-sacrifice, fragility, passivity—to which Clara ascribes. Delivered from walking "like a girl" by her childhood impersonation of a boy, Capitola can draw on the range of human—not only feminine—behaviors.

While Clara makes her escape, Cap enacts a parody of "doing the sentimental" by hiding behind her veil and sobbing as if "she was drowned in tears" (308, 312). Cap continues her act until the crucial moment in the wedding ceremony when the bride is asked to affirm her vows and Cap suddenly reveals her true identity. In a delightful speech that illustrates the freedom of the madcap to throw off the garb of conventional femininity,

Cap put her thumb to the side of her nose and whirling her four fingers, replied:
"It means, your worships' excellences, that—you—can't—come it! it's no go! this chicken won't fight! It means confusion! distraction! perdition! and a tearing off of our wigs! It means the game's up, the play's over, villainy is about to be hanged, and virtue about to be rewarded, and the curtain is going to drop, and the principal performer—that's I—is going to be called out amid the applause of the audience!" Then suddenly changing her mocking tone to one of great severity, she said:
"It means that you have been outwitted by a girl; it means that your proposed victim has fled, and is by this time in safety. It means that you two, precious father and son would be a pair of knaves if you had sense enough; but, failing in that, you are only a pair of fools." (316)

The humor of this passage plays on the sudden change from the sentimental heroine who cries too much to be able to speak to the linguistic facility of the madcap as much as it does to the comic dialogue. Further, the speech articulates two important points about the female trickster: Capitola's description of herself as "the principal performer" and the shift from parodic play to seriousness. First, the trickster tactic of impersonation is analogous to acting and performance; this prefigures the links between femininity and the unladylike profession of actress central to Alcott's *Behind a Mask*. Second, when Cap shifts from her "mocking tone to one of great severity," she exposes how thoroughly she has duped the Le Noirs; despite her playfulness, she is aware of the high stakes in this game.[12] Through her ludic behavior, Cap not only saves her friend and humiliates the villains, but also satisfies her desire for adventure.

Moreover, Southworth shows that sentimentalism is *only* useful as a veil to obscure Capitola's rebellious intent. "Doing the sentimental" is a necessary cover, but in and of itself it is not a course of action that can lead to escape and freedom. Conversely, acting like a madcap without the veil of conventional femininity would be similarly useless in a situation like Clara's imprisonment; until Capitola is in the public place of the church, she does not have the opportunity to escape. The two roles represented by Cap and Clara, Southworth suggests, are each appropriate as tactics in a treacherous world rife with domestic imprisonment and involuntary marriage. In *The Hidden Hand*, it is not only "good to be shifty," but necessary for survival.

In another scene, Capitola uses trickery that plays on notions that women are nurturing and passionless. When the outlaw Black Donald appears in her bedroom, intent on capturing, "marrying," and then murdering her, Capitola once again must "act" to survive. Throughout the novel, there has been a mutual fascination between Capitola Black and Black Donald based on their admiration for each other's rebellious trickery;[13] the important difference, of course, is that Black Donald is a criminal employed by the Le Noirs and Capitola remains within the boundaries of lawful society.

Southworth portrays Black Donald as an attractive and erotic figure as well as a mercenary bandit; his personification of contradiction, mastery of disguise and impersonation, and outlaw status mark him as a liminal character who, like Capitola, is a trickster moving "betwixt and between" culturally defined categories. Just as Black Donald's goal is to capture Capitola (because he was hired by the Le Noirs to murder her so she won't inherit the fortune they want for themselves and also because he has fallen in love with her), Capitola "would like the glory of capturing Black Donald . . . by stratagem I mean, not by force" (111).

When Capitola finds Black Donald in her bedroom, she tells herself, "nothing on earth will save you, Cap, but your own wits! . . . Now, Cap, my little man, be a woman! don't you stick at trifles! Think of Jael and Sisera! Think of Judith and Holofernes!" (385). That Southworth alludes to these biblical heroines in Cap's exhortation to "be a woman" is significant: Jael and Judith can both be seen as female tricksters who use deception to kill their enemies (Camp 19; Fontaine 85; Good 126). Jael and Judith encourage Sisera and Holofernes, respectively, to enter their tents and let down their guard. By appearing to proffer food, shelter, and sexual availability, Jael and Judith lull these leaders of enemy forces with their femininity and, when the men do not expect it, kill them: Jael impales Sisera's head with a tent peg, and Judith cuts off Holofernes's head. Both women perform violent acts under the guise of feminine hospitality to further the political and military causes of the Hebrews. These acts are typical of how female trickery is represented in the Bible, which, theologian Carole Fontaine explains, often couples deception "with the motif of sexual exchange, or takes place in contexts where 'Woman the Provider,' associated with food, drink, and shelter, turns deceiver, thereby rendering the familiar nurturing figure suddenly dangerous to unsuspecting males who fall into her 'snares'" (Fontaine 85).

Capitola follows the specifically female mode of trickery described by Fontaine; she enacts the role of woman as "Provider," offering Black Donald bread and cheese, making him eggnog, and scurrying around the room tidying up. She calls him "my hero" to appeal to his ego and convince him of her guilelessness (387). After giving him a look of "humor, mischief and roguery" (386), Capitola claims that earlier she had wanted him to capture her because she "was tired of hum-drum life, and I wanted to see adventures" (387). Here Capitola hints at a transgressive sexual willingness antithetical to "passionlessness." And there *is* a sense in which Cap's confession of her desire for him rings true; she has been attracted to him all along. Moreover, Capitola tells him that what he thought was an attempt to capture him was really an indication of her favor, traditionally the claim made by the rapacious villain of melodrama. By exploiting his obvious attraction to her, Cap lulls him into a false sense of security, pretending to tidy the room as she maneuvers closer to the lever that opens the (conveniently placed) trapdoor in the floor of her room. After failing to convince Black Donald to leave, or even to pray for mercy on his soul, she opens the trapdoor and sends him to what she thinks is his death.

Although Black Donald survives his fall and Capitola helps him escape hanging by bringing his burglar's tools to his jail cell, Southworth stops short of transgressing the line of propriety that separates Capitola Black and Black Donald. Nevertheless, Capitola's ability to outwit and capture the bandit and her willingness to free him align her more with Black Donald than with her fiancé Herbert Greyson. The triple wedding with which the novel concludes (Cap and Herbert, the long-suffering Marah Rocke and Old Hurricane, and the sentimental Clara and Traverse Rocke) does not resolve Capitola's quarrel with conventional femininity. Here, as in other texts featuring female tricksters, narrative closure is not necessarily ideological closure. Black Donald's survival—reminiscent of the disruptive middle of the narrative—undercuts the conventional ending of marriage.

Perhaps the unresolved tensions between madcap freedom and sentimental captivity contributed to the popularity of the work. Readers demanded that *The Hidden Hand* be reprinted three times serially in the *Ledger*; it achieved wide circulation as a bound volume well into the early twentieth century, and was dramatized in over forty versions in America and England (including one in which actor John Wilkes Booth played Black Donald). As Dobson concludes, "In her own comic way, Capitola Black captured the imagination of the American public and, as much as the women's right's activists, she marched in the vanguard of the struggle to destroy old texts for women's lives" ("Hidden Hand" 236). Further, as a madcap, Capitola articulated a model of woman's nature as so rebellious and independent that she could not help but bristle against the limitations of Victorian femininity.

The Con Woman "Behind a Mask" of the Little Woman

In contrast to Capitola's deployment of the veil of femininity in the pursuit of madcap adventure, Jean Muir, the heroine of Louisa May Alcott's thriller *Behind a Mask, or A Woman's Power*, uses femininity to mask the con game she plays in the "love economy" of Romantic conventions of gentility. Jean, an actress by profession, plays the part of a governess to the wealthy Coventry family. By enacting one ideal role in the "love economy"—the ideal submissive and self-sacrificing female servant—Jean entices all the men in the house to fall in love with her. As Judith Fetterley comments, the story "articulates a radical critique of the cultural constructs of 'femininity' and 'little womanhood,' exposing them as roles women must play, masks they must put on, in order to survive" (2). Further, as the subtitle suggests, female power is covert: sexual and emotional manipulation emanating from behind the mask of femininity.

Alcott reveals how this female power is based on women's performance and appearance in the private sphere of domesticity. In her successful masquerade, Jean appears young and sweet, assessing and serving the needs of the family almost magically in the full expression of her good and loving personality. She thus impersonates the opposite of what she really is: a hardened actress for whom every gesture or facial expression is artifice. Off the "stage" of the Coventry home, in the privacy of her room, Jean drops her mask:

When alone Miss Muir's conduct was decidedly peculiar. Her first act was to clench her hands and mutter between her teeth, with passionate force, "I'll not fail again if there is power in a woman's wit and will!" . . .

Still sitting on the floor, she unbound and removed the long abundant braids from her head, wiped the pink from her face, took out several pearly teeth, and slipping off her dress appeared herself indeed, a haggard, worn, and moody woman of thirty at least. The metamorphosis was wonderful, but the disguise was more in the expression she assumed than in any art of costume or false adornment. Now she was alone, and her mobile features settled into their natural expression, weary, hard, bitter. (11–12)

Although the detail of the "several pearly teeth" is a sardonic touch, Alcott points out that Jean's impersonation goes beyond the commodified trappings of femininity to encompass her facial expression and bodily comportment. In other words, Jean's tactics are those of the con artist who, historian Karen Halttunen explains in *Confidence Men and Painted Women*, "could manipulate facial expression, manner, and personal appearance in a calculated effort to lure the guileless into granting them confidence" (xv). In her description of Jean Muir, Alcott closed the gap between the "painted lady" (with its connotations of prostitution) and the covert power of the con woman.

Through her female trickery, Jean successfully transforms herself from the liminal position of governess, "betwixt and between" servant and lady, into Lady Coventry, wife of the elderly uncle of the family. Jean's carefully controlled masquerade results in the satisfaction of her desires, which are primarily economic and social; she wants the wealth, status, and respect of a noblewoman. She does not "fall" at the end of the story, and even sneakily burns the letters in which she explicitly relates her deliberate deceptions and manipulations, destroying the only tangible evidence of her trick. Significantly, Jean succeeds. Alcott's assessment of the cultural demands of femininity includes an understanding that playing the role of the guileless, self-sacrificing, sentimental, and moral "little woman"—a woman's power exercised covertly—is the *only* way to succeed and survive.[14]

Jean exemplifies the female trickster as con woman; significantly, she is not a comic figure nor the heroine of a comic text. *Behind a Mask* is a thriller meant to provide "psychological catharsis" with the subject matter of "wronged women wreaking violent vengeance on evil men," as literary historian David S. Reynolds explains in *Beneath the American Renaissance: The Subversive Imagination in the Age of Emerson and Melville* (408). Although many mid-nineteenth-century plots turned on their heroine's deployment of social masks and roles, it is only in what Reynolds calls the "subversive" genre of the lurid thriller that such manipulations emerge as the activity of a con woman. In more comic works like

Fanny Fern's [Sara Willis Parton's] *Ruth Hall* (1855) and *The Hidden Hand*, the heroines hide behind the mask of a literary pseudonym (Reynolds 406) and the veil of "doing the sentimental," but in the thriller *Behind a Mask*, Alcott can render the darker motivations and implications of impersonations of femininity.[15] Jean's successful transformation of the conventions of gender into a rewarding con game demonstrates how "little woman"-hood can and often must be used to mask women's ambition and power. Alcott's depiction of the Victorian con woman demonstrates the chilling realization that, rather than subverting the "love economy," the con woman ends up ensconced in the very confines of femininity she deplores.

Old Maid to New Woman

In between the cold calculation of the con woman and the irrepressible impulse of the madcap lies a recognition and manipulation of social roles that characterizes the screwball heroine, a twentieth-century manifestation of the female trickster. An example of a prototypical screwball heroine occurs in Mary Wilkins Freeman's chapter in the multiauthored novel *The Whole Family: A Novel by Twelve Authors* (1908). Aunt Elizabeth, considered an "old maid" by her family, is really an independent new woman who refuses to be marginalized as a spinster. But before I discuss Aunt Elizabeth as a female trickster, there is a strange piece of literary history to relate: how Mary Wilkins Freeman pulled off what might be the best act of female trickery in American literature—the subversion of *The Whole Family*.

The novel, as conceived by the influential author and editor William Dean Howells, was to consist of chapters by different *Harper's* magazine authors, each written from the perspective of members of a family. Howells envisioned the novel as a realistic portrayal of the daily life of a family preparing for a wedding, an occasion he perceived as "much more a family affair, and much less a personal affair than Americans usually suppose."[16]

The project that Howells imagined certainly is a fascinating one that raises formal issues about individual and collaborative authorship, narrative subjectivity, seriality, and the centrality of character to plot development, issues that are increasingly important in the development of twentieth-century media such as radio, film, television, and video. The execution of the novel, however, was hardly smooth; in her autobiography, Elizabeth Jordan, who had the unenviable task of soliciting and editing chapters and juggling the idiosyncrasies of often unruly authors, documented a process rife with conflict, not familial harmony. But the logistical problems paled beside the controversy caused by Mary Wilkins Freeman's chapter, "The Old Maid Aunt."

In brief, Freeman hijacked the novel with her characterization of Elizabeth as a new woman, not an old maid. In contrast to the New England spinsters in Freeman's popular short stories, Elizabeth is a vibrant modern woman who plays the role of old maid aunt only to fulfill her family's expectations; she has another life unimagined by her family as Lily, an attractive and flirtatious pleasure-seeker. And if that was not enough, Freeman shattered Howells's vision of the family with the revelation that the groom-to-be was actually madly in love with the aunt. In a funny detail that borders on spite, Freeman gave Elizabeth and the narrator of Howells's chapter a past in which she scorned his affections, causing him to threaten to shoot himself.

The other authors had a range of reactions to the proofs of Freeman's chapter. According to Jordan, it caused "the explosion of a bombshell on our literary hearthstone" (quoted in Bendixen xxiii). Howells pleaded with her not to publish the chapter: "Don't, *don't* let her ruin our beautiful story!" (quoted in Bendixen xxiii). Other authors wrote to Jordan expressing concern about the disruptions Freeman's characters caused. Alice Brown almost quit the "family," mourning the loss of one of Howells's "dear entirely natural families of 'folk' we should all delight living with. . . . But in Mrs. Freeman's chapter I had a facer" (quoted in Bendixen xxiv). Despite the consternation of her coauthors, Freeman succeeded in having her chapter accepted as written. Each author had to take a stance on the question of Aunt Elizabeth's self-appraisal raised in but not answered by Freeman's chapter: is Aunt Elizabeth crazy, a madwoman parading around in a cloud of self-delusion, or a new woman accurately assessing the gap between her own and her family's perception of her social role?

Freeman's subversive trick shifted the novel from the quiet field of literary realism to the contested terrain of societal definitions of femininity, indeed a "facer" that forced the writers to confront representations of older single women. By taking advantage of the autonomy given to the participating authors and changing the old maid into a new woman, Freeman exposed the sexism and willful idealization of the family prevalent in literary realism, which denied complex female subjectivity to women who did not fit societal categories.[17]

On the level of the narrative, Aunt Elizabeth functions as a female trickster who disrupts the wedding preparations, causes strife between the narrator of Howells's chapter and his wife, sends the groom a cryptic telegram that precipitates a series of miscommunications, disappears to New York, prompting family members to search for her, and generally ends up in the center of the narrative instead of on the margins to which she was relegated by Howells's conception of her as an old maid. As critic Dale M. Bauer suggests, Aunt Elizabeth "overthrows the custom of silence, insisting that she have a voice in the family" (112).

In Freeman's chapter, Aunt Elizabeth is a liminal character who self-consciously shifts between different social roles. The chapter begins with Elizabeth's statement, "I am relegated here in Eastridge to the position in which I suppose I properly belong. . . . Here I am the old-maid aunt. Not a day, not an hour, not a minute, when I am with other people, passes that I do not see myself in their estimation playing that role as plainly as if I saw myself in a looking-glass" (30). She considers this clash between her perception of herself and that of her family to be "amusing . . . sort of a joke on other people" (31). She dresses in pink instead of the black silk of an old maid, a costume that causes "quite a commotion, and they all saw me through their eyes of prejudice. . . . If I had been Godiva, going for my sacrificial ride through the town, it could not have been much worse" (45). Elizabeth's inability to be herself within the socially sanctioned roles of femininity prompts her to maintain her sense of humor and interact with the family as a trickster who provides comic pleasure for herself if for no one else.

Like Aunt Elizabeth, the female tricksters in the examples of nineteenth-century fiction by American women I have discussed recognize and exploit the limitations of cultural definitions of femininity, defying expectations that they will conform to social roles in their pursuit of autonomy and satisfaction. From veil to mask to social role, femininity is used as a cover for the exertion of female power. The characters who are comic heroines, such as Capitola and Elizabeth, articulate the madcap and screwball sensibility that facilitates their rejection of societal dictates and the preservation of their unconventional individualism. The cynical, borderline evil con woman Jean Muir impersonates a "little woman" in order to get the rewards of good femininity—the class privilege of a lady—without paying the price of self-sacrifice.

Capitola, Jean, and Aunt Elizabeth prefigure the twentieth-century female tricksters who will be the focus of the rest of this book. Capitola's happy rejection of convention is paradigmatic of the adventurous individualism of madcap heroines; Jean's conflation of economic and erotic motives exemplifies the con woman's exploitation of the sociosexual marketplace of marriage; and Aunt Elizabeth's recognition and playful manipulation of different feminine roles illustrates the screwball heroine's ability to construct tactically appropriate or inappropriate public personas. Jean's economic and erotic trickery shows how woman's ability to fit the type of femininity valorized by a society may be her best asset in the sociosexual marketplace; Aunt Elizabeth's preoccupation with her appearance reinforces the sense that playing feminine roles buys into (so to speak) the equation of women's attractiveness and worth prevalent in the emerging culture of consumption.

In these nineteenth-century texts and the twentieth-century examples they prefigure, the tactics of female trickery are represented as successful and necessary for women's survival; by flouting—and exploiting—social conventions of female behavior and character, these characters articulate the power to hop over, slip through, wiggle under, and splinter the ideological and material fences surrounding woman's sphere, all the while illustrating the usefulness of being "shifty"—flexible as well as tricky—a character trait crucial to survival in the rapidly modernizing culture of twentieth-century America.

Chapter 2
Economics and Erotics
The Female Trickster in the Jazz Age

The woman in Florine Stettheimer's painting *Portrait of Myself* (1923) stares blankly at the viewer with vacant, red-rimmed eyes (Fig. 2.1). Their emptiness is reinforced by the exaggerated red eyelashes, which draw attention away from the center of the unfocused eyes and epitomize this depiction of a feminine public self. Judging from these eyes, there is little behind the feminine form on display. The figure reclines in a position of repose, her lower half covered by elaborate flowers, which contrast with the revealing transparency of the dress. The flowers are rendered in greater detail than the face, which further diverts the viewer's attention. We would expect to be able to glimpse the "self" in the face, but the slightly smiling, accommodating lips only give us another site of surface appearance without revealing an inner self. In this painting, Stettheimer subverts our expectations of seeing a representation of the artist as a subject, presenting instead a portrait of the female artist as object. In contrast to the static figure of the woman, however, is a small mayfly floating airily toward the sun in the upper right-hand corner of the painting; this suggests that the energetic flying soul of the artist cannot be contained in a traditional representation of a woman's body. Stettheimer's biographer claims that "The mayfly was Florine's private *persona*, her *anima*, which she projected in this self-portrait into a dimension of metamorphosis: air's magic mirror where 'society' becomes pure space. The mayfly's identity with her is clearly given by the resemblance between its figure and the swirling, slender calligraphy of her white signature across the painting's top" (Tyler 41). Stettheimer confounds our viewerly expectations by locating her self in her signature and in the mayfly, not in the lackluster female figure on display as an object, even in a woman artist's self-portrait.

That Stettheimer chose not to invest the figure of her body with energy, movement, and life (yet did include those aspects of her self-

Figure 2.1. In Florine Stettheimer's painting *Portrait of Myself* (1923), modern feminine consciousness is split between the passive object at the center and the active subject of the mayfly in the upper right-hand corner. Oil on canvas. Gift of the Estate of Ettie Stettheimer, 1967. Courtesy Columbia University.

representation in other parts of the painting) illustrates the unbreachable split between women's experience as the "surveyed" and as the "surveyor," to use John Berger's terms (cf. Berger et al. 46–47). If, as Berger contends, women's self-surveillance means that "she turns herself into an object—and most particularly an object of vision: a sight" (Berger et al. 47), then a female artist's self-portrait is indeed a vexed enterprise. Stettheimer's solution to the problem of female self-representation—rendering the female body as passive object of display and locating the active, surveying self elsewhere—illustrates what literary critics Sandra M. Gilbert and Susan Gubar call "female female impersonation," a strategy that empowered modern women poets such as Edna St. Vincent Millay and Marianne Moore "to move from what was in the nineteenth century an aesthetic of renunciation underlying women's poetry to a twentieth-century aesthetic of self-dramatization" (*No Man's Land* 3:111). Using their consciousness of the "masquerade" of femininity to deliberately construct what I am terming a feminine public self, women deployed costume, makeup, behavior, and comportment to create a mask from behind which to negotiate the public sphere.[1] Because it is a construction and not the "true" or complete self (whatever that might be), women can dissociate themselves from the feminine public self that is surveyed, judged, discriminated against. The viewer looking at the "portrait" of Florine Stettheimer will find nothing but an image staring back blankly; in contrast, the mayfly, unconcerned with the viewer, gravitates toward the brilliance of the sun. The tactic of the private self operating in the pursuit of her desires while the public self impersonates an appropriate spectacle of femininity is indicative of the strategy of the female trickster in the 1920s. The issue of specularity—of what is seen and what is hidden—is at the center of Jazz Age discourses of femininity.

Even more explicitly than in her self-portrait, Florine Stettheimer articulated the modern woman's experience of the split between object and subject, surveyed and surveyor, in her poem "Occasionally":

OCCASIONALLY
A human being
Saw my light
Rushed in
Got singed
Got scared
Rushed out
Called fire
Or it happened
That he tried

To subdue it
Or it happened
He tried to extinguish it
Never did a friend
Enjoy it
The way it was
So I learned to
Turn it low
Turn it out
When I meet a stranger —
Out of courtesy
I turn on a soft
Pink light
Which is found modest
Even charming
It is a protection
Against wear
And tears
And when
I am rid of
The Always-to-be-Stranger
I turn on my light
And become myself
        (*Crystal Flowers* 42)

The speaker in Stettheimer's poem responds to external judgment by retreating behind an acceptably "soft" and feminine public self, and relegating her full self to private isolation. Hiding her "light" is a necessary trick because the "stranger," the surveyor to whom she defers, either is hurt by her strength or, worse, tries to hurt her. Because the speaker wants the company of the "Always-to-be-Stranger," she both accommodates him and protects herself by turning on the "soft / Pink light" of femininity.

The word "courtesy," with its implications of societal propriety and deference to the needs of others, is particularly ironic here as the motivation for subjugating the strength and brilliance of her "light" and indicates the depth of accommodation implicit in female female impersonation: instead of trying to transform society by refusing to turn on the soft pink light of femininity—as, for example, Emma Goldman did—the female female impersonator does not challenge the accepted ideology of gender except in a private, tricky way. Female female impersonation is more a strategy of individual survival than of social transformation; in fact, like so many of the tactics of female trickery, which exercise power covertly, it only serves the individual who practices it.

In this poem, Stettheimer suggests that there is no place for women's undiminished artistic and individualistic light in the public sphere. Not surprisingly, the speaker takes refuge in the most private of spheres, the self in isolation, and thus participates in the tradition of women hiding the "light" of their selves and their art, playing "the angel of the house" out of fear and unwillingness to be perceived and treated as a monster. By playing on the traditional and modern connotations of candlelight (which can be snuffed out) and electric light (which can be turned on and manipulated through the filter of a pink light bulb), Stettheimer extends the nineteenth-century trope of being imprisoned, albeit in a prison of her own making, to encompass the twentieth-century consciousness of the artifice of public presentation, limited not by woman's sphere but by female female impersonation. If femininity is the armor women must wear in order to withstand the public (surveying, judging, restricting) eye, at least the artist Stettheimer can allow her light to shine and, in the image of the mayfly if not as the body of a woman, fly spritely toward the even more brilliant sun.[2]

Popular culture texts, such as the advertisements, novels, and films discussed in the rest of this chapter, also addressed these issues of specularity, subjectivity, and oneness. Look, for example, at a 1927 Winx mascara advertisement with the slogan "Make Your *Eyes* Irresistible!" (Fig. 2.2). The image of the woman echoes Stettheimer's self-portrait. We can see a similar tilt of the head, an equally vacant stare, pursed lipsticked lips, exaggerated lashes around large eyes. The copy reads, "More than any other feature, eyes that *speak* create charm and wonder." Unlike Stettheimer's painting, where the mayfly offers an alternate locus of subjectivity and agency that contradicts the passivity of the woman's face and body, the advertisement equates blankness with "irresistible loveliness." Instead of representing the split, the ad only shows the woman as object, and redefines the passivity and silence in the woman's face as an active expression of "irresistibility." The ad tries to capitalize upon and channel the discomfort and repression of living as the surveyed into the desire to buy a product that will make eyes "speak"—a powerful metaphor in the era of silent film. Like the "Danger—woman at work" swimsuit ad (analyzed in the Introduction), this ad shows the cultural work that advertising attempted to do in representations that obscure social realities by creating and playing upon public fantasies.[3] You, the ad implies, can have the enormous power of "irresistibility" if you augment your appearance in certain ways. The ad addresses what theorist Jürgen Habermas has termed a "legitimation crisis"—consumer con-

Make your *Eyes*
IRRESISTIBLE!

The appeal of *eyes* is Beauty's ace-of-hearts. More than any other feature, eyes that *speak* create charm and wonder. And it is the effect of long, luxuriant lashes that heightens the play of lights and shadows in the eyes and gives them that irresistible loveliness.

Winx will impart to your eyes this fascinating beauty, in this simple way: Just darken your lashes with this waterproof liquid. At once your lashes appear longer and thicker and your eyes become strikingly appealing in every glance. Easily applied with the brush attached to the stopper of the bottle, Winx dries instantly and will not rub or smear—and it is harmless. At drug or department stores or by mail. *Black or brown* 75c. U.S. or Canada.

OFFER! *Mail 12c. for a generous sample of Winx. Another 12c. brings a sample of Pert, the waterproof Rouge.*

ROSS COMPANY
240-B West 17th St.
New York

Figure 2.2. Compare the eyes in this advertisement with those in Stettheimer's *Portrait of Myself* (Figure 2.1). If these are "eyes that *speak*," what are they saying? How might Stettheimer's self-portrait comment on images in popular culture? *Cosmopolitan*, February 1927.

sciousness is predicated upon people defining themselves as consumers, not as members of families, communities, or society, except as those social units are defined in relation to consumption. In the example I am exploring here, the contradictions, discomfort, and self-repression created by women's self-surveillance results in a need for images and discourses that assure people that consumption is a legitimate, modern, good way of living. Where Stettheimer's painting and poem probe the split, the Winx ad offers the power of "irresistibility"—priced at seventy-five cents—as compensation and legitimation for the problems in self-definition reinforced by the art and copy of the ad.

Another Stettheimer painting represents the centrality of women's acquisitive zeal in modern culture. *Spring Sale* (1922), which shows many women actively participating in the public sphere of mass consumption, is anchored by the same rich reds, pinks, and golds as *Portrait of Myself,* but here the human figures are kinetic (Fig. 2.3). Their curving bodies lunge for the items of fashion, stand back to admire the fabric; their gazes are riveted upon the clothes or linger critically on their images in the many mirrors. The composition of the painting is balanced, with activity in each corner.

In *Spring Sale,* the focus is as much on the public persona and the trappings of female trickery as *Portrait of Myself* and "Occasionally" are about the private self and the feelings that prompt female trickery. Taken together, Stettheimer's poetic and artistic strategies exemplify the pervasiveness of female trickery in emerging cultural definitions of femininity in the Jazz Age.

The "Acquisitive" Intelligence of Lorelei Lee

Lorelei Lee, the female trickster whose "diary" entries comprise Anita Loos's comic novel *Gentlemen Prefer Blondes* (1925), recasts the feminine cover of the "soft pink light" as the "pink negligay" she wears to trick Sir Francis Beekman, or Piggie as she calls him, into buying her a diamond tiara. For Lorelei, whose only desires are material, turning on the pink light of femininity means turning Piggie on sexually with her blend of sexual allure and innocence. Despite her ignorance (she is, after all, the quintessential "dumb blonde"), she is fully cognizant of the social capital of her appearance and of the tricks she can pull off because of the emphasis "gentlemen" place on it. She is a modern day "Lorelei," the mythic German siren who lured sailors to their deaths by combing her beautiful hair. To illustrate, here is Lorelei's diary entry for April 20: "Yesterday afternoon I really thought I ought to begin to educate Piggie how to act with a girl like American gentlemen act with a girl. So I asked him to come up to have tea in our sitting room in the hotel because I

Figure 2.3. Kinetic movement in mass consumer culture in Stettheimer's *Spring Sale* (1922). Contrast this painting's representation of the zeal for fashion and consumption with the tension between activity and passivity in the previous two illustrations. Oil on canvas. Gift of Miss Ettie Stettheimer. Courtesy Philadelphia Museum of Art.

had quite a headache. I mean I really look quite cute in my pink negligay [*sic*]" (80). Welcome to the world of Lorelei Lee, consummate Jazz Age female trickster. The manipulation, deception, and self-objectification in this passage typify her modus operandi of the cons she plays on the egocentric dupes she terms "gentlemen." That the seductive costume Lorelei chooses is pink is significant because it shows her exploitation of cultural cues of femininity; as Lorelei explains in *But Gentlemen Marry Brunettes*, Loos's 1927 sequel, "red may make gentlemen look, but nothing holds their interest like pink and blue" (317). Loos's clever rendering of the blonde's inner thought process reveals the deception that Lorelei practices regularly. She doesn't "really" have a headache; the next sentence beginning with "I mean" tells us that what she "really" wants is to have Piggie see her provocatively dressed in her "cute" attire. Her lie enables her to lure Piggie into the private sphere of her hotel suite, where, cloaked by the blend of femininity and sexual promise conveyed by the "pink negligay," she can "educate" him so that, like American gentlemen, he will spend money on her.

Briefly, the plot of *Gentlemen Prefer Blondes* follows Lorelei and her brunette friend Dorothy on a trip through Europe (paid for by Mr. Eisman) and back to New York, where Lorelei marries Henry Spoffard and begins a career in the movies. In Lorelei, Loos gave voice to the ideal female consumer, whose acquisitive ethic is summarized in the line "[a man] kissing your hand may make you feel very very good but a diamond and safire [*sic*] bracelet lasts forever" (100). All Lorelei's energy is focused on the attainable goal of embellishing her public self so her appearance will indicate her "value." Nothing else—not sex, love, talent, fun—is as pleasurable as satisfying her gem-lust, which conflates economic exchange with erotic desire. As she confides to her diary, "I mean I always seem to think that when a girl really enjoys being with a gentleman, it puts her to quite a disadvantage and no real good can come of it" (77). The only "real good" for Lorelei is the material good.

In effect, by constructing a feminine public self that is literally covered in the gleam and sparkle of expensive jewelry, Lorelei makes herself into the most conspicuous physical symbol of wealth and luxury—the diamond. As an influential 1920s advertising industry tactician explained, an ad for pearls that showed a woman fondling a breast-length necklace worked because the pearls "center attention on those parts of the feminine body which they encircle and touch," and thus the ad "ingeniously compares women with these precious adornments, attributing to the former the qualities possessed by the latter" (quoted in Ewen 180). Ads like one for Traub rings explain that jewelry is seen as an indicator of the wearer's status: "You notice other women's rings . . . other women will notice yours. By the smartness, beauty, and correctness of engagement and wedding rings, the taste of the viewer is judged."

Lorelei's gem-lust is an internalization of the Jazz Age equation of female beauty—and worth—and expensive commodities, as well as a desire for increased hedonic power. Because Lorelei is an economic vampire, producing nothing herself yet profiting by siphoning off the surplus accrued by rich gentlemen, she is indeed the embodiment of female consumption, spending all the money the male earns. Her self-transformation into a luxury item represents "the separation of the ideological world of women (consumption) from that of men (production)" (Ewen 173), and thus reflects the perpetuation of separate spheres for men and women in the emerging mass consumer society.[4]

An example of the conflation of the economic and the erotic is a diary entry from the first chapter of the novel (the original story published in *Harper's*), which demonstrates how Lorelei uses the covert tactic of withholding affection and sex to motivate Mr. Eisman, her principal benefactor, into satisfying her gem-lust:

Well, my birthday has come and gone but it was really quite depressing. I mean it seems to me a gentleman who has a friendly interest in educating a girl, like Gus Eisman, would want her to have the biggest square cut diamond in New York. I mean I must say I was quite disappointed when he came to the apartment with a little thing you could hardly see. So I told him it was quite cute, but I had quite a headache and I had better stay in a dark room all day and I told him I would see him the next day, perhaps. . . . But he came in at dinner time with really a very very beautiful bracelet of square cut diamonds so I was quite cheered up. (18–19)

This passage, like the one quoted earlier, shows Lorelei's almost monomaniacal focus on precious stones and the manipulative tactic of withdrawing favor she uses to entice men into fulfilling her never-ending acquisitive zeal. Even though she participates in the cover story of Mr. Eisman's "friendly interest" in "educating" her, the bottom line is the size of the rock.

To convey the artifice with which Lorelei operates, Loos cleverly places Lorelei in the tradition of first-person vernacular narrators of American literary humor, whose linguistic quirks often reveal more to the reader than the narrator is aware. This gap between what Lorelei sees and understands and what the reader sees and understands is at the root of the novel's irony.[5] Loos continually reinforces the gap between the reader and Lorelei through Lorelei's euphemistic lexicon. Lorelei practices a linguistic trickery that the reader recognizes as duplicitous at the same time that she enacts social trickery that her gentlemen dupes do not see through.

Loos invests words such as "gentlemen," "refined," "friendly," and "educate" with layers of ironic meaning, so that over the course of the novel they constitute a euphemistic code from behind which emerges the true economic nature of the social relations of the sexes that Loos satirizes. Because Lorelei likes to think of herself as "refined," she casts the various men in her life in the role of "gentleman" so they can bestow upon her the class privilege and status of being a "lady." Of course, Loos's irony undercuts Lorelei's version of events and makes it clear to the reader that Mr. Eisman, the "Button King," and the other men who keep her are not gentlemen, and that she is a "kept woman," not a lady. Loos makes sure that the reader sees the inaccuracy of Lorelei's subjective (and limited) perspective; Lorelei's language reveals more than she understands.

In her instinctive if unreflexive manner, Lorelei refuses to read the gentlemen's sexual subtext. Instead, she takes what they say at face value and converts their duplicity into a base from which to redefine relationships to better suit her material wants. At some level, of course, she realizes that there is a game of trickery being played and does use this to her advantage, but her diary entries keep her consciousness on the most superficial of levels and her trickery on the level of getting the goods, not on the sexual level of the men's desires. Here, Loos plays out her satire on the terrain of women's intelligence; as Loos wrote in a later (1953) Lorelei Lee sketch, men want women "to provide an indication of brains as an alibi for enjoying our company" ("But Dr. Kinsey, What About Romance," *Fate Keeps on Happening* 36). In *Gentlemen Prefer Blondes*, Loos makes the same point more subtly when Lorelei explains that Mr. Eisman, who "spends quite a lot of money educating a girl" (15), "always has something quite interesting to talk about, as for instants [*sic*] the last time he was here he presented me with quite a beautiful emerald bracelet" (16). Here Loos uses Lorelei's lack of self-consciousness to show that despite discussing her relationships with men in terms of education, intellectual conversation, and literariness, money and commodities are really the foundation of these relationships.

Loos's satire resonated among other 1920s discourses that sought to shape Americans into eager participants in the emerging mass consumer culture. Loos uses the word "educate" in the same way as Edward Filene, the businessman with the international reputation as "the mouthpiece of industrial America" (Ewen 54). Filene espoused a form of education that would teach the masses a thought paradigm that "limited the concept of social change and betterment to those commodified answers rolling off American conveyor belts" (Ewen 54). Lorelei's gentlemen provide an education limited to encouraging Lorelei to refine herself as a commodity for their pleasure and status, not for her own independent betterment. Because she has internalized the values of consumerism so completely (in her limited intellectual fashion), she is assured of satisfying her material wants; because of the sociosexual market in which she pursues the objects of her desire, she finds it most profitable to practice female trickery.

In order to understand the centrality of female trickery in *Gentlemen Prefer Blondes*, we must return to Lorelei, whom we left standing in her hotel suite in her "pink negligay," deliberately poised as the object of Piggie's fascinated gaze. In what is the most telling use of "educate" in the novel, Lorelei decides that "it would be nice for an American girl like I to educate an English gentleman like Piggie" (75). And so she embarks on a plan to trick Piggie into buying her the $7,500 diamond tiara, which she wants "because it is a place where I really never thought of wearing diamonds before" (68). When Lorelei writes "educate," she really means *trick*; for example, when she begins to "educate Piggie how to act with a girl like American gentlemen act with a girl," she pays the bellhop to bring a dozen orchids when Piggie is in her hotel room. When they arrive, she hugs Piggie in thanks, and despite his protestations that he did not send the expensive flowers, she continues to thank and hug him. She performs the age-old act of buttressing and massaging the male ego, pointing out that he is the only generous and sweet gentleman in London who would send her a dozen orchids every day and that she would have to give him another big hug. Loos explicitly renders the tactics of flattery and sexual promise that Lorelei uses to trick Piggie: "So Piggie blushed quite a lot and he was really very very pleased and he did not say any more that it was not him. So then I started to make quite a fuss over him and I told him he would have to look out because he was so good-looking and I was so full of impulses that I might even lose my mind and give him a kiss" (82). This successful trick, of course, is only a prelude to her real objective: the diamond tiara. She reasons, "by the time Piggie pays for a few dozen orchids, the diamond tiara will really seem like quite a bargain" (83).

Lorelei continues to use the tactics of trickery—deception, disguise, theft, and impersonation—to acquire the tiara. She "educates" Piggie into paying for the tiara with more flattery and "hugs," telling him she "only felt fit to be with him in a diamond tiara" (86). As she confides to her diary, she and Dorothy are planning to leave London for Paris, diamond tiara in hand, but she tells Piggie the opposite. In true con-artist fashion, Lorelei has tricked him by playing on his weaknesses and vanity. In Ralph Barton's witty illustrations as well as in the writing, Piggie is a ludicrous figure, all puffed up in his uniform, believing he has captured Lorelei's affection. He has made a fool of himself over her, while she has been playing him for all he's worth—about $7,500.

Lorelei further shows her "acquisitive intelligence" as the saga of the tiara continues in Paris.[6] Her next dupes are "Louie and Robber," the two French men Piggie's wife hires to distract Lorelei and Dorothy and thus create an opportunity to steal the tiara. When the women figure out their plan, Lorelei's startling cleverness at swindling men (and, in this case, Lady Beekman) leads her to substitute a paste tiara for the real one, all the while spending Lady Beekman's money. Each of the men offers Dorothy money for stealing the tiara and not telling the other man, but after she does sell the paste tiara to Robber, Lorelei "really got to thinking that an imitation of a diamond tiara was quite a good thing to have after all," and pinches it from Robber's pocket. When the men realize the tiara is gone, Lorelei sympathizes with them and together they get another paste imitation made, charge it to Lady Beekman, and everyone is satisfied.

In this episode, then, Loos pushes Lorelei beyond the sociosexual market of her gentlemen into a classic con game, complete with the substitution of an imitation for the real thing, a trope that spotlights the role of artifice in obscuring the differences between appearance and reality. Lorelei not only holds her own against two professional con men, but teams up with them to spite Lady Beekman and emerges with one fake and one real diamond tiara. Lorelei baits Louie and Robber into spending money with the object of their desire—the tiara—the same way she baits the gentlemen with her insincere promises that they will be able to acquire her:

So then I would leave the imitation of the diamond tiara lying around, so Louie and Robber could see how careless I seem to be with it so then they would get full of encouradgement [sic]. So when we go out with Louie and Robber I could put it in my hand bag and I could take it with me so Louie and Robber could always feel that the diamond tiara was within reach. So then Dorothy and I could get them to go shopping and we could spend quite a lot and every time they seemed to get discouradged [sic], I could open my hand and let them get a glimpse of the imitation of a diamond tiara and they would become more encouradged [sic] and then they would spend some more money. Because I even might let them steal it at the last . . . I mean it would be quite amusing for them to steal it for Lady Francis Beekman and she would have to pay them quite a lot and then she would find out it was only made out of paste after all. (115)

This episode marks a shift in Loos's representation of her heroine: Loos makes explicit Lorelei's pleasure in her carefully planned trickery. By describing Lorelei's self-conscious artifice and implying Lorelei's conflation of herself and the material goods, Loos downplays Lorelei as a "dumb blonde" and foregrounds her material savvy, her "acquisitive" intelligence.[7] The last section of the novel shifts the representation of Lorelei once more to foreground her mastery of female female impersonation.

In her alternating pursuit of and withdrawal from the rich Henry Spoffard Jr., Lorelei changes her feminine public self from a diamond-covered flapper to a marriageable "old fashioned girl" (139)—and back again—several times. When she meets Henry on the train (en route to meet with Mr. Eisman in "the Central of Europe"), she accurately sees him as susceptible to conventional, conservative ideals of femininity and immediately impersonates his ideal. She tells him "I always seem to think that a penny earned was a penny saved" to indicate her values (137), shifting her definition of "refined" from materialism to the morality she senses is so important to Henry. In order to explain what "such an old fashioned girl as I was doing with such a girl as Dorothy," she informs Henry that she is "reforming" her (139–40). And, most telling of all, she charms his mother in a "tatatate" by mirroring her disapproval of "flappers." Being a consummate female female impersonator, Lorelei dresses the part in "a simple little organdy gown that I had ripped all the trimming off of" and shoes without heels (163–64); his mother deems her "the most sunshine that she ever had in all her life" (166). Meanwhile, Lorelei (who has been juggling Henry and Mr. Eisman by spending days with the former and nights with the latter and getting no sleep at all) convinces Mr. Eisman to take her away from Vienna so Henry will have to propose marriage in a letter, which she plans to use as evidence in a breach of promise suit if (when) he breaks off their engagement. So, although Henry is not the type to spend money lavishly and participate in mass consumer culture, she intends to get something—money—from him, and perhaps she will decide to marry him. By impersonating an "old fashioned girl," she secures a written proposal that she can cash in, one way or the other.

Although Lorelei certainly measures her self-worth in terms of diamonds and other commodities, she is interested in more than self-esteem; she makes decisions based on preserving her autonomy and reducing boredom (by ensuring that her "brains" are stimulated). For example, when she contemplates marriage to movie censor Henry Spoffard, she fears that because Henry does not work, he will be "always on the verge of coming in and out of the house. And a girl could not really say that her time was her own" (170). Because the boring Henry and his eccentric family members will intrude on her autonomy, she decides to get out of the engagement by having Dorothy tell Henry all about her exorbitant shopping habits. But just as Dorothy is delighting in chasing away Henry for her friend, Lorelei—who has been spending time with Mr. Montrose, a screenwriter who wants her to star in his movie about Bulgaria—"suddenly decided that if I married Henry and worked in the motion pictures at the same time, society life with Henry would not really be so bad. Because if a girl was so busy as all that, it really would not seem to matter so much if she had to stand Henry when she was not busy" (206). Even her explanation to him of Dorothy's "lies" about her shopping—a test of his love for her—reinforces the image she has created for herself to fit Henry's Victorian ideal of the blonde: an old-fashioned, selfless, socially conscious woman who "is nothing but sunshine" (196).

By the end of *Gentlemen Prefer Blondes*, Lorelei parlays her female female impersonation into both marriage and a career as an actress in the movies. Although Dorothy articulates doubts about Lorelei's acting ability (Lorelei would be successful if someone wrote her "a part that only had three expressions, Joy, Sorrow, and Indigestion" [214]), Lorelei has been acting with her gentlemen all along, feigning interest in them, impersonating their particular ideal of a woman, while calculating what she could acquire before disappearing. As an actress, Lorelei could continue to be admired for her cuteness and continue to surround herself with money, glamour, and activity. She could avoid the mundane realm of the domestic and the private and remain in the public sphere, able to meet new men (an activity she does not intend to give up for marriage).

Lorelei's simultaneous entrance into the movies and marriage is the ironic finale of the novel. Indeed, the film industry in the mid-twenties was a contested terrain in which competing images of feminine public selves articulated women's negotiation between private and public senses of self. For Lorelei, the embodiment of self-commodification, becoming a film image is the ultimate step in capitalizing on her masquerade of femininity by extending it further into the public sphere; getting married represents Lorelei's selling of herself as a commodity. As Loos makes clear, female female impersonation and trickster tactics are necessary to both.

The heroine type that Lorelei portrays in the movies is the Lillian Gish sweetheart, as good inside as she is blonde and demure on the outside. Of course, the sentimental heroine is also the role she plays to secure marriage to Henry Spoffard. But in 1925, the primacy of the sentimental heroine in film was already challenged by the screen image of the flapper, the pleasure-seeking, independent modern woman of mass consumer culture. *Gentlemen Prefer Blondes* ends on an ironic note: its heroine finds success impersonating the antithesis of her modern acquisitive nature in a medium that screenwriter Loos knew very well to be based on artifice and public personas.

Discourses of Blondeness and Beauty

The ending of *Gentlemen Prefer Blondes* calls attention to "the blonde" as a type: instead of being an adjective, it is a noun. The meaning of the cultural sign "blonde" shifted radically from the Victorian-sentimental notion of goodness to a consumer-hedonist symbol of gold. In a 1936 scholarly article coyly titled "Puritans Preferred Blondes," Frederick I. Carpenter claims that 1840 is when darkness and blondeness "come to connote distinct types of character" (quoted in Fryer, *Faces of Eve* 85). Like other writers of the American Renaissance such as Nathaniel Hawthorne and Herman Melville, Harriet Beecher Stowe used blondeness as a sign of goodness. In her sentimental tour de force, *Uncle Tom's Cabin* (1852), a novel that inspired a cultural phenomenon that redefined what it meant for a text to be popular for its era in a way parallel to that of *Gentlemen Prefer Blondes* in the Jazz Age and *I Love Lucy* in the 1950s, the evil Simon Legree is tormented psychologically by locks of hair from Eva and his mother, the two good blondes whose sentimental power lives on in their curls after their deaths. When Legree confiscates Tom's possessions, he finds a curl of Eva's hair (which she lovingly doled out to her friends before she died), "a long, shining curl of fair hair—hair, which like a living thing, twined itself around Legree's fingers" (369). Eva's curl, and the chilling effect it has on Legree, has precedent in a similarly blonde lock of his mother's hair that accompanies a letter:

> He opened it, and a lock of long, curling hair fell from it, and twined about his fingers. The letter told him his mother was dead, and that dying, she blest and forgave him. . . . Legree burned the hair, and burned the letter, and when he saw them hissing and crackling in the flame, inly shuddered as he thought of everlasting fires . . . often, in the deep night . . . he had seen that pale mother rising by his bedside, and felt the soft twining of that hair around his fingers, till the cold sweat would roll down his face, and he would spring from his bed in horror. (370)

For Legree, these curls of blonde hair reach beyond death with a menacing, wrathful key to his unconscious. Although the powers ascribed to blondeness by Stowe and Loos are radically different, they each occupy the same kind of place in the cultural mythos. In Stowe's religious-sentimental world view, the horror inspired by blonde goodness in the hands of an evil man is a metaphor of a fantasy of female power as moral influence; in Loos's ironic perspective on modern commodified culture, the malleability that Lorelei's blondeness causes in her gentlemen is also a fantasy of female power. As Loos concludes in her comic introduction to a reprint of *Gentlemen Prefer Blondes*, "The Biography of a Book" (1979), the men in her social group were eager to perform gallantries for a blonde, while they ignored her: "Obviously there was some radical difference between that girl and me. But what was it? We were both in the pristine years of early youth; we were about the same degree of comeliness; as to our mental acumen, there was nothing to discuss: I was the smarter. Then why did that girl so far outdistance me in feminine allure? Could her strength possibly be rooted (like that of Samson) in her hair? She was a natural blonde and I was a brunette" (*Fate* 53–54). Of course, this "important scientific fact" that gentlemen prefer blondes is couched in our understanding that the appeal stems as much from the blonde's lack of intelligence as from her appearance. Nevertheless, Loos—like Stowe—reinscribes blondeness as the physical attribute that best expresses the feminine ideal of her time. As an example of how cultural values are contained, transmitted, and transformed in visual images, the change from "blonde=good" to "blonde=gold" articulates the many facets of the shift from Victorian sentimentalism to modern consumerism (good=gold).

How did blonde move from signifying angelic morality and sexual purity to material desire and the lure of sexuality? Historian Lois Banner asserts that blonde hair eclipsed dark hair as the preferred color in the late 1860s.[8] "Earlier in the [nineteenth] century dark hair had been popular partly because blonde hair, according to the theory of the physiognomists, indicated an uninteresting personality. But once the new trends towards open sensual expression began to permeate the transatlantic world [c. 1870], blonde hair was seen in a different way. Its old associations with innocence now became both a way of legitimizing the new sensuality and of heightening it by combining both purity and voluptuousness" (Banner 124). Tinting hair brown had been socially acceptable since the early decades of the nineteenth century; copy in a 1843 ad announced, "Unrivalled Circassian Hair Dye for changing Light, Red or Grey Hair to a beautiful Brown or Black."

Actresses and performers were the first to peroxide their hair blonde. Banner locates the origin of the fashion in the influence of the Lydia Thompson burlesque-style dance troupe, known as the British Blondes, who toured the United States from 1869 to the turn of the century.[9] The association of blondeness with burlesque explains the centrality of sexuality to the image of the blonde and suggests why blondeness and stupidity came to be so tightly linked. Of course, the advent of the blonde in popular culture never completely overshadowed the connection of dark hair with sexuality; rather, it gave the old dark/light dichotomy a new twist as the blonde sex goddess represented a kind of sexuality that was distinctly Anglo-Saxon and eventually distinctly American and the dark-haired voluptuous woman evolved into the exotic vamp embodied by actresses such as Theda Bara. Darkness seemed to imply inherent sexuality, whereas blondeness implied the more superficial sexual allure of the gold digger and the showgirl, whose real motives are economic and not erotic.

Perhaps, blondeness is the ideal physical attribute for mass consumer culture because it can be commodified. In the context of the emerging commodity culture of the early twentieth century, blondeness no longer signifies moral and/or racial purity, but a consumer choice. Given the availability of peroxide bleach and the widespread cultural acceptance of cosmetically altering one's appearance by the turn of the century, anyone could be a blonde if she desired and dared. The hair-color sector of the beauty industry, with its emphasis on how easily the artificial can appear natural, promoted female trickery as the social practice of femininity in everyday life. But, like other aspects of the beauty myth, bleaching blonde has its dangers. Jean Harlow's platinum blonde hair was so popular—and so hazardous to achieve—that *Photoplay* published an article entitled "Don't Go Platinum Yet! Read before You Dye!" in November 1931 that detailed the long, expensive, and often dangerous procedure. Despite such a warning, changing hair color based on images and styles from the movies became one of the cornerstones of the commodified beauty culture.

Racial Implications and Intrafeminine Fascinations

The qualities attached to darkness and lightness have racial implications, especially in the Harlem-fascinated Jazz Age. Despite the fascination with the "exotic primitive" that whites projected onto Harlem's inhabitants, standards of beauty were codified as white. In the context of race and beauty, the belief that gentlemen prefer blondes sets up a sinister rubric that, as represented in Nella Larsen's novel *Passing* (1929), leads to self-hatred, jealousy, and murder. Unlike the complementary friendship of Loos's Lorelei and Dorothy, the relationship between Irene and Clare, *Passing*'s dual protagonists, is one of mistrust, envy, and an idealization of the other woman that inflects their self-definitions. Both women are light-skinned enough to "pass" as white, but Clare has gone over the color line to live as a white woman in a marriage to a racist, and Irene is part of the black upper-middle professional class in Harlem. Irene passes only occasionally, to gain access to a segregated restaurant like the one where she bumps into her childhood friend Clare after many years.

The narrative in *Passing* is acutely aware of the split in feminine consciousness between the surveyor and the surveyed, and Irene's fault-finding self-surveillance bleeds into her critical assessment of Clare, who Irene thinks is the woman that gentlemen, including her husband, prefer. In the novel, Irene and Clare engage in an intrafeminine fascination like the ones popular culture scholar Jackie Stacey finds between the double heroines in the films *All About Eve* and *Desperately Seeking Susan*. Like the female spectator of the films, the novel's reader is "invited to look at or gaze with one female character at another, in an interchange of feminine fascinations. This fascination is neither purely identification with the other woman, nor desire for her in the strictly erotic sense of the word. It is a desire to see, to know and to become more like an idealized feminine other, in a context where the difference between the two women is repeatedly re-established" (115). Throughout the novel, Irene looks at Clare with the judging gaze that beauty industry ads threatened, and, at the end of their first meeting, finds her to still have the same insolence.

> Just as she'd always had that pale gold hair, which unsheared still, was drawn loosely back from a broad brow, partly hidden by the small close hat. Her lips, painted a brilliant geranium red, were sweet and sensitive and a little obstinate. A tempting mouth. The face across the forehead and cheeks was a trifle too wide, but the ivory skin had a peculiar soft lustre. And the eyes were magnificent! Dark, sometimes absolutely black, always luminous, and set in long, black lashes. Arresting eyes, slow and mesmeric, and with, for all their warmth, something withdrawn and secret about them.
> Ah! Surely! They were Negro eyes! Mysterious and concealing. And set in that ivory face under that bright hair, there was about them something exotic. (161)

The complexion and hair of the blonde, the eyes of the "exotic" Negro: Larsen has created a character whose beauty takes on mythic proportions in the racial fascinations of the age of the film close-up and the cosmetics ad. The hedonic power ascribed to Clare's eyes is similar to an ad for Maybelline "eyelash beautifier": "Let your eyes speak the full measure of their beauty. . . . What a world of meaning the eyes can express—but not with light, scanty eyelashes!" (*Cosmopolitan*, June 1932, 152). Clare's eyes "speak" her hidden blackness in the context of her visible whiteness.

Significantly, the speech that Larsen describes in Clare's eyes is because she embodies the paradox of black and white, of being "betwixt and between." Carefully watching the movements of Clare's body, face, and especially eyes, Irene feels increasingly worse about herself in contrast to Clare's "vivid beauty" and her "trick of sliding down ivory lids over astonishing black eyes and then lifting them suddenly and turning on a caressing smile" (221). Larsen's description of Clare's "trick" reveals the racial boundary Clare's *appearance* crosses again and again: black masked by white, white pulling back to reveal black, always accompanied by "turning on" what Stettheimer called "the soft pink light" of the feminine smile. But, as I argued in the Introduction, the heroines of passing novels are not comic. Their trickery, their exploitation of the sociosexual marketplace, is complicated by the genre's view of them as race traitors, a view that aligns them more closely with the "fallen women" of silent film and prefigures the femmes fatales of film noir.

The two heroines are con artists in differing ways, but both have paid the price of living according to materialistic values. Irene uses the cover of her light skin in order to participate in white privileges and luxuries; she uses passing as a tactic to lessen the restriction of the color bar. Clare, however, uses passing as a strategy, permanently fixing herself in the white world, where she finds herself in a racial closet created by her own greed. Both women are primarily concerned with material possessions, wealth, status, and appearances. As Clare says to Irene, "Money's awfully nice to have. In fact, all things considered, I think, 'Rene, that it's even worth the price" (160). The price, for Clare, is marriage to a man whose nickname for her is "Nig," which he calls her in front of Irene and another of their fair friends.

As I have suggested, *Passing* takes up many of the same cultural discourses that inflect *Gentlemen Prefer Blondes*—and Fitzgerald's *The Great Gatsby*, as well. When I have taught the three novels beside each other in courses on the Jazz Age, the cultural import signified by "blondeness" emerges in terms of class, ethnicity, and gender. The point is that the blonde is both the beauty and the material, and, in a context mad for materialism and eager for gold, women as well as men embraced the conflation of economics and erotics in the image of the blonde.

In the same way that the blonde was codified as a type in the emerging mass consumer culture of the twenties, so too was the redhead. Novelist, screenwriter, film producer, and celebrity "Madame" Elinor Glyn, who will be discussed more fully in the section on the silent movie *It*, was quite fond of her own red hair and, in this and many other ways, wished to make over America in her own image. Her movies starring red-haired Clara Bow, *It* (1927) and *Red Hair* (1928), propelled her agenda into the mainstream, and in *Red-Headed Woman* (1932) starring Jean Harlow, Anita Loos jumped on the titian bandwagon with a script that began, "Gentlemen prefer blondes???"

The ability to change hair color also meant that women could choose which type of woman they wanted to be: a blonde, a brunette, or a redhead, the three categories with which advertisements and films hailed women consumers visually and textually.[10] As we will see in Chapter 3, Tangee cosmetics ads described a "magic lipstick" that would turn whatever color best suited its wearer. Although Tangee's rhetorical strategy was to appeal to women's desire for individuality with a lipstick that magically adapts to each woman, it still addresses women as blonde, brunette, or redhead (see Figure 3.7). Unlike the nineteenth-century idea of "moral cosmetics," which suggested that inner nature manifested itself in appearance, the modern equation of external and internal hinged on the notion that, whether it is fair or not, people are judged by their appearance, so they better pay enormous attention to it. Historian Roland

Marchand terms this "the parable of the first impression" and presents a brilliant analysis of many examples of advertisers creating, reinforcing, and playing off anxieties about being judged superficially (208–17).

> Ads with such leading questions as "Do you know how to be yourself?" and "Can a woman change a man's idea of her personality?" had explained how a perfume or nail polish might resolve a woman's identity crisis. Like other versions of the parable of the First Impression [in advice manuals and popular journalism], such ads reinforced Americans' growing perception that they must create their own identities in the face of superficial and unsympathetic judgements by impersonal others. Advertisers did not create the modern "identity crisis," but they welcomed the opportunity to dramatize it. They then stepped forward as personal counselors on how to meet the scrutiny of judgemental others and how to succeed by "looking the part." (Marchand 216)

In this context, women's hair color could be a telling factor in the all-important superficial judgment of a woman's appearance. The dark-haired and exotic vamp, the golden-haired and gold-digging girl, the fiery and unconventional redhead were the types reinforced in ads, movies, books, and magazines. The three types were played off each other in a constant battle over which was the most attractive. In 1925 the phrase "Gentlemen Prefer Blondes" mocked and yet reinforced that debate.

In order for the use of makeup to become the norm, advertisers had to overcome the historic association of cosmetics with "bad women," such as prostitutes and actresses, who sought the public gaze. Indeed, as we will see in the following discussion of the silent movie *It* (1927), flapper heroines legitimized practices of self-adornment that were previously reviled as immoral artifice; they functioned as symbols of and models for the rejection of Victorian notions of femininity. In the emerging mass consumer society, this acceptance of makeup and fashion constitutes, of course, an endorsement of consumption. Paradoxically, the acceptance of cosmetics and the rise of the beauty industry extended women's reliance on covert rather than overt modes of power by locating the source of a woman's power—in both public and private contexts—in her appearance.[11]

Hedonic power—the covert mode of power exercised through display and adornment—was irrevocably conflated with commodification, as the use of cosmetics was deemed acceptable and then necessary to fulfill dictates of female beauty. This is in marked contrast to mid-nineteenth-century definitions of femininity, which valorized the concept of "moral cosmetics" rather than "paint." As historian Karen Halttunen summarizes, in sentimental culture "[t]he practitioner of moral cosmetics focused her beauty ritual not on her person but on her soul. Shunning the cosmetic arts of that feminine version of the confidence man, the painted woman, she cultivated physical beauty through moral self-improvement. Her beauty was not the deceitful product of surface work, but the transparent outward reflection of her inner mind and heart; she was beautiful because she was sincere" (88–89). We can see that the rejection of "moral cosmetics" in favor of commodified ones is part of the shift in cultural values from Victorian-sentimental to consumer-hedonist. Not surprisingly, the cosmetics industry originated with face creams and lotions,[12] and advertisements for soap, face creams, eyedrops, toothpaste, and olive tablets (taken internally) combined the rhetoric of moral cosmetics with the appeal to the modern individual seeking to manipulate the all-important First Impression.

The success of the beauty and cosmetics industries depended on defining beauty as artifice, not nature or morality. By 1925, there were twenty-five thousand beauty parlors nationwide; by 1930, the number had increased to forty thousand, and American cosmetics companies sold almost $180 million worth of products (Banner 271–72). In the same period, only food companies spent more money on advertising (Banner 273).

Popular discourses about beauty and sexual allure supported the beauty industries by appealing to women's continued domestic orientation, as well as to their increased independence and individualism. Women were encouraged to express themselves by constructing an image that would set them apart from other women and also conform to socially created standards of beauty and attractiveness. More importantly, however, many ads presented their products as tools for women to exert power, to demonstrate how the social practice of female trickery belonged in women's everyday life.

Further, ads cast consumers as potential film actresses, offering a fantasy subject position from which to interpret the powers ascribed to the product. Consider a Winx ad featuring Goldwyn star Colleen Moore with the slogan, "The Girl with the Wonderful Eyes" that asked, "Are you that girl—the charming person who fascinates by a mere glance? You could be, if you had long dark lashes to emphasize the depth of your eyes" (Fig. 2.4). Another in the series of Winx ads with photographs of "famous" stars presents a similar rhetorical strategy; under the slogan "Eyes that Capture and Detain," it asked, "Are your eyes like that? Do they challenge with a look, tantalize with a glance?" These ads place the power to affect the world in a body part that is enhanced with a product. Again and again silent film era ads tout the "speech" and "bewitching" nature of the eyes, surely a form of female trickery in everyday life.

Ads for other products also placed women consumers in the position of a film actress. A Lux toilet soap ad announced, "Clara Bow—Betty Bronson—Janet Gaynor—You—Every woman must face her own

The Girl with the Wonderful Eyes

ARE you that girl—the charming person who fascinates by a mere glance? You could be, if you had long dark lashes to emphasize the depth of your eyes.

Use WINX, the Liquid Lashlux. It will bead your lashes and make them appear darker and heavier. Easily applied with the glass rod attached to the stopper, it lasts all day, unaffected even by swimming or weeping at the theatre. Absolutely harmless.

WINX, the Liquid Lashlux (black or brown) 75c. To nourish the lashes and promote their growth, apply Cream Lashlux at night. Cream Lashlux (black, brown or colorless) 50c. At drug or department stores, or by mail.

Send a dime for a sample of WINX, the Liquid Lashlux. And for another dime we will mail you a sample of Pert, the waterproof rouge.

ROSS COMPANY

74 Grand Street   New York

WINX
The Liquid Lashlux

Colleen Moore,
Goldwyn Star,
famous for her
expressive eyes.

Figure 2.4. This ad uses the rhetoric of the power of the glance and the image of a film star to create consumer demand for an early mascara. *Cosmopolitan*, April 1923.

particular *Close-up Test*" (Fig. 2.5). This ad takes the parable of the First Impression and inflects it with the particular circumstance of women's attractiveness in the caption for an inset photograph of an anonymous woman in close proximity to a critical man: "In a flood of revealing light YOUR skin can be flawlessly lovely to closely observant eyes." The ad implies that the gaze of the cinema spectator catches the star in "revealing" light, when of course film close-ups were lit and photographed with techniques that flattered and enhanced the star. By making the comparison between "you" in everyday life and the audience who "is swept

Clara Bow—
Betty Bronson—
Janet Gaynor—
You —

In a flood of revealing light YOUR skin can be flawlessly lovely to close observant eyes

Every woman must face
her own particular *Close-up Test*

SMOOTH SKIN *instantly attracts, say 45 Hollywood directors . . .*

A GIRL'S lovely skin is an instant attraction. A whole audience is swept by enthusiasm when the close-up brings the radiant loveliness of a star near to them.

And every woman must meet the scrutiny of close appraising eyes. Does your skin quicken the heart with its loveliness like Clara Bow's, Betty Bronson's, Janet Gaynor's? It can.

For the lovely screen stars have

discovered a sure way to complexion beauty. Clara Bow, the bewitching little Paramount star, beguiling Betty Bronson, Janet Gaynor, the beloved Fox star, are among 511 of the 521 important actresses in Hollywood who jealously guard their smooth skin with Lux Toilet Soap. Their enthusiasm has made it official in all studio dressing rooms.

Hollywood — Broadway — Europe
the favorite beauty care

Not only the stars in Hollywood, but the famous Broadway stage stars, too, have enthusiastically adopted this gentle beauty care. So devoted

are they to this fragrant white soap that it is in 71 of the 71 legitimate theaters in New York. And even in Europe, the beautiful screen stars insist on this soap for *their* beauty.

MARY BRIAN
beloved Paramount star, says "It's certainly a wonderful soap. I always use it"

98% of the lovely complexions on the screen and radiant skin of girls everywhere are cared for with . . . Lux Toilet Soap-10¢

Figure 2.5. By claiming that every woman is judged as if she were a film star, this ad blurs the line between women's appearance in film and everyday life. *Cosmopolitan*, September 1930.

by enthusiasm when the close-up brings the radiant loveliness of a star to them," the ad encourages women to believe that the men in their everyday lives see them with the same gaze with which the women view film actresses. Rather than placing women spectators in the position of the "male gaze," as influential feminist film critics from Laura Mulvey to E. Ann Kaplan have argued, this strategy encourages women to think of men as seeing women as women see women. As we will see in the discussion of Tangee ads in the 1930s in Chapter 3, ads encouraged women to think of themselves as men see them—or rather in the construction of the male gaze that is highly critical of women's use of cosmetics. "You" look at Bow, Bronson, and Gaynor; both "you" and the man in the inset look at the woman, who is also "you."

The close-up test, which was a convention in cosmetics and beauty advertising well into the fifties, is an explicit exhortation for women to survey themselves being surveyed—and to be as critical as the imagined (male) viewer will be. As such, it extends anxieties created by the idea of the importance of the First Impression into a daily self-surveillance and judgment that is panoptic indeed. The trope of the close-up externalizes the split between woman as surveyor and surveyed into the relationship between the cinematic image of woman and the film spectator. Another ad, this time for shoes, also uses the metaphor of the close-up to, interestingly, call attention to the artifice of beauty and style. Under the drawing of Mary Phalbin being filmed in a scene from *Love Me and the World Is Mine*, the copy reads: "She was born the true artist. But the 'Close-up' revealed her use of every material aid to supplement her art and enhance her appearance. Her footwear, for example, was faultless— possessing not only beauty, but those unseen qualities which gave to her every movement a captivating grace" (Fig. 2.6).

The close-up builds on artistic and advertising conventions of depicting women looking into mirrors. These images refer to ideas about female vanity and also reinforce the idea that, to quote a 1928 cosmetics ad, "personal charm and attractiveness form the ruling power of a woman's destiny" (Fig. 2.7). Like portrayals of close-ups, advertisers' depictions of mirror-looking reinforce ideas about the value of women's appearance stated so explicitly in the copy for Miss Hopper's cosmetics.

For example, a striking 1923 Palmolive ad depicts a woman looking into a mirror (Fig. 2.8). The spectator position created by this ad brings the potential consumer into a triangle of looking: the woman looks at her reflection, which looks back at her; the spectator looks both at the woman and her reflection from over her shoulder. By looking over the woman's shoulder, we are invited to imagine our own image in the mirror. The ad also connects the modern with the ancient in the beautiful

Figure 2.6. In contrast to Figure 2.5, here the close-up calls attention to the role of artifice in creating appearance and performance. *Cosmopolitan*, May 1927.

She was born the true artist.

But the "Close-up" revealed her use of every material aid to supplement her art and enhance her appearance.

Her footwear, for example, was faultless—possessing not only beauty, but those unseen qualities which give to her every movement a captivating grace.

You, too, may enhance your natural grace—have footwear that will fit you superbly—be admired for its distinctive beauty—by wearing FOOT SAVER SHOES.

Foot Saver's exclusive, patented features fit and support the arch—give you an ease—poise—lightness of step—you never before experienced.

Visit the Foot Saver Store in your town—and know the luxury of wearing this perfect-fitting, grace-giving footwear.

Handsome Style Book and name of your nearest Foot Saver dealer on request.

THE JULIAN & KOKENGE CO.
Makers of the famous J & K Arch Fitting Shoes for Women
Dept. C-5   Cincinnati, Ohio

Beauty Appeal and Charm— Woman's Greatest Need

IN any story, true or otherwise, there is always another possible ending.

With a little foresight any girl or woman may completely change the course of her life. But she must know this one thing—that personal charm and attractiveness form the ruling power of a woman's destiny. Yet how few women seem to observe it.

Personal beauty is the guiding star in the life of Edna Wallace Hopper. She knows the importance of feminine appeal. Today, when most women of her age consider beauty a vanished dream, she looks like a girl.

She has made numerous trips abroad for the best creams and powders that science could produce to refresh the cherished bloom of youth. No effort was too great, as she was determined to find the best beauty aids.

Miss Hopper now shares her discoveries with other women. Because of the large quantities sold, her cosmetics are available on any toilet counter at prices all women can afford.

An Invitation

Every girl and woman is urged to accept Miss Hopper's special introductory offer as below. Note the beauty box filled with Edna Wallace Hopper's own beauty builders, which is yours at trifling cost. Send Coupon for liberal trial sizes of seven Beauty Aids. Full size packages would cost you over $4.

FREE Certificate for full fifty-cent tube of exquisite Quindent toothpaste will be included, so this week-end beauty case really costs you nothing!

Photograph by Alfred Cheney Johnston showing how Miss Hopper looks today.

Complete Beauty Outfit

Containing Every Beauty Need

Mail this special-offer coupon at once to Edna Wallace Hopper, 536 Lake Shore Drive, Chicago—enclosing 50c (stamps accepted) for liberal trial sizes of all seven of these beauty aids, Miss Hopper's own beauty book, also certificate good for Free 50c tube of Quindent toothpaste.

5-C

Name ....

Street ....

City .... State ....

Figure 2.7. The ad copy explicitly states many principles of the importance of women's appearance in modern American culture. *Cosmopolitan*, May 1928.

Face to Face
—as if you were another girl

WHAT do the eyes of others see? This is a question every girl should be able to answer. Do the glances which rest upon your face express admiration, or turn away with indifference?

Meet yourself face to face in your mirror and pass judgment upon what you see as critically as if you were some other girl. Take note of every fault and learn the remedy

The First Step

Whether your problem is the improvement of a poor complexion or to keep a good one, this first step is the same. The network of tiny pores which compose the surface of the skin must, every day, be cleansed from clogging accumulations.

Soap and water is the only effective means of cleansing yet discovered. Cold cream alone only increases the clogging, while other remedies are often unnecessarily harsh. The selection of the soap you use is the only problem and this is easily solved. Facial soap must be pure, mild and soothing in its action. Thus

you should select Palmolive. Once a day, and the best time is bedtime, wash your face thoroughly with the profuse, creamy Palmolive lather. Massage it thoroughly into the skin. Then rinse thoroughly and dry with a fine soft towel.

The blend of palm and olive oils has produced the mildest cleanser science can produce.

These rare oriental oils impart their rich, green color to the attractive Palmolive cake. Palmolive green is as natural as the color of grass and leaves.

A 10c Soap

If Palmolive cost many times this modest price it would be considered worth it by the millions of users who find it the only satisfactory soap. But it is these millions who make it possible for us to offer Palmolive at a popular price. The gigantic demand keeps the Palmolive factories working day and night and allows manufacturing economies which makes the 10c price possible.

THE PALMOLIVE COMPANY, MILWAUKEE, U.S.A.
The Palmolive Company of Canada, Limited, Toronto, Canada
Also manufacturers of Palmolive, Shaving Cream and Palmolive Shampoo

Volume and Efficiency
Produce 25c Quality
for
10c

Figure 2.8. Employing images of ancient and modern women, this ad portrays the critical gaze at the mirror as a timeless feminine activity. *Cosmopolitan*, May 1923.

drawing of an ancient Egyptian woman looking in a mirror, admiring the effects of palm and olive oils (bottom left). In both drawings, the women are satisfied with their reflections, and so the visual facets of the ad offer a fantasy of self-approval. The Cleopatra-like figure in particular does not seem concerned with how others see her, and, like so many other Jazz Age representations, the ad equates the attainment of female beauty with class privilege. The rhetorical strategy employed in the copy picks up on and extends how Jazz Age popular culture encouraged consumers to imagine the way they appeared to others. Like silent film, the Palmolive ad and others discussed here call attention to the importance of "reading" how a person is looked at and treated by others, and the ability to change those looks and treatment by using consumer products. The idea that, in order to catch flaws, the consumer must see herself with the critical gaze of "some other girl" dramatizes the split in female subjectivity that characterizes the Jazz Age.

Of course, the belief that a woman could control and change her appearance can be optimistic and empowering as well as narcissistic and self-defeating; this is the contradiction of modernity. On the one hand, cosmetics gave the New Woman a creative way to make up her own mask in as sexy and modern an image as she desired, but on the other hand, the cosmetics, advertising, film, and magazine industries codified impossible standards of beauty, played on intense self-scrutiny, and deliberately blurred distinctions between woman as object and subject.

It is within these contradictions that female trickery in the Jazz Age thrived. Like the character Lorelei, film and fiction heroines made female trickery seem like the obvious extension of modern definitions of femininity. Texts like *Gentlemen Prefer Blondes* presented the comic premise that, to quote the same ad that called beauty and charm "Woman's Greatest Need," "In any story, true or otherwise, there is always another possible ending." The discourses of beauty, which implied that any woman could be attractive if she bought the right products and worked hard and skillfully enough with them, do suggest "another possible ending," but in the movies as in the ads, the happy ending was always the same: marriage that fused economics and erotics.

Getting "It"

The silent movie *It* (1927) is a modern fairy tale about a working girl employed in a New York department store whose marriage means erotic fun based on "It" and economic plenty based on the man being the boss's son. But before and after the movie that made Clara Bow the "It" girl, British romance novelist turned Jazz Age media star Elinor Glyn had created and perpetuated the cultural phenomenon of "It."

The most common definition of "It" is sex appeal, and yet originally Glyn meant something closer to a magnetic, irresistible force so elusive that it could not be fabricated or learned, but also so desirable that it became for decades a topic of discussion. The cultural phenomenon she started demonstrates the commodification of ideas and feminine public personas in the emerging mass consumer culture of the 1920s.

Glyn first used the term in a 1915 novel and then bandied it about in popular magazines like *Photoplay* in order to strengthen her celebrity status as arbiter of sexiness and romance. By January 1923, Glyn published a series of advice columns in Hearst's *Cosmopolitan*. One particularly evocative graphic shows a huge woman playing chess with several men under the title "Elinor Glyn on Living with a Difficult Husband" (Fig. 2.9).

Glyn was particularly adept at parlaying her words and persona into commodities. In a manner similar to how Anita Loos parlayed the phrase "Gentlemen Prefer Blondes" into a lifelong career, Glyn held forth on "It" in fiction, in magazine articles, on lecture tours, and on film. By the time her 1926 novella "It" was published in two parts in *Cosmopolitan*, Glyn was a self-appointed judge of what and who was sexy and romantic; not only did she claim authorship of the term "It" to describe personal and sexual allure, but she supplemented her romantic fiction (which included the sensationalistic 1907 novel *Three Weeks*) and nonfiction treatises such as *The Philosophy of Love* (1920) with international lecture tours and cameo appearances in her movies *It* and *Red Hair* (Rosen 122–23). *The Philosophy of Love*, full of practical advice on how to make love last and how to inject more romance into life, sold a quarter of a million copies in the first six months after publication. By 1923, Madame Elinor Glyn was well known as the national "directrice of feminine *affairs de coeur*" (Rosen 122), and she was an international expert on, to use the title of one of her lectures in Sweden, "woman's place in modern civilization" (Elinor Glyn, *Romantic Adventure* 314). Samuel Goldwyn summarized Glyn's influence in Hollywood when he wrote, "Elinor Glyn's name is synonymous with the discovery of sex appeal in the cinema" (quoted in Anthony Glyn 279). Glyn's notoriety—and association with sex—is indicated in the popular anonymous verse that memorializes the shocking sex scene that takes place on a tiger-skin rug in her novel *Three Weeks* (1907):

Would you like to sin
With Elinor Glyn
On a tiger-skin?
Or would you prefer
To err

ELINOR GLYN *on*

Living *With a* Difficult Husband

WHOEVER has a "difficult" husband has to humor him. The tragedy which very few men realize is that the moment a woman has to humor a man she unconsciously loses respect for him, even if she goes on loving him in a protective sort of way; because the possibility of his answering to humoring implies either vanity or weakness, and however tolerant of his faults the conscious mind may be, the subconscious mind recognizes the truth and feels contempt. A man might very well ask himself, therefore, whether he wants his wife to despise him before he permits himself to become "difficult."

When a woman marries a man, even after the shortest acquaintance, she must have some idea of what his character is. It seems to me that it can be only in books where situations are created to meet the exigencies of the story that total changes in men occur after marriage, and that simple lambs turn into Bluebeards and delightful companions become morose tyrants.

In real life surely any observant person could get the general "hang"—so to speak—of the character of an ordinary man; and as we are considering the question broadly, it is of the ordinary man we must judge.

I do not mean that the troubles of matrimony or the waning of love do not alter people, because of course they do. What I mean is that there are certain fundamental qualities which remain, and these, except in the cases of deliberate arch deceivers, must have been evident in the beginning; such qualities as generosity, jealousy, arrogance, egotism, vanity pettiness. About truth or honor a woman could hardly be certain because both these qualities are looked at by the male mind from a different standpoint when dealing with women to what they are in the abstract, or when dealing with men.

But to discuss that interesting point would be a long story.

Therefore we must start this discussion by supposing that

Margaret has a general idea of George—greatly exaggerated as to the good side if she is in love—when she marries him. But although she may have remarked that he is mean over little things, or selfish to others even though he may be a slave to herself, or easily flattered, or avaricious, or weak of will—still, she has glossed over all his faults and so has not faced the idea that he is going to turn into a "difficult" husband. She marries him; and afterwards becomes this tiresome bore, making the days uncomfortable and filling the atmosphere with discontent.

Now what is she to do about it?

Every woman has some grain of tact because it goes back to the self preservation instinct, which through the ages has instilled cunning into woman to oppose the brute force she had to fight.

Therefore that sixth sense, that intuition, is in every female in some degree, and she can never be so completely impervious to things, people or events as man can.

But the subconscious and basic motive of all human actions is to follow nature's laws; in the case of woman, this means to secure a mate and to reproduce. Civilization is responsible for countless diversifications and perversions, and for atrophying or exaggerating these instincts, but they can always be found if the probe goes deep enough.

So that once the woman has fulfilled the first of them—that is, secured the mate—her sixth sense in regard to him automatically loses its alertness, and indeed is often allowed to sleep.

Thus a girl seemingly tactful during the engagement can become an apparently tactless woman so far as her husband is concerned. All this quite unconsciously; but that in itself may cause some of his "difficulties."

The case with man is different, because nature is continually prompting him to be unfaithful, and it is only the effects of civilization and custom upon the subconscious mind for generations

Figure 2.9. A fantasy of female power illustrates Elinor Glyn's advice that married women should self-consciously draw on the hedonic and covert tactics they used to "secure a mate" to deal with a man who has become "difficult." *Cosmopolitan*, January 1923. Article reproduced with the permission of *Cosmopolitan*.

With her
On some other fur?
            (quoted in Slide 70)

Anita Loos also commented on Glyn's influential—and artificial—persona: "Had Hollywood never existed, Elinor Glyn would have invented it. Her appearance was bizarre; the make-up she wore might have been scraped off the white cliffs of Dover, and it provided a startling contrast to her dyed red hair, green eyes, and mouth of vivid crimson. She jangled with long earrings, economically set with second-rate gems" (Loos, *A Girl Like I* 119).

Loos's bemusement at Madame Glyn (who seems to have resembled the Joker in *Batman*) is echoed by Dorothy Parker in an acerbic *New Yorker* book review that ridicules the excess of Glyn's prose and reveals Parker's irritation at Glyn's persona; she imagines Madame Glyn "drawing her emeralds warmly about her" as she holds forth on "It." Confessing her previous (and blessed) ignorance of Glyn's fiction, Parker ironically states, "When I think of all those hours I flung away in reading William James and Santayana, when I might have been reading of life, throbbing, beating, perfumed life, I practically break down" (Parker 465).[13]

In the novel *It*, the male character John Gaunt is the one with "It"; as Parker observes, "Madame Glyn, in fact, has interestingly entangled his It with sadism all through the book" (467). Parker's astute comment that Glyn's definition of sexual allurement has more to do with reifying male dominance and female submission drives to the heart of the twentieth-century romance plot based on female enthrallment to male domination; in her participation in the construction of the mythos of romance, Glyn defined "It" as based on the magnetic pull of a male sexuality that verges on sadism. Although the movie replaced the finer details of Glyn's portrayal of romance with characters and plot designed to showcase Bow, Glyn nevertheless was influential as the mother of twentieth-century sentimentalism-romance—a rationalizing schema that explains away the inequalities between men and women rather than confronting them.

But in the process of creating and consolidating her public persona in the Hollywood scene, Glyn redefined "It" to embrace both male and female sexual allure and continued to capitalize on her image as the judge of sexiness. Glyn used her celebrity to opine on a variety of topics, including style, as in this 1921 article from *Photoplay*, titled "In Filmdom's Boudoir": "I would like to start a 'Charm School' . . . in which I could teach [actresses] how to acquire individuality and fascination and attraction. I would teach them never to be restless—above all, to learn repose. A woman's greatest charm is repose. Men are worried and irritated by constant vivacious movement, just as they never can love a cold or vain woman" (Slide 78). That Elinor Glyn wanted to teach women to sit still and make sure they did not annoy men is indicative of her view of the social relations of the sexes. Although she certainly wanted to be a public figure and be involved in creative endeavors, her ideas about romance and femininity were reactionary. Of course, this was in keeping with her stated life's goal, "the glorification of romance," which motivated Glyn's desire to "teach all gold-digging girls that true love meant giving unconditionally and not receiving or bargaining" (quoted in Anthony Glyn 279). Because romance depends on defining male and female as opposite poles that will harmonize in marriage, but not as equals, and represents women as objects who find safety and satisfaction when they are possessed by a strong man, romance plays on women's "desire to be valued, which is a direct consequence of their devalued position in society as a whole."[14]

The romance genre that Glyn was so influential in extending into the mass consumer culture of the early twentieth century defines female sexuality as responsive to aggressive male sexuality. In the words of cultural critic Rosalind Coward, the "fantasy" of romance "maintains men as actually powerful, 'out there in the world,' and maintains women as passive, gaining their power only through their relations with men/children. The fantasy secures women's desire *for* a form of heterosexual domination and *against* active sexual identity" (196).

It is particularly ironic, then, that Clara Bow—the "Northwest Mounted policeman of sex" (because she always got her man)—became the embodiment of Elinor Glyn's romantic term "It." Bow's wild flapper persona—on and off screen—was the antithesis of the enthralled ladylike heroines of Glyn's romantic fiction. Rather, Bow's flapper heroine embodied precisely the active female sexuality that is impossible in the power relations of romance. One of Bow's most compelling characteristics was her restless, constant movement. As historian George Douglas puts it, "Throughout *It*, Clara is in a constant state of sensual activity, bouncing, blooping, giggling. She commands and demands the whole screen" (24).

The movie *It* represents the intersection of two competing definitions of the ideal public feminine self around which the plots of self-satisfaction and romance are organized: the active flapper represented by Clara Bow, and the stylish lady advocated by Elinor Glyn, analogous to the split between the woman of "repose" and the mayfly in Florine Stettheimer's *Portrait of Myself* discussed at the beginning of the chapter. Clara Bow rejected Glyn's traditionalism and asserted a modern image of public femininity: "The 'It' Mme. Glyn attributes to me is something of which I am not aware. As far as I know I think it must be my vivacity, my fearlessness and perhaps that I'm just a regular girl or tom-girl, one that doesn't think of men much; maybe it's my indifference to them. I really don't care particularly about men" (quoted in Rosen 89–90). The contradictions between the antisentimental and pleasure-seeking flapper and the sentimental, man-pleasing woman implicit in the clash between Bow's and Glyn's definitions of "It" are indicative of the conflict between modern and Victorian ideologies of the social relations between the sexes. The two definitions also cast men either as dominating husbands who want their women to keep still or as modern men looking for interesting female companionship to share leisure. Clara Bow and the other actresses who portrayed new women on the screen therefore helped construct a female attractiveness based on activity, independence, strength, autonomy, as opposed to weakness, submissiveness, passivity.

So, in the film *It*, Glyn's reactionary fetishization of asymmetrical power relations between men and women as the basis of "It" sits uneasily beside Clara Bow's modern incarnation of "It." Instead of the "repose" Glyn believed women should cultivate because it would please men, Bow conveyed motion and autonomy, which were defined by her own desires, not by accommodation to men. *It* participated in the construction of a public femininity that depended on women's active satisfaction of their desires, an ideal that encouraged women to participate in the public sphere as consumers as well as commodities. From the moment that Betty Lou's gaze finds and latches onto Waltham, the object of her desire, she is determined to have him, to make him want her. And she gets him by being a female trickster. Bow was "the flaming incarnation of the flapper spirit,"[15] as feminist film historian Molly Haskell explains eloquently. "She is the twentieth century pitted against the nineteenth, urban against rural society, the liberated working girl against the Victorian valentine, the boisterous flapper against Lillian Gish's whispering wildflower" (Haskell 79). This dichotomy is enacted most explicitly in the movie when Waltham (the boss) chooses Betty over Adela, the wealthy (and boring) blonde fiancée of his own class. As the movie implies, his choice centers not only on who is attractive, but also on the more active kind of relationship that the modern woman has with men. The fiancée is associated with the private sphere and represented as static and dependent on men for her self-image, in sharp contrast to the public, active, independent, and self-conscious modern woman. The quality of being conscious of oneself as a participant in societal relationships—of being a female trickster who resourcefully manipulates her costume, comportment, and expression depending on the situation—is at the core of the representation of the modern woman in *It*.

One of the subplots of the movie clearly concerns the shift from Victorian to modern values. Betty lives with Mary, a friend who had a baby out of wedlock. Seduced and abandoned, unable to keep her job at a department store, Mary is the "fallen woman" who represents the specter of the personal ruin that results from extramarital sex. The sentimental Mary is constantly weeping and is unable to stand up to the dour Victorian spinsters who report her to social services. But our heroine Betty is strong and brave and claims the baby is hers; she defends the baby like a "tigress" (as she is described in the newspaper article that makes Waltham think that Betty has a baby), and the social service workers leave her alone. Betty is not afraid to impersonate an unwed mother and does not reject Mary; in close-up after close-up, Bow's expressive face shows that Betty doesn't care about standards of conventional morality. Her heroism in protecting her friend, however, does lead to the misunderstanding that disrupts her courtship with Waltham. But even when Betty learns that Waltham has offered to set her up as his mistress instead of proposing marriage because he thought she was an unwed mother (that is, damaged goods),[16] she does not judge herself according to external standards. Rather, she is infuriated by Waltham's judgment and embarks on a plan of revenge. She crashes a party on his yacht and performs a cross-class female female impersonation of a society woman in order to charm him into proposing marriage. She rejects his proposal out of spite but finds that scorning him is not satisfying. When the yacht crashes, however, the tumult gives the lovers an opportunity to reconcile. Her trick, therefore, succeeds in securing the object of her desire in marriage.

It dramatizes the process of catching a man. When Betty, a clerk in the Macy's-like Waltham's department store, sees Waltham on the day he takes over his father's store, she implores (in the intertitle that follows a shot of her gaze riveted on him), "Sweet Santa Claus, give *him* to me!" and starts fantasizing about marriage. The camera offers up the handsome Antonio Moreno to our gaze, mimicking Betty's point of view. Her co-workers scoff at her, but that only fuels her determination to possess him, or rather, to finagle him into wanting to possess her in marriage. Betty actively pursues the object of her affection, an endeavor she accomplishes by the tactics of female trickery: impersonation, deception, duplicity, and disruption. In its representation of trickery as an acceptable and fruitful part of modern femininity, *It* both reflects and shapes a modern—more equal—style of negotiating relationships between men and women.

The change in American models of courtship from "calling" in the nineteenth-century to "dating" in the early twentieth century was, of course, influenced by the changing economic and social conditions.

Cultural historian Beth L. Bailey argues in *From Front Porch to Backseat: Courtship in Twentieth Century America* that, in contrast to courtship, which takes place in "woman's sphere," dating "moved courtship into the world of the economy" (21), into the public sphere. The Coney Island scenes in *It* demonstrate the public date, which revolved around "fun." In contrast to the stuffiness of the Ritz dining room, the Coney Island scenes provide a montage of Betty and Waltham eating hot dogs while gazing into each other's eyes and going on rides like the "Social Mixer" that jostle them and send them crashing into each other's arms, often with Bow losing the struggle to keep her skirt down. *It*'s portrayal of the date—unchaperoned, each amusement purchased with the man's money and resulting in laughter and physical closeness—is visceral, joyful, and unconnected to the class-bound social mores of the Ritz. In the democratic, populist realm of the amusement park, the shopgirl and the boss can find common ground.

This shift in the site of courtship is indicative of the shift in control over the courtship process from women's families in the domestic sphere to independent young individuals in the public sphere, where men's money became the definitive factor. The comparison between dating and prostitution, both institutions based on exchange, is tempting but, as Bailey explains:

> In dating, though, the exchange was less direct and less clear than in prostitution. One author, in 1924, made sense of it this way. In dating, he reasoned, a man is responsible for all expenses. The woman is responsible for nothing— she contributes only her company. Of course, the man contributes his company, too, but since he must "add money to balance the bargain" his company must be worth less than hers. Thus, according to this economic understanding, she is selling her company to him. In his eyes, dating didn't even involve an exchange; it was a direct purchase. (23)

But, as Bailey continues, men purchased not only female company, but obligation, power, and control. Further, there is the murky territory of sex: were men purchasing that, too?

In the movie *It*, the less romantic, more economic aspects of the sociosexual market are overlooked in favor of focusing on Betty's independence, autonomy, and control. When Waltham tries to kiss her after their date at the Coney Island amusement park, Betty slaps him and runs up to the window seat in her room, where she dreamily watches Waltham drive away. It is clear that she is not insulted but pleased by his advance, but it is also clear that her sexual favor is not easily purchased and that she will hold out for marriage. The viewer seeing the weeping Mary and her hyperactive baby is reminded of the consequences of giving in; although romance is clearly desired by the single girl, sex is safe only within the confines of marriage.

Both *It* and *Gentlemen Prefer Blondes* depict marriage as an economic exchange, but there are telling differences between the two texts' representations of love and marriage. In contrast to *It*, *Gentlemen Prefer Blondes* is not about romance but about the conflation of economics and erotics; the sociosexual system is represented as the "new country" in which the female trickster finds it profitable to be "shifty." As the antics of Lorelei Lee show, a clever flapper could really clean up by manipulating the affections and gifts of "gentlemen." Because Loos casts Lorelei as thoroughly antisentimental in her use of men as instruments, not romantic partners, Loos's novel presents the negotiation of the sociosexual market as a simple strategy. But for the majority of women in the 1920s, the link between economics and erotics was obfuscated by contradictory mass consumer culture representations of romance, sexual desire, and consumption.

The movie *It* portrays male-female sexual relationships in a far more romantic (and obfuscating) way than *Gentlemen Prefer Blondes* by focusing on attraction, dating, and love that leads to marriage. *It* is a commodified fantasy of female power within the modern sociosexual market portrayed as romance, whereas *Blondes* is an ironic indictment of the materialism of the Jazz Age and the economic basis of the social relations of the sexes.

As the example of *Gentlemen Prefer Blondes* reminds us, one aspect of the new dating system was perfectly clear: men and women increasingly perceived each other as commodities, thus removing the sentimental veneer that obscured the realities of the economic and power bases of male-female relationships. Dating encouraged both men and women to assess their worth in terms of money, status, and pleasure. If a man's worth was measured by money—what kind of date event he could provide for the woman and the economic value of gifts he could afford to purchase—a woman's worth was measured by the price she could demand based on her appearance, social status, sexual availability, and manipulation of the man. The economic power that was the province of men (whether women earned their own living or not) because men instigated and paid for dates encouraged women to create their own power base out of the limited resources they had, making feminine wiles an attractive tactic. To use historian Stuart Ewen's evocative phrase, women relied on "the survival tactic of allurement" (*Captains of Consciousness* 182).

Because of the very Victorian ideology of gender that Glyn advocates, Betty can't saunter up to Waltham and tap him on the shoulder; instead she must try to get his attention indirectly by dropping her purse, a gesture of submission and helplessness which calls up traditional codes of chivalry. (Interestingly, it is not a handkerchief that she drops, but her purse, a detail that signifies the economic terrain on which the transaction occurs.) She puts herself in the submissive position so that Waltham will see her from the vantage point of rescuer, a move calculated to make him place her in the category of desirable sexual object.

When this conventional trick fails because Waltham does not *notice* her as a woman with "It," but sees her only as a clerk in his store, Betty moves on to a more modern approach, transforming her appearance so that when she presents herself to Waltham's gaze again, he won't see "employee" but a possible object of his desire. Betty gets his attention when she has Monty, Waltham's "It"-less friend, take her to the Ritz for dinner because she overheard Waltham discussing his plans to dine there. Again, Betty relies on a covert tactic—eavesdropping—to gain the knowledge she can exploit only by finagling Monty. At home, she and her friend Mary alter her work dress into an outfit Betty thinks is appropriate evening wear for the dining room of the Ritz. With her bricolage, Betty embodies the possibility and optimism of the trickster, and although her ensemble is clearly makeshift, Bow's vibrancy transcends the class boundaries her character faces.

Significantly, it is at this point in the movie that Clara Bow's flapper "It" and Madame Elinor Glyn's refined "It" intersect. While Betty tries to catch Waltham's eye, the people at Waltham's table discuss "It." This scene is not the first in which the characters discuss Glyn's term; the opening scene of the movie shows Monty reading "It" in *Cosmopolitan*, and the camera dwells on the text: "'IT' is that quality possessed by some which draws all others with its magnetic force. With 'IT' you win all men if you are a woman—and all women if you are a man. 'IT' can be a quality of the mind as well as a physical attraction." Monty and the viewer read on to learn that "The possessor of 'IT' must be absolutely un-selfconscious, and must have that magnetic 'sex-appeal,' which is irresistible."

In a truly bizarre clash of "reality" and artifice, when Waltham asks his friends (including his fiancée Adela) to define "It," one replies, "There's Madame Glyn. Let's ask her." And there *is* Madame Elinor Glyn, decked out and poised at the top of the stairs (Fig. 2.10a). The camera follows her as she promenades over to Waltham's table, where she happily explains that "It" is "Self-confidence and indifference to whether you are pleasing or not—and something in you that gives the impression that you are not all cold. That's 'IT'" (Fig. 2.10c–d). Glyn has revised her original concept into one that would buttress Hollywood's construction of a modern public femininity.

When Glyn entered into the mass consumer culture as a screenwriter and celebrity, she adapted her ideas, took a $50,000 endorsement, and willingly shifted the locus of "It" from the male sadism of John Gaunt to the wild self-satisfaction of Clara Bow. Her concept was transformed into a product of mass culture (a movie under the control of Paramount) and the ideological terrain on which the cultural work of "It" was performed shifted from romance (an explanation for male sadism and indifference that does not disrupt the power relations between men and women) to an ideal of femininity that propels mass consumer society. Clara Bow, the flapper-working girl, pursues fun and leisure through consumption. Her modern attitude of being unconcerned about whether she is pleasing or not (a quality in Betty that does not manifest clearly until the misunderstanding about the baby) proves her "It" when (after she "accidentally" bumps into him) Waltham does notice her, and their romance begins. The two competing modes of public self-presentation, one based on trickery (Bow's personification of "It") and the other based on submission (subsumed by Elinor Glyn's reification of herself as Madame Glyn), intersect in the scene in the Ritz dining room. The moment in the film when Waltham's gaze settles on Betty heralds the triumph of the modern flapper over the Victorian lady.

The movie *It* portrays its triumphant flapper heroine as a public woman, active and mobile in both her employment and leisure activities. The date Betty and Waltham have at Coney Island characterizes her as fun-loving, physical, and informal. The realm of mass consumption and leisure is represented as Betty's terrain, and by doing what she enjoys she charms Waltham.

Moreover, Betty's physicality is representative of the modern woman's participation in the public sphere. The focus on the physical was reinforced by the popularity of frenetic dancing and women's increasing participation in sports. Instead of women's bodies being weak vessels, held together by tightly laced corsets, through which spirituality flowed unencumbered by muscle or activity, modern women's bodies were seen as strong and interesting, vehicles for pleasure or economic gain (Brown 42–45). Women in the 1920s reached a new level of mobility, driving cars and flying airplanes; the mechanization and commodification of transportation and the propriety of a woman going places unescorted meant new public freedom for Jazz Age women. During the previous decade, unprecedented numbers of women had marched through the streets in support of suffrage. In 1915, for example, there were twenty-eight suffrage parades. In the postsuffrage twenties, even more women participated in union agitation, which was prompted in part by increased public access for women (Matthews, *Public Woman* 212).

Women's increased public access also had a negative aspect. Accord-

b

a

c

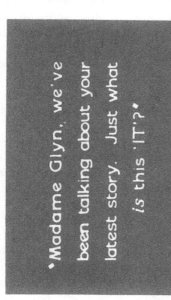

d

> "Madame Glyn., we've been talking about your latest story. Just what *is* this 'IT'?"

Figure 2.10. In the dining room of the *Ritz*, Waltham (Antonio Moreno) and his guests discuss Elinor Glyn's new story, "It," which was published in *Cosmopolitan* in 1926. *a.* Suddenly, there *is* Madame Glyn descending the stairs. *b.* Medium close-up of Glyn and her escort. *c.* Intertitle. *d.* Waltham graciously thanks Glyn for explaining "It." During Glyn's cameo, Betty (Clara Bow) watches from another table, trying to lock eyes with Waltham. Frame enlargements from *It* (1927).

ing to historian Stephen Norwood's study of the Telephone Operators Union in the early twenties, although the consumer culture brought women into the public space of downtown areas and allowed women an increased level of experience and sensual gratification, it also influenced the women workers to overemphasize their appearance and participate in the commodification of femininity (Norwood 311).

A 1927 advertisement for Murine eyedrops uses the cultural idea of "It" to capitalize on the popular film and channel women's anxieties about their appearance into consumption (Fig. 2.11a). The word "IT" is the dominant part of the ad, which claims that " 'IT' . . . usually lies in the eyes." Here we see yet another reinterpretation of the term "It," this time so that "It" not only is commodified, but has a precise location—in the eyes. "Don't be discouraged if your own eyes are dull, lifeless and unattractive," the ad continues. "A few drops of harmless *Murine* will brighten them up and cause them to radiate 'IT'." Given Clara Bow's ability to use her eyes to convey emotion and internal thought processes and, most famously, to flirt, it is not surprising that "It" would weave its way through the culture and emerge in an eyedrop advertisement. Other products also jumped on the "It" bandwagon: Glazo nail polish has "It" (Fig. 2.11b), and an ad for Heinz rice flakes quipped, "You Need This 'It'!"—meaning fiber. These ads show the pervasiveness of the term and how far "It" had traveled from Glyn's original meaning.

The Murine ad associates women's sexual allure with the use of a commodity, a link that a contemporaneous perfume ad makes explicit: "Woman's deep-seated instinct urging her to the use of perfumes is a manifestation of a fundamental law of biology. *The first duty of a woman is to attract.* . . . It does not matter how clever or independent you may be, if you fail to influence the men you meet, consciously or unconsciously, you are not fulfilling your fundamental duty as a woman" (quoted in Ewen, *Captains of Consciousness* 182). Like Figures 2.2 and 2.4–2.8, this ad illustrates the primacy placed on women's ability—or *duty*—to attract men despite increased representations of women's autonomy and intelligence. In order to convince women that they needed to consume the products churned out by the cosmetics and beauty industries, advertisers not only reinforced traditional reliance on the covert power of "influence," but transformed women's covert power from morality to the trick of attracting a man by employing a commodity like Murine or perfume. This is how "It" is filtered through mass consumer culture as a commodifiable and attainable way of executing the tricks necessary to "influence the men you meet, consciously or *unconsciously*" (emphasis added); by purchasing and using Murine, women will make their eyes "radiate 'IT' " and be able to attract men who will satisfy their wants.

One of the most striking aspects of the emerging mass consumer culture was its ability to funnel social discontent into consumption. The location of women's power in a few drops of Murine is a far cry from both the moral superiority of Victorian notions of gender and the vote of suffrage agitators. Where *does* feminism, or any political manifestation of the modern woman's freedom, figure in the mass consumer culture's representations of mobility, increased participation in the public sphere, economic power, and self-development? Although flapper heroines such as Lorelei Lee and Betty articulated fantasies of autonomy from the submission of romance and economic uncertainty, respectively, neither one expresses political consciousness. As historian William H. Chafe explains, "The flapper might be seen by some as reflecting a 'feminist' rebellion against convention, but the revolt was for the most part superficial, not structural. It focused on style, not substance—on the appearance of sexual liberation, not on the radical restructuring of all relationships. . . . Nothing did more to eviscerate feminism of the radical potential than this popular tendency to equate 'freedom' with the life-style of the flapper" (106).

Looking at the ads of the 1920s, one sees how the feminist demand for equality and freedom for women was appropriated into the jargon of consumerism. A classic example of commercialized feminism was a 1929 campaign in which the American Tobacco Company attempted to encourage women to smoke in public. George W. Hill, owner of American Tobacco, had contracted Edward Bernays to run the campaign, hoping to expunge the "hussy" label from women who smoked publicly. The smoking taboo among women, Bernays reasoned, was of deep psychological significance. Accordingly, he consulted the psychoanalyst A. A. Brill for advice. Brill's explanation was this: "Some women regard cigarettes as symbols of freedom. . . . Smoking is a sublimation of oral eroticism; holding a cigarette in the mouth excites the oral zone. It is perfectly normal for women to want to smoke cigarettes. . . . Cigarettes, which are equated with men, become torches of freedom." Bernays needed to break the taboo against women smoking in public: "Why not a parade of women lighting torches of freedom—smoking cigarettes." Utilizing the feminist motif and enlisting the support of a "leading feminist," Ruth Hale, Bernays had a contingent of cigarette-puffing women march down New York's Fifth Avenue in the 1929 Easter parade. "Our parade of ten young women lighting 'torches of freedom' on Fifth Avenue on Easter Sunday as a protest against women's inequality caused a national stir," Bernays proclaimed. "Front-page stories in newspapers reported the freedom march in words and pictures" (Ewen, *Captains*, 160–61).

That cigarettes, the ultimate product of addictive commodification, were associated with feminist freedom is an irony almost too sharp to

Figure 2.11. The commodification of a concept: Get "It" in a bottle. *a*. This ad plays on the power ascribed to the eyes and the gaze in advertising, romantic fiction, and films such as *It*. *Cosmopolitan*, May 1927. Advertising reproduction courtesy of Ross Products Division, Abbott Industries. *b*. Here the product itself has "It." *Cosmopolitan*, March 1928.

Eyes that have
"IT"

"IT". . . that subtle something which attracts others . . . usually lies in the eyes. Don't be discouraged if your own eyes are dull, lifeless and unattractive. A few drops of harmless *Murine* will brighten them up and cause them to radiate "IT".

Thousands upon thousands of clever women use *Murine* daily and thus keep their eyes *always* clear, bright and alluring. A month's supply of this long-trusted lotion costs but 60c. Try it!

MURINE
FOR YOUR EYES

Free

Mail this coupon to Murine Co., Dept. 22.9 E. Ohio St., Chicago, for book checked: "Eye Beauty" "Eye Care"

Name

Address

City   State

Please PRINT your name and address in PENCIL.

a

Glazo has IT
by Rosaline Dunn

In 3 Brief Steps . . . This Marvelous Glazo Method Bestows on Hands The Enchanting Loveliness I Have Sought for 15 Years

THE smartest women in New York's social group have adopted me as their personal manicurist. Naturally, I am jealous of this reputation. And to aid me in my work I use only the finest accessories money can buy.

Until recently, my one despair has been polishes. I think I can truthfully say I have experimented with every one that has come to my attention. I had even vainly tried to produce the perfect polish that I had looked to others for, so many years.

When Paris ushered in the sensible vogue of liquid polishes, I breathed a sigh of relief. But even the most expensive imported polishes failed to live up to my expectations.

I began to believe I was looking for the impossible, that I had an ideal too high ever to be realized—when I discovered Glazo Manicure.

Perfection at last!

Imagine my delight when I found the lovely Glazo package—two phials containing the solution of my problem. At last I had found the perfect polish for the nails.

Glazo has IT.

Every quality that I have sought, it has in abundance. It is lasting. Its tint is that of beautiful, healthy nails. And from one appointment to the next, it holds its soft patina, its perfect lustre.

Then there is Glazo Cuticle Oil to frame the nails in exquisite pink cuticle ovals which are the perfect setting for dainty, white half-moons. For those who prefer a cream to an oil, Glazo Cuticle Cream is a marvelously healing preparation.

I would like to show you how I keep the nails of my patrons forever smart and correctly manicured.

The coupon will bring you the lesson book I have prepared. It tells you how to keep busy hands young.

Of course you can obtain Glazo at all the better shops and stores. Its price including the Remover 50c.

Lovely, Elegant Hands in 3 Brief Steps

1. Work Glazo Cuticle Oil into the skin that borders the nail. It smoothes the cuticle and keeps it soft and clean. It fashions the cuticle curve of beauty.
2. Cleanse the nail surface with Glazo Remover to prepare for polish.
3. Apply Glazo Liquid Polish. Even so quickly it gives to nails a lovely lustre that lasts a whole week.

Miss Rosaline Dunn
205 Blair Ave.
Cincinnati, Ohio.

Please send me your booklet and miniature Glazo manicure set. 10c enclosed.

Name ....

Street ....

City ....

b

bear. But because the tobacco industry had the resources and motivation to appropriate the desire for women's increased freedom in the public sphere and offer its product as both symbolic and actual satisfaction, feminist impulses led not to political power, but to nicotine addiction, a symbol of the enslavement of mass consumer culture.

But mass consumer culture is not simply enslaving, just as it is not unequivocally liberating. Advertisers and the corporate interests they advanced tried to exploit anxieties, desires, and beliefs in such a way as to link cultural issues to their specific product. To use an example from historian Nancy F. Cott's study of postsuffrage feminist consciousness, *The Grounding of Modern Feminism*, General Electric juxtaposed "the suffrage and the switch" as part of their project to reify women's traditional place in the domestic sphere in modern modes of consumption. Cott summarizes the internalization of a female modernity that was the cultural work of advertising directed toward constructing women as consumers:

Not duty imposed by church or state but personal "adjustment" and "fulfillment," demanded from within, called women to the performance. What was unprecedented here was less the didacticism, or sense of knowing best (which traditional sources had shared), than the way in which women's household status and heterosexual service were now defended—even aggressively marketed—in terms of women's choice, freedom, and rationality. . . . The culture of modernity and urbanity absorbed the messages of Feminism and re-presented them. Feminist intents and rhetoric were not ignored but appropriated. Advertising collapsed the emphasis on women's range and choice to individual consumerism. . . . Feminists' defiance of the sexual division of labor was swept under the rug. Establishing new formalism, these adaptations disarmed Feminism's challenges in the guise of enacting them. (174)

The image of a modern public femininity represented by Clara Bow in *It*, then, is both liberatory—expressing women's independence, active participation in the public sphere, assertiveness in pursuing erotic and economic satisfaction, and the desire for "companionate marriage" based on a mutual recognition of each other's "It"—and containing—the legitimation of marriage as women's goal, substitution of commodified pleasure for political freedom, and reification of the sexual division of labor.

The social practice of female trickery functions in the popular culture of the twenties as a way of escaping traditional confines of gender, as a group of tactics for negotiating the public sphere, and as practices appropriated by mass consumer culture in the legitimation of the cosmetics, beauty, and fashion industries (as well as the primacy of women's appearance). The female trickster, therefore, can be seen as an articulation of the contradictory position in which women were placed by the processes of modernity. Despite the enormous gains in women's freedom, covert exercises of power were still necessary for women to satisfy

Figure 2.12. In the lobby of the Ritz, Betty (Clara Bow) pretends to talk on the telephone while she poses for Waltham's gaze. Frame enlargement from *It* (1927).

their desires (economic and erotic); because of the triumph of mass consumer culture over, say, socialism, women's covert power shifted from morality to "It." The tactics of female trickery that constitute the self-conscious construction of a feminine public self—disguise, female female impersonation, split of the self into surveyor and surveyed, duplicity, deception, and theft—illustrate the difficulties and rewards of women's entrance into the public sphere, a place where neither the figure of "repose" in Florine Stettheimer's *Portrait of Myself* nor the activity and flight of the mayfly can exist without the other. When Clara Bow glances off to the side, eyes sparkling as she presents herself for the gaze of her object of desire and her willing audience, she incorporates the objectification of the female form and the embodiment of active female participation, both inescapable tenets of modernity (Fig. 2.12).

Chapter 3
Out of the Garden and into the War
Female Tricksters in the Depression and War Years

The Cultural Work of Mae West, or, Doin' Culture

On a Sunday evening in December 1937, Mae West played the part of Eve in a comic radio sketch introduced as "what might have taken place in the Garden of Eden."[1] The nine-minute interchange between Eve (West), Adam (Don Ameche), and the snake (the voice of Charlie McCarthy, ventriloquist Edgar Bergen's "dummy" sidekick) retells the story of how Eve's trickery of the "long, lazy, and lukewarm" Adam allowed her to escape the boredom of Eden. The ironic fit of Mae West, the modern female trickster and self-proclaimed "bad girl," playing Eve, the archetypal female trickster, failed to amuse the organized forces of moralistic censorship in the listening audience. They objected to the sketch as obscene and blasphemous, and their outcry provoked heated debate about the moral standards of radio in newspapers, the Federal Communications Commission, and the House of Representatives. As a result, West was blacklisted from radio well into the fifties, and even the mention of her name was forbidden on NBC radio.

That the popular Mae West was a target of the social purity movement is hardly surprising; her bawdy humor and sexually provocative dialogue played with the limits of propriety. In fact, many film scholars have pointed to West's wisecracking endorsements of sex for pleasure as an impetus for the movie industry's Production Code. The Production Code consisted of a list of moral proscriptions; not only were some representations forbidden (nudity, miscegenation, the details of how to commit crimes), but the code dictated a moral stance that forced Hollywood to tack on endings in which any and all villains and sinners were duly punished and the institutions of society (marriage, religion, the legal system, the police) were upheld. Although the code addressed violence, its main focus was on sex, which, in the eloquent words of critic

Molly Haskell, was "an activity both sinful and, from the moral referees' point of view, contagious, since it could be transmitted by the image on a screen like sperm on a toilet seat" (118).

The controversial sketch comically recast the biblical story of Eve's transgression in terms of Depression-era issues such as dispossession, optimism, and the changing social relations of the sexes caused by the economic crisis. The sketch was broadcast on NBC radio's weekly show *The Chase and Sanborn Hour.* The author of the sketch, veteran radio writer Arch Oboler, characterized Eve as a female trickster who unsuccessfully implores Adam to "break the lease" with the "landlord" (*the* Lord!): "take me outta this dismal dump and give me the chance to develop my personality." Adam replies that leaving the Garden—"dispossession"[2]—is impossible, because the only way out involves eating the apple from the tree that the "landlord" forbade, a transgression in which he will not participate. After a parodic domestic squabble about Eve's assessment of life in Eden as "too safe," Adam leaves to pursue his only interest, fishing. In his absence, Eve cajoles the snake into helping her escape and tricks Adam out of the stultifying stasis of Eden and into the outside world, where they find the common ground of sex.

Not only does the controversy over the sketch provide a useful illustration of the cultural clash over the meanings of female trickery and sexuality, but the sketch itself is exemplary of Depression comic representations of female trickery as pragmatic, home as emotional and social rather than material and economic, and marriage as an equal nondomestic arrangement based on fun and pleasure—issues that find their fullest expression in the film genre of screwball comedy. But before turning to film comedy, a little more on the sketch's positive depiction of Eve as a female trickster is in order.

The sketch's dialogue alone constitutes a provocative reinterpretation of Eve as the instigator who taunts the snake into doing her bidding:

SNAKE: That's the forbidden tree.
EVE: Oh, don't be technical. Answer me this—my palpitatin' python— would you like to have this whole Paradise to yourself?
SNAKE: Certainly.
EVE: Okay, then pick me a handful of fruit—Adam and I'll eat it—and the Garden of Eden is all yours. What do ya say?
SNAKE: Sssounds all right . . . but it's forbidden fruit.
EVE: Listen, what are you—my friend in the grass or a snake in the grass?
SNAKE: But forbidden fruit.
EVE: Are you a snake or are you a mouse?
SNAKE: I'll—I'll do it. (hissing laugh)

EVE: Oh—shake your hips. There, there now, you're through.

SNAKE: I shouldn't be doing this.

EVE: Yeah, but you're doing all right now. Get me a big one. . . . I feel like doin' a big apple.

SNAKE: Here you are, Missus Eve.

EVE: Mm—oh, I see—huh—nice goin', swivel hips.

SNAKE: Wait a minute. It won't work. Adam'll never eat that forbidden apple.

EVE: Oh, yes, he will—when I'm through with it.

SNAKE: Nonsense. He won't.

EVE: He will if I feed it to him like women are gonna feed men for the rest of time.

SNAKE: What's that?

EVE: Applesauce.

The irreverence of the sketch is obvious from the dialogue, but what is impossible to render in print is what West termed her "characteristic delivery," which sexualized even the most innocuous utterance. West's goading of "swivel hips" was embellished by what radio historian Arthur Frank Wertheim describes as "West's love-groans and promiscuity in interpreting Eve's seduction of Adam [which] definitely overstepped radio's sexual boundaries" (Wertheim 106). Because West's intonations (as well as the unseen but perhaps imagined bodily comportment, facial expressions, and mannerisms) were virtually dripping with sexual innuendo, she undoubtedly highlighted the sexual implications of the story. To West's Eve, the Garden was not a paradise but a cage, a prison, a place of domestic entrapment from which to escape. And, in true trickster fashion, the tactic she uses—disguising the apple as sauce—draws on the domestic role that traps her.

The ending of the sketch reinforces Eve's motives—and rewards. She proudly calls herself "the first woman to have her own way, and a snake'll take the rap for it." "Dispossessed" from the Garden, Adam and Eve have the following concluding dialogue:

ADAM: Eve, it's as if I see you for the first time. You're beautiful.

EVE: Mmmm. And you fascinate me.

ADAM: Your eyes!

EVE: Ahhhh. Tell me more.

ADAM: Your, your lips. Come closer. I wanna hold you closer. I wanna . . .

EVE: You wanna what?

(Sound of two loud kisses followed by trumpets and thunder.)

ADAM: Eve, wha, what was that?

EVE: That was the original kiss!

Thus, this sketch replaces original sin with a kiss; instead of feeling shame after eating the apple, Adam finally pays attention to his wife's sexiness (always the most important quality of the West heroine), and the couple together feels the sexual pleasure that Eve had been aware of all along.

Oboler's sketch ends on a note of complete comic reversal from traditional renderings of both "what happened" in the Garden of Eden and its ramifications; instead of the list of punishments (mortality, labor, women's subordination, pain in childbirth) that usually concludes this Ur-text of misogyny, the sketch offers instead a world outside the Garden that has distinct benefits. This hilarious revision of the "fortunate fall" offers sex as the reward for female trickery. Pleading and bickering with Adam is fruitless (so to speak); only by being a female trickster can Eve pull off the shift from domestic drudgery in which she and Adam have nothing in common to the worldly paradise in which she and Adam meet on the common ground of sex, hinting at pleasurable cooperation between the sexes.[3]

The sketch's rendering of change, marriage, woman's place, and female trickery is typical of thirties' comedy. By calling the Garden "too safe" and "disgustin'," by rejecting conventional domesticity in her willingness to "break the lease" and join the ranks of the dispossessed, Eve articulates an optimistic response to the turmoil of the Depression. "If trouble means something that makes you catch your breath," Eve declares, "if trouble makes your blood run through your veins like seltzer water, mmmmm, Adam my man, give me trouble." In this way, the sketch participates in the "celebration of *change*" that film historian John Belton finds at the center of American comedy (144); as he argues in *American Cinema/American Culture*, comedy "endorses change as a positive feature of history, unlike tragedy, which conceives of change negatively" (145). By presenting change and "trouble" as preferable to stability, Depression-era comedy participated in the cultural work of disseminating the optimism necessary for the acceptance of the New Deal. As catalysts of change, female tricksters such as West's Eve and the screwball heroines embodied that cultural work.

The sketch's ultimate comic endorsement of change is evident in the consequences of leaving the Garden; by replacing shame and fear—those quintessential Depression-era responses[4]—with pleasure and opportunity, the sketch offers a positive way of looking at changes in the social relations of the sexes resulting from the Depression. Historian Elaine Tyler May explains that the Depression "opened the way for a new type of family based on shared breadwinning and equality of the sexes. But it also created nostalgia for a mythic past in which male breadwinners provided a decent living, and homemakers were freed from outside employment" (38). America did not take the path of equal partnership but instead one of polarized gender roles (which, as May argues, resulted in the domestic ideology of the cold war era). However, the possibility of equality between men and women was portrayed in thirties' comedy, as it was in the Adam and Eve sketch.

The sketch sets up a dichotomy that underlies representations of trickery in Depression-era culture at large. On the one hand, deception and role playing are depicted as necessary to the modern personality who can adapt and thrive in an unstable social system, one that includes changing social relations of the sexes. Dale Carnegie's influential book *How to Win Friends and Influence People* (1936) exemplifies the Depression-era advocacy of feigned submission as a kind of trickery necessary to succeed in the interpersonal relationships of the business world. On the other hand, however, trickery contributes to the discomfort of social change, and therefore causes anxiety. The screwball comedies of the decade play on ambivalence about individual adaptation to change. When we put this dichotomy into the charged terrain of "good" and "evil" set up by the Christian interpretation of the Adam and Eve story, trickery takes on sinister implications. Judgment of trickery, like rebellion, power reversals, and insubordination, depends on what side of the fence—or Garden—one is on.

Certainly, from the beginning of her career in vaudeville and on Broadway to her successful film career, West deliberately constructed a public persona that transgressed cultural definitions of gender, especially those surrounding the "goodness" and "badness" of sexuality. Her famous one-liner, "When I'm good, I'm good, but when I'm bad, I'm better," and the title of her autobiography, *Goodness Had Nothing to Do with It*, encapsulate West's celebration of the aggressive female sexuality she achieved by tapping the label of "bad girl." West was aware and, to a large extent, in control of the cultural work she performed in discourses of sexuality, femininity, and censorship. As West explains in her autobiography:

I had a proper understanding which grew stronger; that behind the symbol I was becoming, there was much good material for drama, satire, and some kind of ironic comment on the wars of sexes and the eternal engagement and grappling between men and women in a battle that never ends. I did not perhaps treat the subject as seriously as Havelock Ellis, or as deeply as Sigmund Freud, Adler, Jung or Dr. Kinsey, but I think if we all could have sat down and discussed the subject fully, my ideas would have been listened to with some sense of awe. They may have been the generals, but I was in the front lines—out in an emotional No Man's Land, engaged in dangerous hand-to-hand, lip-to-lip raiding parties. (73)

And of course the title of her movie *I'm No Angel* (1933) is an explicit renunciation of the role of the Victorian "angel in the house." By reversing the morally charged terms of "good" and "bad," West performed important cultural work that articulated the "modern" sexual liberalism prevalent in the twenties against which the organized forces of conventional morality (such as the Legion of Decency) reacted. The Adam and Eve sketch plays on such a reversal of good and bad.

Although West's female female impersonation cast West as a sex object, it also recast the sex object as an active, self-interested subject who retained control over her own objectification and commodification, making sure no one ever got the better of her.

By refusing to keep sex hidden and writing plays and movies that infused sex into American culture, West performed important cultural work that articulated "modern" liberal attitudes toward sex. West doesn't hide her strength, desire, intelligence, or self-control behind what artist Florine Stettheimer called "the soft pink light," which I argued in the previous chapter was symbolic of the cover of a submissive, pleasing femininity that hides the true self; but in stepping away from the pink light of good womanhood, West steps into its shadow, where the only light is the often-garish red light that defines a sexual woman as a "bad girl." As Elizabeth Janeway explains in her classic feminist book *Man's World, Woman's Place*, "Old, accepted roles throw shadows, and when the role-player steps away, he [or she] will find him [or her] self engulfed in the shadow role which is the reverse, or the negative role from the one he [or she] has left" (118).

The public persona of Mae West was not only a shadow-dweller but also a celebrant of the opportunities available in the underside of American society. When West constructed her female female impersonation of the bad girl, she created for herself a social and linguistic space in which she could be a woman who was not submissive or subordinate. West's engagement in the battle of the sexes is illustrated by the final scene of her 1933 movie *She Done Him Wrong*. Lady Lou (West) is in a carriage with Cummings (Cary Grant), who has just revealed himself to be a federal agent, not the Salvation Army officer he was impersonating. Lou thinks Cummings is taking her to jail, but instead (or rather, analogously) he wants her to marry him. He takes away her spectacular diamond collection and gives her a (small) diamond as an engagement ring. When Cummings attempts to set the terms of their relationship with lines like "I'll be your jailer from now on," Lou resists submission. When Cummings asks if he can hold her hand, she replies, "It ain't heavy. I can hold it myself," an explicit reversal of the expected feminine response. And in the final interchange of the movie, Cummings says, "You bad girl," and Lou's reply resonates with implications of her continued refusal to submit: "You'll find out." Marriage—or jail—will not end her "badness." A similar point is made at the end of West's other movie with Cary Grant,

I'm No Angel. Tira (the circus performer who does a lion taming act) clinches her reconciliation with her wealthy lover Clayton by reprising the title song, "I'm No Angel." A more explicit renunciation of the role of "angel in the house" is hard to imagine.

West's famous wisecracks depend on the shadow world of double entendre and sexual innuendo. What she says is a kind of trick, and an essential part of her "camp sensibility" is calling our attention to her clever artifice.[5] West's linguistic facility is exemplary of what anthropologist Robert Pelton terms the "polyvalent" quality of trickster utterance in *The Trickster in West Africa: A Study of Mythic Irony and Sacred Delight.* Her clever exploitation of language and meaning as a source of power and control undercuts attempts to censor and restrict sexual expression. By investing nonsexual comments and situations with sexual innuendo, West shows how futile and ridiculous the cultural work of censorship is.

West also manipulated her physical appearance in a female female impersonation designed to encapsulate the contradictions of femininity. In the twenties, an era that fetishized the boyish silhouette of the flapper, West turned to the fin de siècle image of the voluptuous woman for her Gay Nineties Bowery prostitute with the hourglass figure. In a move away from the indifference of the flapper, which was represented by "modern" clothes made for ease of motion, West's costumes were restrictive and called attention to the female body as sexual object. West looked back to the 1890s, the fin de siècle transition period between the agrarian society of the past and the mechanization that formed the modern era. She based her persona on the liminality of the Gay Nineties, which evoked images of the frontier, of a premodern simplicity, and a less restricted female sexuality.

By drawing on the liminal decade "betwixt and between" the nineteenth and twentieth centuries, West articulates the contradictions of gender constructs in the shift from Victorian morality to modern consumer-hedonistic values. West's costumes were restrictive, but her behavior in them contradicted the image of imprisoned femininity. West commented, "What can be accomplished by the feminine figure, once it is nipped here and there, but allowed free reign elsewhere, would surprise" (quoted in Ward 56).

By juxtaposing restraint and "free reign," West embodied not only female sexual objectification, but also a female subjectivity based on sexual pleasure. Her comportment expressed a self-control that also characterized her verbal and physical behavior. She relies on men for sexual gratification, but if a specific man will not meet her terms, she will find another. West conveyed this attitude every time she made men the object of her assessing gaze, with every mincing step toward or away from the object of her desire, with each beckoning gesture of hand, hip, or head. As West explained in a 1979 interview, her persona was based on her unshakable sense of self: "I've always looked out for Number One. Men have structured society to make a woman feel guilty if she looks after herself. Well, I beat men at their own game. I don't look down on men but I certainly don't look up to them either. I never found a man I could love—or trust—the way I loved myself" (quoted in Ward 61). It is hard to think of another woman in mainstream American culture—then or now—who presented such an individualistic image. In a publicity still, West strikes a pose looking at herself in the mirror, an image reminiscent of the trope of the mirror in beauty advertisements discussed in the last chapter (Fig. 3.1). But West exudes such control and satisfaction over her image that this photograph, narcissistic to be sure, demonstrates a self-love that doesn't depend on how anyone else sees her.

From her vaudeville and stage beginnings to her successful film career, West deliberately constructed a public persona that played on contradictions of cultural definitions of ideal and shadow femininity. Her independent and fulfilled characters rejected conventional moral standards that deemed sex outside of marriage "impure" and preserved their autonomy by refusing to submit to male dominance. From Diamond Lil in her stage plays to Lady Lou in *She Done Him Wrong*, Tira in *I'm No Angel*, Ruby Carter in *Belle of the Nineties*, and Cleo Borden in *Goin' to Town*, West's characters depict the link between economics and erotics and are "tricky" in the sense that they recognize and profit from the sociosexual market.

The heroine as successful and happy prostitute was an image that reformers could not tolerate, and as Ramona Curry explains in her insightful study *Too Much of a Good Thing: Mae West as Cultural Icon*, these four films "suggest in dialogue, performance, and narrative that virtually all relations between men and women, within or outside marriage, operate in terms of the exchange of sex for money" without depicting it as wrong or leading to unhappiness (53). Like the Anita Loos-scripted *Red-Headed Woman* (1932) and other pre-Production Code films about "kept women," West's movies presented fantasy figures who were financially independent, lived in luxury, and enjoyed their sexual activities.

However, *Klondike Annie* (1936), West's next film, reflects increased Production Code enforcement in its portrayal of a West protagonist who does not happily get rich through the exchange of sex for money. As Curry shows, a case study of the film reveals "how industry censorship worked *not* to eradicate depictions of illicit sexuality, but rather to suppress the power and pleasure that West's characters derived from such sexuality" (56). Production Code Administration correspondence insisted that the sexual knowledge and enjoyment of the heroine be toned down and was particularly concerned with the film's portrayal of

Figure 3.1. West looks out for Number One and enacts her self-reflexive manner as a public woman who controls her image and enjoys the gaze of others as well as her own. Compare this photograph to Figure 2.8. Publicity still courtesy of Museum of Modern Art/Film Stills Archive.

how West's character, the San Francisco Doll, impersonated Klondike Annie, a missionary worker.

What is significant here is that the first West film to really show the constraints of the Production Code is the one in which the main character performs a female female impersonation of a woman who, in the polarized ideas of "good" and "bad" women, is her moral opposite. Further, this is the first West vehicle to suggest that the West persona was divided into public and private, an external body distinct from an inner "soul."

The censorship of the Production Code transforms the transgressive West star persona into the kind of female trickster who emerged as the screwball heroine in Depression-era film comedy. Although the sexually active heroines in films like West's first five, Ernst Lubitsch's *Trouble in Paradise* (1932), and *Red-Headed Woman* (1932) yielded to the more sexually restrained heroines in *It Happened One Night* (1934), *Twentieth Century* (1934), *The Gay Divorcee* (1934), *Sylvia Scarlett* (1935), *My Man Godfrey* (1936), and *Theodora Goes Wild* (1936), the genre that evolved into screwball comedy continued to present unconventional heroines who engaged in the social relations of the sexes as equals to men. Sexually active heroines were moved from the comic terrain of West and Harlow into the genre of the melodrama, where sexuality and transgression were punished. In off-screen publicity, the film industry in the thirties characterized stars as independent; career and marriage as compatible albeit challenging; and heterosexual relationships as based on the equality of the sexes (Elaine Tyler May 41).

These attitudes were prevalent in the genre of screwball comedy, which philosopher Stanley Cavell describes as "the comedy of equality, evoking laughter equally at the idea that men and women are different *and* at the idea that they are not" (122). In a similar vein, film scholar Elizabeth Kendall argues that romantic comedy directors "brought a style of male-female collaboration into the movies that hadn't yet been seen. . . . Capra and company treated their leading ladies not as icons of femininity but as companions. The choice wasn't so much a question of methodology as of psychology: these were men who didn't shrink from imagining what it might feel like to be a woman" (xvi).[6] From behind the "smoke screen for seriousness" that comedy provided, the directors dealt with the issues about women's status and equality raised by Jazz Age discourses of sex and the "woman question" (Kendall 63). As movie censorship limited representations of sexuality from the mid-1934 enforcement of the Production Code (in response to threats of boycotts by the Legion of Decency), screwball comedy diverted sexual energy into the less private arenas of the private sphere: the parlor and workplace instead of the bedroom. As Molly Haskell explains, the Production Code and the advent of sound "gave birth to new forms and figures of speech: to romantic comedies in which love was disguised as antagonism and sexual readiness as repartee" (124).[7]

Predicated upon what humor theorist Jerry Palmer terms "the logic of the absurd," screwball comedy set up and followed through the comedy surrounding the premise that "The love impulse in man frequently reveals itself in terms of conflict," to quote the psychiatrist "expert" in *Bringing Up Baby* (1938). Once that contradiction is accepted, the screwball world spins around similar kinds of "topsyturvyism," as humor theorist Henri Bergson terms the inverted world that comedy portrays. Because the genre of comedy means that we get the desirable ending and because the creation of a couple provides the narrative closure for the vast majority of Hollywood films,[8] the screwball comedy can take its audience on a wild trip through fantasies that trespass the very boundaries the trickster traverses: class, gender, animal and human, public and private selves, lawful and outlaw.

In particular, the screwball genre favorably portrayed unconventional female behavior, including female trickery as a strategy for fighting the battle of the sexes. The title of *Theodora Goes Wild* (1936) summarizes the story of the screwball heroine. Theodora Lynn (Irene Dunne) appears to be on her way to joining the ranks of Lynnfield's spinsters, but secretly she writes sexy best-selling novels under the name Caroline Adams (Fig. 3.2). When the book jacket painter (played by Melvyn Douglas) follows her to Connecticut, he convinces her to "break loose"; she rebels against the dowagers of the Literary Circle and declares her love for the painter. When he disappears, she follows him back to New York and, as the outrageous "public woman" Caroline Adams, forces him to end his unhappy marriage. The film strikes a blow against the Depression-era forces of censorship that would erupt scarcely a year later when Mae West did Eve. But, most interestingly, the film lingers on Theodora's double life, giving Dunne the opportunity to perform private restraint and public wildness, with female trickery as the common link between the two personas.

Sparked by the success of Dunne in *Theodora Goes Wild*, movies like *The Awful Truth* (1937) with Dunne and Cary Grant, *Bringing Up Baby* (1938) with Katharine Hepburn and Grant, and *The Lady Eve* (1941) with Barbara Stanwyck and Henry Fonda portrayed heroines that used disguise, impersonation, deceit, and (small) theft. From the planned female female impersonation of Lucy in *The Awful Truth* and the relentlessly madcap personality of Susan in *Bringing Up Baby* to the jilted Jean's sardonic impersonation of *The Lady Eve*, screwball heroines successfully employ the tactics of female trickery to get what they want. *The Awful Truth* presents female transgression and trickery as useful strategies to

Figure 3.2. The ladies of the Lynnfield sewing circle would never imagine that mild Theodora (Irene Dunne, seated in the center) is secretly the best-selling author of the racy novels that scandalize them. Publicity still from *Theodora Goes Wild* (1936) courtesy of Museum of Modern/Art Film Stills Archive.

gain equal footing in the battle of the sexes. *Bringing Up Baby* uses the female trickster to advocate the adoption of a flexible social self that can survive the speed of obsolescence (which characterized discourses of mass consumption in the Depression.) In *The Lady Eve*, the deployment of covert power through female trickery is again the only strategy that works. However, instead of taking on the Depression-era valorization of flexibility, the manipulations of the female trickster on the brink of wartime in *The Lady Eve* are presented as more darkly destructive. As fantasy figures of strong women who assert their individual will (rather than submit to men's) and who participate equally on the slippery terrain of comic pratfalls and humiliations, the screwball heroines cross the boundaries between "good" and "bad" femininity, elite and common class, and honest and deceptive behavior with their female trickery.

The Truth of Style

"What wives don't know won't hurt them," proclaims Jerry Warriner (Cary Grant) as he props himself in front of a sunlamp so his wife Lucy (Irene Dunne) will believe that he has been in Florida for two weeks. From this endorsement of deception at the beginning of *The Awful Truth* to the confusing doublespeak of the final reconciliation scene, the characters operate within a web of duplicity in which whoever is the trickier controls the situation. In general, then, this film represents marriage as a series of tricks; in order to meet the screwball hero on level ground, the screwball heroine must create for herself a social self that practices trickery.

Briefly, the plot of *The Awful Truth* follows Lucy and Jerry during the ninety-day waiting period before their divorce is final. Brought together by Jerry's visitation rights to their dog, they sabotage each other's new relationships and reconcile moments before the divorce would be final. Perhaps the most ironic of the subgenre of the "comedy of remarriage" discussed by Stanley Cavell and others, *The Awful Truth* is an antisentimental and hilarious exegesis on truth and style. The movie was based on a popular 1922 play by Arthur Richman, and in many ways expresses a Jazz Age mentality of game-playing and "terrible honesty" underlying the deception.[9]

When Jerry comes home from "Florida," appropriately tan and bearing a basket of oranges (which, unfortunately for him, have California stamped on them), Lucy is not there. She enters in an evening gown with her handsome voice teacher Armand; his car broke down and they had to spend the night at a roadside inn. Jerry is immediately suspicious (prompted perhaps by his own guilt), and their fight ends with a blithe decision to divorce. In court, they maintain their distant tone of sophisticated irony as they tell the judge how they met (they both wanted to buy Mr. Smith, their dog) and each asks for custody of the dog. It is at this point that Lucy first uses a trick to get what she wants. As both people call to the dog, Lucy slyly shows Mr. Smith the toy that Jerry brought him from "Florida," and he runs to her. It is ironic that she uses one of the props of his deception as the basis for her trickery.

Significantly (in its ludicrous way), the dog keeps Jerry and Lucy in contact. Mr. Smith (played by Asta, the famous Hollywood dog of the *Thin Man* series and the "fiend" George in *Bringing Up Baby*) is remarkable for his ability to perform the tricks Jerry and Lucy have taught him; he symbolizes the spirit of play on which their relationship is based. Jerry's court-ordered visits to the dog give him the opportunity to interfere with Lucy's relationship with Dan (Ralph Bellamy), a dull millionaire from Oklahoma who offers Lucy a life of rural security. Jerry's tricks point out Dan's innate lack of the urbane wit and sophisticated charm that Lucy and Jerry share: he pays the orchestra leader to play the song to which the cloddish Dan dances, and he tickles Lucy from his hiding place behind a door while Dan proposes in a poem he wrote, "Oh you would make my life divine / If you would change your name to mine." In the scenes in which Lucy, Jerry, and Dan interact, it is obvious that Lucy and Jerry belong together, but Lucy's pride prohibits her from reconciling with Jerry until it is almost too late.

Director Leo McCarey expresses the connection between Lucy and Jerry visually as well as narratively and comically. For example, when Jerry and his companion, Dixie Belle Lee (Joyce Compton), bump into Lucy and Dan at a nightclub, McCarey directs the actors, positions the camera, and edits the shots in such a way that the viewer is encouraged to be sympathetic to Lucy and Jerry's relationship. That the two couples meet up is a narrative choice, but the comic effect of the dialogueless exchange of looks among the four characters is an example of the meaning created by the language of film.

In the frame enlargements from this scene (Fig. 3.3 a–h), McCarey exhibits a playful formalism. After a four-shot (Fig. 3a) that gives the viewer the positions of the characters around the table, the composition of shots unite Lucy and Jerry while isolating Dixie Belle and Dan. In Figure 3.3b, Lucy and Jerry meet each other's gaze, two equals facing off with amused detachment. In Figure 3.3c, the viewer still sees Lucy and Jerry, but now they look into the camera, a perspective revealed as a subjective shot from Dixie Belle's point of view in the next cut to Figure 3.3d, the reverse-shot, a close-up of Dixie Belle. Coyly, Lucy and Jerry exchange a look of mutual recognition in Figure 3.3e and then, simultaneously turn to glance at Dan in Figure 3.3f. In Figure 3.3g, a puzzled Dan looks back at them, and in Figure 3.3h, the final frame in this series, Lucy looks down, betraying the emotion that Jerry has been hoping for. The direction underlines the self-conscious irony that Lucy and Jerry share. The spectator is invited to share in this elegant "looking-dance," to see Dixie Belle and Dan as the odd people out, to recognize—as Lucy and Jerry do—who the real couple is.

Dixie Belle is the performer in the club and has adopted a Southern accent and persona that contrast with Lucy and Jerry's elegantly mocking politeness (based, of course, on their mutual class privilege). Dixie Belle is honest about putting on an act as a singer and in creating her public persona, but the film treats her with contempt, making her the butt of the joke. When Dixie Belle takes the stage, she sings the first verse of a poignant song about loss (Fig. 3.4), but at the line "My dreams are gone with the wind," the skirt of her dress is lifted by a wind effect despite her mock protestations and exaggerated attempts to keep

b

a

c

d

Figure 3.3. These frame enlargements from *The Awful Truth* show the editing, camera position, and blocking that create comedy out of the uncomfortable moment when Jerry invites himself and Dixie Belle to join Lucy and Dan for a drink. The point-of-view and use of subjective shots help to make the viewer sympathetic to Lucy and Jerry. The lack of dialogue in this part of the scene calls attention to the formalist use of the language of film. *a.* Four-shot of Jerry (Cary Grant) and Dixie Belle (Joyce Compton) joining Lucy (Irene Dunne) and Dan (Ralph Bellamy) at the nightclub; *b.* Jerry and Lucy look at each other; *c.* at Dixie Belle; *d.* close-up of Dixie Belle.

f

e

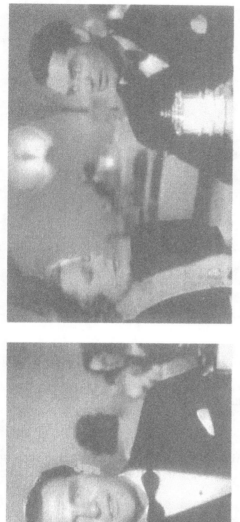

g

h

Figure 3.3 (cont.). *e.* Jerry and Lucy look at each other; *f.* Jerry and Lucy look at Dan; *g.* close-up of Dan; *h.* Lucy glances down and ends the looking game.

Figure 3.4. The calm before the storm. In the nightclub scene of *The Awful Truth* (1937), Dixie Belle (Joyce Compton) sings "My Dreams Are Gone with the Wind"—right before the wind effect lifts her skirts. Publicity still courtesy of Museum of Modern Art/Film Stills Archive.

it down. What begins as a sentimental Depression-era ballad of dispossession ends up as a lampoon of popular culture as her skirt flies up triumphantly, and she runs off the stage.

Jerry and Lucy's response to the risqué nature of the act is a funny combination of trying to maintain composure, feeling embarrassment (Jerry leans over and says, "I just met her"), and being very amused by the many levels of humor in the situation. Lucy has caught Jerry with just the kind of woman she suspected he would take up with: a floozy. Dan does not share their ironic detachment, and his leer shows his enjoyment of the "low" entertainment before him. The comic timing of the editing in this scene includes the spectator in the amusement Lucy and Jerry share, which excludes Dixie Belle and Dan; this invites the spectator to imagine a subjective position from the point of view of Lucy and

Jerry's stylish class, and the viewer who resists is placed in the same category as the other outsiders.

The elitism at the center of *The Awful Truth* comes through loud and clear here in what romantic comedy scholar Elizabeth Kendall judges as "ungenerous." "Underneath the parody, Dixie Belle is being blamed for the bad taste of the nightclub owner who hired her, the hack who wrote her song, and Jerry Warriner himself, who asked her out" (203–4). Not only is she the butt of the joke in the nightclub scene, but Lucy also reprises the song and dance to humiliate Jerry. As Kendall points out, Dixie Belle is a mockery of a Ginger Rogers heroine, and when Lucy performs the same song and dance routine later in the film, it completes the film's snobbish self-centeredness.

Despite its distinctly undemocratic tendencies—which were rare in screwball comedy—the movie is wickedly, viciously funny. For example, while researching advertising strategies in *Cosmopolitan*, I found an advertisement for Dixie Belle gin with the slogan "The Good Companion" (Fig. 3.5). The copy reads, "Such refinement of bouquet, such gracious smoothness, such readiness to merge discreetly with your chosen cocktails and highballs, are instant tokens of a gin of the highest character." The joke is on Dixie Belle, because she "picked out the name" herself and, it is implied, thought it would confer "refinement," but it only aligns her with the good time of a drink for "Jerry the Nipper." The character's name must have been improvised on the set (like much of the movie), because in the Viña Delmar script, the character was named Toots Binswanger. Of course, the "good companion" for Jerry is Lucy; together they emulate the elegant style of the gin ad's drawing. In marked contrast to Lucy, who studies opera and performs in *private* recitals, Dixie Belle's public performance, her display of her body, and her inability to get the joke make her common and fair game as a pawn in Lucy and Jerry's class-inflected competition.

In screwball comedy, the female trickster's impersonations, like the actresses' performances, are metaphors for the necessary duplicity caused by the subject/object split and by women's having to act in such a way as to be preferred by gentlemen. The wealthy women don't need to rely on men for money; these economically independent heroines disentangle their erotic and economic happiness, although they certainly create new entanglements, some economic. The masquerade of femininity becomes a cross-class impersonation that calls attention to how female identity is constructed through appearance and behavior. Further, the impersonations of women who stand in contrast to the character and the actor's star persona in *The Awful Truth* (and *It, Bringing Up Baby*, and *The Lady Eve*) are examples of how, according to James Naremore, clas-

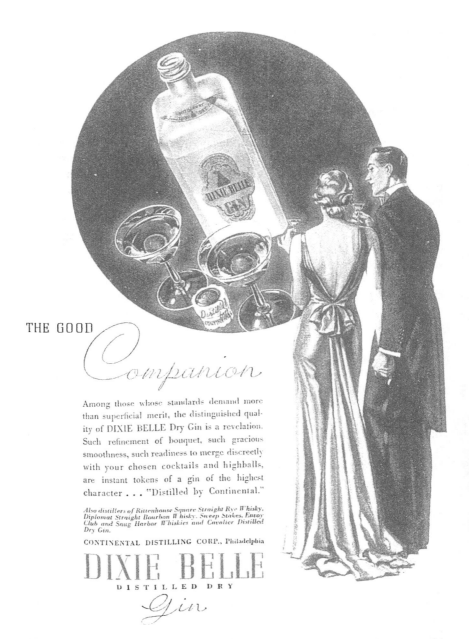

THE GOOD

Companion

Among those whose standards demand more than superficial merit, the distinguished quality of DIXIE BELLE Dry Gin is a revelation. Such refinement of bouquet, such gracious smoothness, such readiness to merge discreetly with your chosen cocktails and highballs, are instant tokens of a gin of the highest character . . . "Distilled by Continental."

Also distillers of Rittenhouse Square Straight Rye Whisky, Diplomat Straight Bourbon Whisky, Sweep Stakes, Envoy Club and Snug Harbor Whiskies and Cavalier Distilled Dry Gin.

CONTINENTAL DISTILLING CORP., Philadelphia

DIXIE BELLE

DISTILLED DRY

Gin

Figure 3.5. The good joke: our knowledge that Dixie Belle was the name of a brand of gin deepens our understanding of the comic bisociation in this scene. *Cosmopolitan,* July 1934.

sical Hollywood narrative often functions to give actors the opportunity to show off their skill by playing roles that run counter to their personas.

In *The Awful Truth*, Lucy parodies Dixie Belle's routine in the first of a series of tricks that sabotage Jerry's engagement to the "madcap heiress," Barbara Vance; these tricks also reconfigure her as an object of his desire. Lucy shows up at Jerry's apartment and, in a painful conversation, tries to remind him of the fun they had together. Even her lie that she is still engaged to Dan fails to make him jealous, and Lucy prepares to leave. Along with the camera work that captures Lucy's emotions, the viewer's privileged information that Lucy is not going to marry Dan makes Lucy more sympathetic, and what happens next reinforces this. When Barbara calls, Lucy unthinkingly picks up the phone. Jerry responds to his fiancée's suspicions with a lie: that the woman who answered was his sister Lola, and no, unfortunately, she cannot accept Barbara's invitation to dinner at the Vance mansion. McCarey places careful emphasis on Lucy's subjective point of view, which encourages the viewer to be sympathetic toward her and to desire the same ending that she does.

Lucy catches Jerry in the "awful truth" that he is deceptive, and we know that despite the earlier montage that shows us newspaper society columns about Barbara and Jerry and footage of them on dates at exciting sporting and social events, the private knowledge that Lucy and Jerry share is more important and real than the public image Jerry and Barbara create together. Moreover, the montage shows Jerry patting Barbara's hand fondly, but he does not return her loving gaze.

Jerry's lie creates the context for the female female impersonation of sister Lola that Lucy performs when she bursts into the Vance parlor that evening. Her arrival puts Jerry in the uncomfortable position of having either to play along with the low-class character she has chosen as his sister or to reveal himself to be the liar he is. She interrupts Jerry's story about his father's activities at Princeton with the information that their father was a gardener there. She horrifies the Vances when she pretends to drink an enormous glass of sherry and suddenly exclaims, "Don't anybody leave this room—I've lost my purse!" She then reprises the song "My Dreams Are Gone with the Wind," which the nightclub singer Dixie Belle Lee performed earlier in the movie. When Lucy (the wife) performs Dixie Belle's (the showgirl's) song as Lola (the sister) in front of Barbara (the future wife), she not only achieves her goal of making Jerry look inappropriate in front of the stuffy Vances but also makes Jerry see her as a clever trickster capable of playing a range of roles. By aligning herself with the low-class Dixie Belle and against the elite Barbara,[10] she puts herself on the side of fun and sex and against rigidity and propriety. That she performs an implied burlesque encourages him to group her with the women he saw while they were married, as opposed to the new "wife" figure, the fiancée. By pretending to be his sister—manifesting herself as the embodiment of his deceit—she reinforces the bond of familiarity between them, a reminder that she knows the "awful truth" about him, but wants him nevertheless. In creating the impression that Lola and Jerry are lower class, she contrasts the stuffiness of the elite Vances with the cool style of the Warriners. And of course, the lyrics of the song take on a more personal meaning as Lucy sings them; if Jerry marries Barbara she will indeed be "out in the cold" emotionally, and who knows what the "stormy weather" will mean for Lucy?

Irene Dunne's performance of Lucy performing Lola is an example of what happens when an actor performs a role within the frame of the movie. Film scholar Charles Affron calls this "performing performing" and argues that although classical Hollywood style obscures artifice and creates verisimilitude (through continuity editing, camera position, and narrative), self-reflexivity makes us reexamine our categories of "real" and representation. In particular, the character who performs as a showgirl "forces us to recognize artifice and the objectification of the performer" (Affron 43).

As a showgirl, Lucy connects herself to the tradition of public women who transgress women's "true" place in the private sphere. The first female celebrities in the 1840s and 1850s, such as Jenny Lind and Harriet Beecher Stowe, were what scholar Richard H. Brodhead calls "Veiled Ladies," in reference to the character who turns out to be the virginal blonde heroine in Hawthorne's novel *The Blithedale Romance* (1852). The Veiled Lady "registers the creation of a newly publicized world of popular entertainment taking place simultaneously with the creation of a newly privatized world of women's domestic life" (Brodhead 277). Female performers on the stage are cultural icons that articulate the position of women as surveyed objects, as watching themselves being looked at, but they are also symbols of erotic and economic independence and public practitioners of the social practices of female trickery. In her article "Private Parts in Public Places: The Case of Actresses," Juliet Blair summarizes, "The actress may be thought to have professionalized the behaviour of all women" (215). Like the "oldest profession," acting involves doing what is inscribed as private in the public sphere doing it and for money. As we saw in Chapter 2, the film actress that Lorelei Lee becomes at the end of *Gentlemen Prefer Blondes* is the comic representation of the conflation of economics and erotics central to definitions of femininity and masculinity in modern consumer culture. As an actress, Lorelei makes a career out of the impersonations and self-objectification she has perfected in her everyday life as a preferred blonde.

When Lucy pretends to be "Lola," when she acts as a female trickster who can take on any role, the attention to performing reminds us that it is sophisticated Irene Dunne who is performing as Lola. As we will see in the discussions of *Bringing Up Baby* and *The Lady Eve*, when screwball comediennes break out of type, they do so with a performance within their performance. Of course, in *The Awful Truth*, Lucy's act is a private one for the benefit/correction of Jerry—only he can get the joke. Her trick aligns the wealthy Vances with Dixie Belle and Dan, as the tricked who never comprehend what is so funny. The spectator, however, is invited to be in on it with Lucy and Jerry, and so we too are welcomed into their elite circle.

Lucy follows her female female impersonation with a series of tricks that precipitate their reconciliation. After her exhibition, Jerry steers her out of the house. Pretending to be too drunk to drive, Lucy manipulates Jerry into driving her to her aunt's cabin in Connecticut, manages en route to push the car into a ravine so Jerry can't go back to the city (forcing them to catch rides on the front of police motorcycles), and sets them up in adjoining rooms separated by a door that is blown open by the wind. It is there that they reconcile, just before the midnight deadline when their divorce would be final.

Despite the accusations of infidelity and duplicity (real and imagined) and the loss of trust between them, Lucy and Jerry are well matched because of their shared outlook (ironic sophistication) and their ability to trick. Elizabeth Kendall comments, "It's as if [director] McCarey had set himself the exercise of creating a female character with the same privileges, the same firm sense of self, as a man, and then engaged her in battle with her 'twin'" (202). Because both characters are unwilling to drop their ironic and distant personas and admit their feelings for the other, the relationship plays out in little deceptions, denials, and tricks. Seen from this perspective, the movie is a study of gender equality based on Lucy and Jerry's mutual trickiness; female trickery is necessary to survive the battle of the sexes. Moreover, the subtext that articulates the Depression-era issues surrounding female trickery, dispossession, and marriage (as represented in the Adam and Eve sketch) implies that marriage can be an emotional and social refuge in times of trouble.

By impersonating a model of inappropriate femininity in a performance that transgresses the boundaries of class, "good" and "bad" public expressions of sexuality, and honesty, Lucy gets her husband back as the escort, playmate, and sexual partner she has missed. Although he is not necessarily more trustworthy (despite his promises in the last scene that he will be different in the future), Lucy wants him as a partner in the life of leisure and style they both enjoy. The representation of their marriage plays on cultural discourses of style and pleasure. Because the Warriner marriage is not based on either female economic dependence or children—two of the conventional tenets of marriage—but on companionship for leisure and "laughs," it is fitting that their reconciliation is based on Lucy's demonstration of their mutual trickiness.

Finally, the most important facet of the life of leisure embodied by the elegant Warriners is a modern style of living. The personas Jerry and Lucy adopt and use to interact with each other and the world masks the less compelling emotions that lurk under the surface; when they do express those emotions of jealousy, love, anger, they do so with panache. Whether it is Cary Grant's unparalleled physical comedy as he not only trips and tips over the furniture at his wife's voice recital but also breaks the chair he sits in, or Irene Dunne's bravado when Jerry and Dan show up while Armand hides in the bedroom, the movie portrays them as unquestionably attractive. As film historian Robert Sklar explains in his discussion of screwball comedy,

> though they never challenged the social order, the pictures gave audiences a whole new vision of social style, a different image of how to be a person: it was okay to be pleasure loving, even if it made you look sexy or odd; it was good to puncture stuffed shirts and be lively, gay, and carefree; it was good to throw decorum to the wind. There's no question but that they made their contribution to cultural change, just by repeating over and over again how attractive it was to be a person who liked to have fun. (188)

Part of Lucy's attractiveness is her willingness to transgress the boundaries of acceptable femininity, which is of course rewarded by her reconciliation with the hero. Her parodic deployment of sexual allurement, the culturally sanctioned means of exerting female power, is in no way submissive either to the dictates of "good" female sexuality or to Jerry's desires. By turning the more staid view of woman's "duty to attract" (the phrase is from an advertisement discussed in Chapter 2) on its head with her female female impersonation, Lucy demonstrates a mode of female power that is attractive because of its unconventionality.

Fashions in Passions

That the heroines of screwball comedy represented a new style of female behavior did not escape the watchful eye of fan magazine writer Ruth Waterbury. In an article evocatively titled "Fashions in Passions: Maybe you movie queens can get away with it, but what about us ordinary gals who must win our men, too?" in the July 1938 issue of *Photoplay* (one of the popular fan magazines that served as important secondary texts in reflecting and shaping the movie audience), Waterbury addresses the screwball actresses with tongue-in-cheek accusations that the tactics they model in the movies are not easily transferable into man-catching strategies in the "real" world. "How can we expect to do anything with the old tricks like eyes shadowed beneath hat brims, mysterious smiles on our lips, or even that mouldy old line about their not thinking we are that kind of girl, do they? Drag those techniques out this spring and it's about as effective as talking about the Oxford movement at the monkey house. And it's all your fault" (Waterbury 251).

Waterbury explains that moviegoing men are so entranced by the images of "goof-nuts" heroines that they expect and desire similar behavior from real women. The article ends with a quasi-threat that if the "mentors" do not provide the eager students in the audience with tactics of allurement that they can copy, the women will be forced to keep their dates at home listening to the radio "because those heroines in the radio stories are still in the old-fashioned lure business. They are still using the skin you love to touch, and the come-hither of perfume, and the charm of good grooming to get their men. So we feel comfortable with them" (325).

Waterbury's complaint—couched in the language made familiar by the advertising industry—points to the discomforting effect of some Depression-era discourses of femininity. Further, it demonstrates a conservative response to changes in representations of female behavior; movie women create the male expectations to which real women should submit if they want to catch and hold onto a man. If on one side of a spectrum of female behavior we have the disorderly conduct of the film female tricksters, then on the other side we have the submissive "old-fashioned lure business" based on the products and practices of mass consumption. Seen from this perspective, the rebellious role playing of female trickery uses and subverts the cosmetics, grooming, and behavior that constitute the social practice of female trickery in everyday life.

As an example of the pervasiveness in American culture of the 1930s of defining acceptable femininity as artifice, we'll turn briefly to the advertising strategies of Tangee lipstick, the "magic" lipstick that is orange in the tube but changes to a "color which is yours and yours alone" when applied to the lips. Like the "close-up test" trope in the Lux soap ad discussed in Chapter 2, Tangee ads also invited women to see themselves as judged by an imaginary, critical, and unforgiving male gaze (Fig. 3.6). A June 1932 ad shows a man pointing a threatening finger at a distressed woman; the heading reads, "Some day . . . I'm going to CLEAN THOSE

Figure 3.6. As part of a rhetorical strategy that calls attention to how men perceive women's use of cosmetics, this Tangee ad implies a male viewer who recognizes the "distinction between art and artifice." Tangee's answer to staying on the right side of this fine line is a lipstick that "magically" turns a color that matches each woman's individual coloring. Note that the illustration depicts the three types of women classified by haircolor: blonde, brunette, and redhead. *Cosmopolitan*, December 1930.

TANGEE
LIKE NATURE'S OWN GLOW

VOGUE TELLS
"WHAT MEN DISLIKE
IN WOMEN"

"Men no longer beam with approval," says this world famous fashion magazine, "at the sight of a schoolgirl complexion guiltless of any make-up. On the contrary they may even find it wan and dull. But there remains always the distinction between art and artifice, and a patently artificial beauty leaves them quite as cold. Avoid therefore lipsticks that do not match one's natural coloring."

Tangee, the world's most famous lipstick, leaves no greasy smear of glaring, flashy color. Tangee is entirely different from any other lipstick. Magically it takes on color after you apply it . . . and blends with your own natural coloring, no matter what your individual complexion. And Tangee never rubs off or looks artificial!

Tangee Lipstick, $1. Rouge Compact, 75¢. Crème Rouge, $1. Face Powder, to match the natural skin tones, $1. *Night Cream*, cleanses and nourishes, $1. *Day Cream*, protects the skin, $1. *Cosmetic*, a new "mascara," will not smart, $1.

SEND 20¢ FOR TANGEE BEAUTY SET

(Six items in miniature and "The Art of Make-Up.") The George W. Luft Co., Dept. C-12 417 Fifth Avenue   New York

Name

Address

"Some Day... I'm going to CLEAN THOSE LIPS!"

"JIM was trying to be nice about it... but that painted look really *repulsed* him. He just had to say something."

Painted lips are one thing a man will *not* stand for. And it's so easy to offend. Colors that you think look well by themselves may look *common* and *cheap* on you.

Be safe. Don't run the risk of having painted lips. Forget your present lipstick at once. From now on, *Tangee* your lips.

Tangee can't make you look painted. It isn't paint. It's a new discovery that changes on your lips to the *one* color best for you. It brings you new loveliness and charm.

Tangee is permanent—waterproof. Its special cold cream base prevents chapping.

Get Tangee at your druggist or cosmetic counter. It costs no more than ordinary lipsticks. And it ends that painted look.

TRY TANGEE LIPSTICK AND ROUGE

- - - - - *Send 10c for Miracle Make-Up Set* - - - - -

The George W. Luft Co.   C 7-6

417 Fifth Avenue, New York, N. Y.

Gentlemen: I enclose 10c. Please send your miracle make-up set to:

Name _____

Address _____

City _____ State _____

Cheeks Mustn't Look Painted, Either
Tangee Rouge changes on the cheeks—just the way Tangee Lipstick changes on your lips. It gives the color most becoming to you... ends that "painted look"! When you get Tangee Lipstick, ask for Tangee Rouge.

Figure 3.7. This ad dramatizes a critical male gaze—and hand. The advertising strategy develops into an exhortation for women to use the lipstick that "ends that painted look." *Cosmopolitan*, June 1932.

LIPS!" (Fig. 3.7). The text of the ad explains, "Painted lips are one thing a man will *not* stand for. And it's so easy to offend. Colors that you think look well by themselves may look *common* and *cheap* on you."

Even in this most conservative context—an advertisement designed to reinforce and play on women's anxieties about the dangers of "that painted look"—makeup is presented as a trick. Women can negotiate the treacherous line between good and bad sexual allure by relying on the "magic" of Tangee to give them the perfect man-pleasing look necessary to female survival, a natural look that can only be achieved through the trick of lipstick. By claiming that the correct deployment of cosmetic trickery can, in the words of a 1934 Tangee ad, "MAKE MEN WANT YOUR KISSES!" Tangee represents its product as a powerful tool in the manipulation of men as long as, paradoxically, it appears natural.

The woman in the 1932 ad can employ the "magic" of Tangee to placate Jim, her irritable judge, so he will get his finger out of her face and, one supposes, provoke affection and respectful lust in place of his possessive display of frustration and impotent anger ("some day" he will wash her lips, but today he is just going to yell at her). By using female trickery, she can better manage him and avoid the ugly scene the ad dramatizes.

In another Tangee ad from the same year, a photograph of the same models shows the man (now called Tom) holding the woman's face close to his disapproving eyes. " 'Tom said . . . my LIPS looked <u>COMMON!</u>' " the slogan shouts. The copy continues, "And that painted look is one thing men *can't* overlook. Don't take chances. Discard your present lipstick . . . *Tangee* your lips!"

A year later in 1933, a slogan for a Tangee ad asked "Lovely Girl *or* just ordinary?" and offered the answer, "MEN CAN TELL by the Smartness of her Make-up!" The rhetorical strategy of a lipstick that defies the look of "paint" and instead would bring out the "natural color hidden in your lips" casts women as the victims of men's judgments. The ads, especially in 1932, give license to men to behave tyrannically; perhaps this is the advertising executives' response to the demasculinization of the Depression era. No matter what the cause, the situations avoidable by using Tangee are sadistic and misogynist.

As Waterbury suggested in her *Photoplay* article, screwball heroines provided a model of female (mis)behavior that was antithetical to the self-surveillance and fear of displeasing men implicit in the Tangee ads. The tricky screwball heroines never give men that much power and, in *Bringing Up Baby* as in *The Awful Truth*, they become the preferred woman by contradicting and frustrating the hero. The power the Tangee ads ascribe to men place the ads in the genre of melodrama, which is the opposite of romantic comedy, as critics like Kathleen Rowe have shown. Melodrama curbs "the feminist potential of the unruly woman. Romantic comedy, on the other hand, takes the 'problem' of female desire to a different conclusion, creating space for the desiring woman's resistance to male control and rewarding her, at least temporarily, for those very qualities that in melodrama lead to her pain" (Rowe 96–97).

Screwball Logic

> [T]he best defense against an illogical world is an illogical nature.
> (Gehring 59)

Like *The Awful Truth*, *Bringing Up Baby* portrays female trickery as a successful strategy. Susan attains the object of her desire by using the trickster tactics of duplicity, deception, theft, impersonation, and subversion. Regardless of David's protestations that he does not want to be involved with Susan, she shows herself to be a talented *bricoleuse*, transforming every situation to keep David close. From their first meeting on a golf course, where David is unable to dissuade Susan from her erroneous insistence that his ball is hers, to the spectacular collapse of the dinosaur skeleton in the final scene, David's rationality, science, and rigidity are no match for the chaos, illogic, and subversion represented by Susan. Through its comic endorsement of "trouble" over stability and the presentation of female trickery as a successful strategy, *Bringing Up Baby* illustrates Depression-era attitudes about the importance of a flexible—and tricky—social self for survival in both the private sphere of relationships and the public sphere symbolized by David's science.

Susan's trickery is successful where David's rigidity is not because she actively manipulates the people and situations around her to her advantage. When David enters her life, she sees him as a handsome and exciting addition to the playground that is her world. So what if he plans to get married as soon as he finishes reconstructing the brontosaurus skeleton he has been working on for years? Susan has other plans for him, one of which concerns the tame leopard she has in her apartment (a gift from her brother Mark to their aunt, Elizabeth Random). When David tries to convince a wealthy patron to donate a million dollars to the museum, he enters her screwball world of the wealthy elite, a world in which chance, people, and even animals conspire to frustrate his desires and further hers.

At first, Susan and David happen to be in the same place at the same time (on the golf course, in the country club dining room), but they are there for opposite reasons. Susan is engaging in her life of leisure and David is attempting to socialize his way to the million-dollar donation. David is merely annoyed by her disruptions of his business, but Susan is intrigued by their antagonistic interactions because, in accordance with screwball (il)logic, she interprets their conflict as indicative of the "love impulse." [11]

In order for the movie to be funny and not merely discomfitting, we the audience have to believe that Susan (being a woman and therefore better at things emotional and social) sees something in her interaction with David that does indicate love, and that David must be rescued from his fiancée, Miss Swallow, who is no fun at all. In addition to the generic and narrative clues that the couple will be romantically involved, director Howard Hawks establishes the connection between Susan and David in a funny bit of physical comedy. When Susan grabs onto the tail of David's dinner jacket to prevent him from leaving, she tears it (Fig. 3.8a); then when *she* tries to leave, he inadvertently stands on the bottom of her skirt and rips the rear panel off her dress. Because he is a gentleman, David tries to save Susan the humiliation of going back into the dining room with her underwear exposed. Unaware that she is no longer fully dressed, she tries to storm off and is too caught up in her

a

b

Figure 3.8 Sublimated sexual desire results in Production Code comedy. *a*. With screwball clumsiness, Susan (Katharine Hepburn) rips David's (Cary Grant's) coat; *b*. with screwball synchronicity, gentlemanly David tries to save Susan from embarrassment after he rips her dress. Frame enlargements from *Bringing Up Baby* (1938).

indignation to listen to him. Still the concerned gentleman, David tries to cover her rear first with his hat and then by standing close behind her (Fig. 3.8b). When she does realize that part of her skirt is missing, she does an about face, and together they lockstep through the dining room, much to the amusement of the crowd. For the second time that day, David fails to make his business connection.

This sequence is important because it shows conflict between the sexes turning to cooperation. Despite David's explicit refusal to interact with Susan, there he is, involved in a collaborative activity that fits them together so well that it reinforces Susan's interpretation that the conflict really means love. And, of course, in this scene the sexual subtext (forced to be a subtext because of the Production Code and the conventions of the genre) emerges hilariously as they rip each other's clothes and respond to the circumstances that cause them to stand and move close together.

The camera and actor movement in the film up to this point contrast smooth horizontal movement with clumsy vertical movement. The tracking shot (with camera positioned ahead of Hepburn and Grant) that captures the characters' comic walk out of the dining room is reminiscent of the characters' exit from the golf course in the disputed car—in both cases, the camera position reinforces David's inability to extricate himself physically from the force that he has become caught up in. In a reverse tracking shot from David and Susan's point of view, we see Peabody's bewilderment as the couple glides by. All David can do is shout the increasingly meaningless, "I'll be with you in a minute, Mr. Peabody!" Words and intentions pale in comparison to the physicality of screwball logic.

Susan does things that, as physical manifestations of the narrative, stop any forward motion that David might take without her. From playing his ball and taking his car to dropping the olive and tearing his coat, the "accidents" that plague Susan and David contrast vertical and horizontal movement. When David slips on Susan's dropped olive, the horizontal quickly turns to the vertical, as does any pratfall. When a person slips on a banana peel—or a more upper-class olive—the premise that there is solid ground beneath our feet suddenly is upended as the person rushes to meet the floor. The pratfall is the great democratic leveler; whether the person is dressed in hat and tails or overalls, he or she falls just the same. Like the pratfall, the accidental clothes-tearing is presented as vertical action by the way it is filmed on the stairs.

As Mast points out, the first close-up of either of the two leads isn't until shot 101, when David tells Susan that he is going to be married the next day (Mast doesn't refer to previous close-ups of minor characters) (12). This means that Hawks has used medium close-ups, medium shots, and long shots up until this scene, a choice that keeps the spectator at a distance from what the characters might be feeling during the initial part of the film. The range between the wide shot and the medium close-up is also the camera position most often used in classical Hollywood comedy, so Hawks's use of the close-up indicates an interest in the emotions of the protagonists that is excluded from, for example, the Laurel and Hardy short in which they move a piano.

Perhaps the most significant aspect to emerge from the sequence that begins in the dining room and ends in Susan's car is that Susan and David's interpretations of their relationship are diametrically opposed. For example, later that night, when David finally takes his leave of Susan, he tells her, "Our relationship has been a series of misadventures from beginning to end . . . I'm gonna say goodnight and I hope that I never set eyes on you again." After he gets up from the pratfall he immediately takes, there is a close-up of Susan (described this way in the screenplay): "Susan watches, smiles, shifts her eyes from side to side, nods her head affirmatively, then leans back out of the light" (67) (Fig. 3.9a). By showing Susan in the act of concocting a plan, screenwriters Dudley Nichols and Hagar Wilde call attention to her deliberate trickiness; the sideways glance connects Susan to female trickster forebears like Clara Bow's "It" girl (discussed in Chapter 2).

It is at this point that Susan intensifies her use of trickster tactics to pursue David. Much to David's surprise, the next morning Susan telephones him and blithely asks for assistance with the tame leopard her brother Mark has sent her. In the frame enlargement (Fig. 3.9b), we can see how the mise-en-scène shows Susan's carefree life in her spacious apartment. Only Hepburn's face and the leopard stand out in this frame of light and white. The contrast between the exotic animal Baby and the refined, robed Susan is central visually as well as narratively. Yet the way that Baby acts as if he were a pet—rubbing up against her leg as she pats him—suggests that both leopard and woman are highly contradictory. As a tame leopard, Baby is a liminal figure like Susan, and is thus unlike the other characters in the film.

Susan is connected to the leopard in her understanding of his tameness and even in her ability to communicate with him. In some of the funniest shots of the movie, Hawks highlights the connections between Susan and Baby in the scene in her apartment. After one of Grant's best physical bits—when David has a spontaneous reaction of surprise at seeing that there really is a leopard in Susan's bathroom (Fig. 3.9c)—Susan demonstrates how Baby responds to the song, "I Can't Give You Anything but Love, Baby." In contrast to his alignment with Susan (or because of it), Baby playfully attaches himself to David's trouser leg. In a telling shot, Hawks focuses on Hepburn, at her eye level as she crouches on the floor, approvingly watching Baby "play." In this shot, Baby seems to be enacting Susan's desires (Fig. 3.9d). In the next sequence, Susan instructs the cat to go after the departing David, "Go on, Baby. Down the stairs." And Baby follows David until Susan convinces him to help her take Baby to Connecticut.

The car ride to Connecticut is where the film is closest to the Hagar Wilde story on which it was based. The story follows the wealthy Suzan Vance and fiancé David as they try to bring a panther from New York to Connecticut. The wit and tone of Wilde's writing shines through the film (she was co-writer with Dudley Nichols) as well as in this highlight from the story:

Hauling a panther seventy miles in a station wagon without bars between you and the panther is no joke. Suzan kept referring to Baby as a lamb because he was quiet but David was aware at all moments during the drive that Baby was no lamb. Those few hours marked a turning point in David's life. He realized that life was not all fun and that it might end in death by drowning or perhaps, through no fault of your own, by having a panther who was in a position of advantage take a dislike to you. (238)

What the story achieves linguistically—the absurdity of the situation and David's disadvantage in it—the film expresses visually. In the frame enlargement of the three-shot in the car, Hawks wittily places Baby between the squabbling people, as if he were participating in the argument (Fig. 3.10a). Baby is both threat and substitute child, and the composition of the frame suggests this. Grant occupies the left third of the frame. Hepburn and Baby share the other two-thirds, looking as if they are having a conversation. In a later shot, Hepburn and Grant try to hold onto the leopard by its tail (it is in fast pursuit of a truck full of ducks and swans that Susan overturns), and Susan and David are united in the frame as they struggle against the animal instinct that motivates Baby (Fig. 3.10b). These frames illustrate critic Gerald Mast's point that Baby "becomes the perfect sexual link between Susan and David, sharing the potential sexual characteristics of both or either" (Mast, "Bringing Up Baby" 294).

At the house in Connecticut, David is relieved of his clothes, bone, identity, and sanity. After they put Baby in the stable (by talking to each other in the Baby-soothing cadences of "I Can't Give You Anything but Love, Baby"), Susan steals David's clothes while he is in the shower. Deftly, she puts on his hat as she completes her theft (Fig. 3.11a). This moment of cross-dressing calls attention to her trickiness and social flexibility. Soon after, the dog George steals the "intercostal clavicle," the final bone needed to complete the brontosaurus skeleton. Without his clothes (the surface signifier of personality and gender) and his bone

a

b

Figure 3.9. *a.* The trickster looks off to the side and decides to proceed with a plan that involves Baby, a tame leopard; *b.* Susan and Baby in her apartment; *c.* Baby surprises David, who thought the leopard was part of Susan's hoax; *d.* the camera, like Susan, "stoops to conquer." Frame enlargements from *Bringing Up Baby.*

c

d

a

b

Figure 3.10. When animals and people share the frame, director Hawks makes the people look particularly ridiculous: *a.* Susan, Baby, and David in the car; *b.* David and Susan unite in their attempt to restrain the animal. Frame enlargements from *Bringing Up Baby*.

(symbolic of both his career as a scientist and possession of the phallus as a man), David appears to be "betwixt and between" social categories.

The next scene is one of the funniest visually and linguistically. David repeats the word "clothes" in almost every line as he runs around the house in a feminine, feathery bathrobe. When he encounters Mrs. Carlton Random, Susan's Aunt Elizabeth, the dialogue reinforces the idea of lost identity:

AUNT: Well, who are you?
DAVID: Who are you?
AUNT: But who are *you?*
DAVID: What do you want?
AUNT: Well, who *are* you?
DAVID: (*sighing deeply*): I don't know. I'm not quite myself today.
AUNT: Well, you look perfectly idiotic in those clothes.
DAVID: These aren't my clothes.
AUNT: Well, where are your clothes?
DAVID: I've lost my clothes.
AUNT: But, why are you wearing these clothes? (97–99)

This prompts the famous jump (Figs. 3.11b and 3.11c) that punctuates David's line, "Because I just went gay . . . all of a sudden." In an interview, Hawks explains the "logic of the absurd" that underlies this and other moments in the film: "It's logical that one of the craziest things was to put him in a woman's negligee. Anything we could do to humiliate him, to put him down and let her sail blithely along, made it what I thought was funny" ("Interview with Joseph McBride," in Mast, *Bringing Up Baby*, 261).

The horizontal sailing along of the woman and the couple, the vertical movements puncturing that fluid and forward progress—these are at the heart of the film's comedy. In depriving David of his clothes and identity (she introduces him as Mr. Bone the gamehunter), Susan pulls him out of his rigid social self and into murkier waters, the realm of the trickster. Here, at the midpoint of the film, the movie has shifted from being about public dignity in the public sphere of New York to being about identity in the private sphere and sanity in the "green world" of Connecticut. So instead of sitting high on his scaffold working on the big brontosaurus skeleton, David is on the ground digging for his bone with the little, live dog George. George is the trickiest character in the movie because he is unaligned and chaotic; the script tips us off to his function when Aunt Elizabeth says, "George is a perfect fiend." He is the type of trickster in comic plots that Northrop Frye identifies as the "vice," who, like Puck, "acts from pure love of mischief" ("Mythos" 151). The

a

b

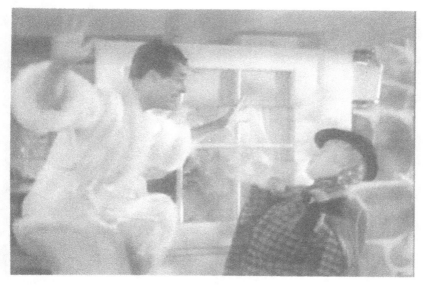

c

Figure 3.11. Susan steals David's clothes to prevent his escape, causing gender-bending hilarity: *a.* Susan looks especially tricky in David's hat; *b,c.* David acts especially loony in Susan's robe when he says, "I've just gone . . . gay all of a sudden!" Frame enlargements from *Bringing Up Baby*.

same dog performed a similar plot function in *The Awful Truth*. Hawks calls attention to George's function by putting him at the center of the composition of a frame (Fig. 3.12) in a scene that bisociates proper and tricky behavior. In contrast to the social motivations of humans, George acts on behalf of the natural world; he has taken the bone and put it back into the earth where it "belongs." Unlike Baby, this animal embodiment of the trickster acts of his own accord—and instinct—to prevent David from attaining his dual goals: completing the skeleton and marrying Miss Swallow.

The ironic understatement of David's intensely serious "I've been unavoidably detained" to Miss Swallow over the phone summarizes his manner of interaction with the zany people and the pursuits with which he has found himself involved. He has no sense of *how* to be a trickster, how to be flexible instead of rigid, how to tailor his response to the situation rather than straight-facedly reporting the objective truth. Even after David begs Susan to hide his identity, he doesn't respond when she calls him "Mr. Bone" (a name fitting for someone obsessed with his missing "intercostal clavicle"). When Susan steals his clothes,

Figure 3.12. In the dinner table scene, David's rigidity curtails his impersonation of "Mr. Bone." Hawks puts the dog in the center of the composition, suggesting perhaps that George is the sanest one in the group. Frame enlargement from *Bringing Up Baby.*

forcing him to wear a woman's feather-trimmed bathrobe, he clings to his rigidity. It is only in the scenes in which they sing (especially the duet of "I Can't Give You Anything but Love, Baby" that turns into a quartet with the participation of Baby and George) that David's enjoyment of himself and of Susan's company occupies him fully; his face changes from exaggerated humorlessness to a softened expression of satisfaction and pleasure. When he participates in this symbolically social moment, David transcends his rigidity and becomes human.

As many critics have noted, the scene in the forest recalls the enchanted forests of Shakespearean romantic comedy where identity and affiliations shift without the logic of daylight and cityscape. In *Bringing Up Baby,* Hawks parallels David and Susan with two other "couples": the elderly Major Applegate and Aunt Elizabeth, and Baby and George. Baby's dangerous double roams the countryside, a dark twin and villain who refuses to participate in a couple.

By depicting the flexibility exhibited by Susan as being better than David's rigidity, the movie participates in Depression-era ideas about the importance of a social self. In the brilliantly funny jail scene (which puts the dull-witted constable in league with the clownish psychiatrist

Dr. Lehman to get Susan and David to confess that they are bank robbers), Susan's cross-class impersonation enables her to escape from jail while David sits frustrated and flabbergasted at her performance of "Swinging Door Susie," a cigarette-smoking gangster's moll. Her sly facial expression and use of language are in sharp contrast to Susan's character; like Lucy's performance as Lola, this gives Hepburn a chance to play against both the character Susan and her own star persona as an upper-class, well-spoken woman. Susan/Hepburn's impersonation of "Swinging Door Susie" frees her from the jail cell as she glides horizontally on the cell door and out of captivity.

In contrast to Hepburn's physical and narrative mobility, Grant remains literally locked up behind bars. From behind the bars of the jail cell/cage, David says, "She's making all this up out of motion pictures she's seen." More accurately, she's making it up from movies that Grant has been in. In this, Susan's most disruptive and tricky scene, David clings to the "truth" that the self-reflexivity of the scene has already fractured. When Susan calls David "Jerry the Nipper"—which is what Lucy calls Jerry during her impersonation of Lola in *The Awful Truth*—it draws attention to the artifice not only of the movie the audience watches, but also of role playing in general. By presenting the constable and psychiatrist with a movie-reality that they will accept as truth, Susan and Hepburn pass in and out of the frames of verisimilitude and artifice that are usually obscured by classical Hollywood style. Susan's trick exemplifies popular discourses of social flexibility propagated by books like Dale Carnegie's *How to Win Friends and Influence People*. The constable and the psychiatrist think she is a bank robber, so she gives them what they want (information about the "Leopard gang") while she gets them to open a window through which she escapes.

Just as the jail scene showcases Susan's flexibility, the final scene in the museum highlights the rigidity that keeps David from the social integration essential to the conclusion of comedy.[12] Specifically, the dinosaur skeleton functions as a symbol of David's inflexible, backward-looking science, which is portrayed as antithetical to the dynamic chaos of the social and emotional world represented by Susan. In a genre that constantly subverts and dismantles any structure it portrays, such an obvious symbol of rigidity, obsolescence, and the long-dead past must come tumbling down, and with the final disruptive vertical movement of the movie, this scene does not disappoint those audience expectations.

But a discomfort lingers at the end of the movie as the skeleton (which also represents hard work, logic, and "man"'s control of nature) collapses; for David, this is truly a dispossession, expelling him from solitary contemplation into the emotional and social realm represented by his relationship with Susan. In the last moments of the movie, David is speechless while Susan carries on both ends of their conversation; all David can do is put his arms around her and accept the inevitability of his union with Susan, taking as his compensation, perhaps, the promise of sex in their embrace. As a symbol of David's rigidity, the destruction of the skeleton marks a new phase in his life; the skeleton he has built must go to make room for Susan.

Moreover, as a symbol of failed masculine achievement, the destruction of the skeleton articulates the way the Depression challenged definitions of manhood based on man's work and his role as breadwinner; all the phallic implications of David's search for his lost "bone" (and Susan's location of it), of David's anxiety about the "erection" of the skeleton, articulate the issue of masculinity in crisis. Further, it illustrates the paradoxical Depression-era attitude toward women and marriage: women's independence is a threat to the status quo, but women's participation as an equal makes the social relations of the sexes more "fun." If Susan brings back David's bone, she also destroys the structure in which it fit. At least she can function as a new partner who is better equipped than he to survive the challenges of the instability of modern life.

Seen from another perspective (and the open-endedness of these comedies invites such speculation), the dinosaur skeleton also represents obsolescence. In 1932, advertising experts Roy Sheldon and Egmont Arens enthusiastically described the speed of obsolescence:

Obsolescence . . . is seething through the life of the nation. Every day the latest fashions in clothes, in furniture, in automobiles, in coiffures is flashed on the screen before 16,000,000 intent watchers. Heralded in the newspapers, illustrated in the magazines, described over the radio, the latest wrinkle and the newest gadget are pushing and crowding into people's lives, not casually or with the leisurely pace of prewar days, but with the hustle and bustle—and also the gaiety—characteristic of the modern American *tempo*. (quoted in Ewen, *All Consuming* 244)

By representing the discomfort resulting from the abandonment of things past in favor of the changes of the future, director Howard Hawks makes a profound comment on modern consumer culture in the Depression era. Surely the idea that things were changing for the better— that, as Susan repeatedly assures David, "Everything's going to be all right"—was particularly attractive. The only response to the disorientation of rapid change is to be flexible like Susan and transform oneself and one's surroundings to further the satisfaction of individual desire. Trickery, then, is not only a symbol of a useful way to manage personal relationships in the private sphere, but also a metaphor of a flexible state of mind to help weather the disruptions in the public sphere, increasingly inseparable from the private.

But there is also a dangerous side to female trickery, one represented by a second leopard loose in the Connecticut countryside. Unlike the tame Baby, this leopard is a "bad cat," a circus animal that clawed a man and is on its way to a gas chamber when Susan and David mistake it for Baby and release it from the truck. The bad leopard is the one Susan finds when she escapes from the jail; unwittingly dragging a "killer" by a rope, she pulls it into the jail (where all the characters have congregated), saying, "I'm just as stubborn as you are."

And indeed she is as stubborn as the bad cat when it comes to her pursuit of David. By linking her with the second leopard, Hawks alludes to the possibilities of Susan putting herself in a dangerous position and of her madcap behavior having fatal consequences. Unlike Baby, the pampered plaything of the rich, the bad cat has endured a life of circus entrapment and rebelled in a way that will cause its own destruction; the second leopard functions as a shadow of the first and, in a move implying that Susan is tame like Baby, is a reminder that female willfulness can nonetheless threaten society.

Hell Hath No Fury Like a Woman Scorned

Although the screwball comedy genre continues into the forties, female trickery now is represented in a more complicated light that shades into the low-key lighting and shadows of film noir. The discomfort present at the end of *Bringing Up Baby* bifurcates into more domesticated, less tricky comic heroines like Irene Dunne's supposed-dead Ellen Arden in *My Favorite Wife* (1940) and into darker, more dangerous precursors of the femme fatale like Barbara Stanwyck's Sugarpuss O'Shea in Hawks's *Ball of Fire* (1941) and Jean in Preston Sturges's *The Lady Eve* (1941).

The destructiveness of the female trickster hinted at in *Bringing Up Baby* is central to the treatment of female power in *The Lady Eve*. In contrast to the Depression-era valorization of change and "trouble" that inflects the treatment of female trickery in *The Awful Truth* and *Bringing Up Baby, The Lady Eve* depicts female trickery as both a useful and a harmful strategy. Jean is a tough con woman in the "racket" of duping men with covert exercises of sexual and emotional power; she manipulates her public persona for economic profit and emotional revenge. Although in all three movies female trickery is the only way for women to achieve their desires, Jean's trickery is self-destructive in a way that Lucy's and Susan's never is.

Moreover, there is a significant difference between leisure-class Lucy and wealthy Susan on the one hand, and criminal-class Jean on the other. Performing their cross-class female female impersonations gives

Lucy and Susan the opportunity to relax the restrictions of femininity and reveals the control they have over their public personas; further, the Depression-era heroines often are fooling not the hero but other people in the hero's presence. When Jean impersonates the Lady Eve, she too demonstrates control and crosses into a different definition of femininity, but she is doing it as revenge, and without the hero's knowledge. Lucy and Susan perform as much for their men as for the audience they trick; Jean, however, plans to entertain or satisfy only herself and to hurt the hero (Henry Fonda) with her impersonation of his ideal. Lucy and Susan have conventional goals—marriage motivated by love and fun—as opposed to Jean's repeated seduction and abandonment of men in her role as the dutiful daughter in the family con business.

By 1941, when *The Lady Eve* was released, the economic crisis of the Depression was on the cusp of being eclipsed by the economy-saving war effort. The war reinforced polarized gender roles—men as "protectors" and women as the "protected"—at the same time that women's war work challenged traditional notions of women's employment (especially of older and married women). As women's economic independence increased, so did the "backlash" images of unhappiness caused by female autonomy and misogynist fears of female power (such as the monstrous "momism" described by writer Philip Wylie in 1942 and the destructive "dames" of forties' films).[13] Anxieties about woman's place and female power reflected and perpetuated the contradictions of the ideology of gender which simultaneously acknowledged and tried to contain women's participation in the "total war" society of the early forties.

Although the film was made before America entered the war, *The Lady Eve* articulates a shift from Depression-era optimism (about change as well as about female trickery and gender equality) to the obligation of the war years. Preston Sturges's satire explores the split self of the screwball heroine in a way that anticipates cultural discourses about the need for containing female sexuality, ambition, and power. In *The Lady Eve*, female power is dangerous and self-destructive; the female trickery Jean uses to avenge Hopsie's moralistic rejection of her takes on the sardonic cast associated with the femme fatale while, paradoxically, it gaily follows the conventions of romantic comedy on which the screwball genre is based.

The Lady Eve was based on a short story called "Two Bad Hats," which was about a shipboard romance between an English aristocrat and the American girl he decides is too common for him. She creates and impersonates a sophisticated twin and wins him back. Stanwyck—who had been paired with Fonda before in the 1938 *The Mad Miss Manton* as a madcap heiress who solves a crime, and with Fred MacMurray as a shoplifter with a heart of gold in the Sturges-written *Remember the Night* (1940) — plays a cross between these two roles in *The Lady Eve*.

The plot of *The Lady Eve* revolves around Jean's changing feelings toward the wealthy Hopsie.[14] On a transatlantic cruise ship, the con woman Jean falls in love with her wealthy "mark," but before she can tell him, he discovers that she is a con artist and rejects her. Seeking revenge, Jean goes to his hometown and impersonates the British Lady Eve, a persona based on his ideal woman. Motivated by her hatred of him, she marries him, and on their wedding night confesses to a decidedly unladylike promiscuous past. But Jean is not satisfied with her revenge and, reverting to her original persona, follows him to the ship. After the torture inflicted upon him by Eve, Hopsie is relieved to find Jean; enthusiastically, they run to his cabin, where the film ends right before Jean reveals that they are already married.

The innocent Hopsie doesn't have a chance against Jean from the moment he steps onto the ship and she drops an apple on his head, a gag that begins the movie-long allusion to the biblical Adam and Eve story. Hopsie, heir to the Pike's Pale Ale fortune, has been "up the Amazon" on a scientific expedition studying snakes for a year. From this moment, we realize that Jean has good aim, and that Hopsie's fate is sealed. When this Eve tricks her Adam, he deserves it because he judges her according to the conventional morality about women that is the legacy of the story of Eve's transgression. In *The Lady Eve*, Jean plays on Hopsie's acceptance of that morality and his class bias to construct an aristocratic alter ego that embodies his ideals of femininity; just when he thinks he has everything he has ever wanted, she dashes his hopes and beliefs as swiftly as he did hers. The female female impersonation in this movie, then, is not a showcase for the heroine's attractive trickiness, but a trick on the hero born out of hatred and revenge.

But at first Hopsie is just another "mark" she will manipulate emotionally and sexually. In a scene that Stanley Cavell analyzes in detail as "woman-as-director," Jean observes Hopsie in her makeup mirror and, in a voice-over narration, analyzes his obliviousness to all the women trying to get his attention. No subtle primper herself, Jean trips him — causing this Adam's "fall" — and accuses him of breaking her shoe. Before he knows what has happened, she guides him through the dining room in a triumphant march to her cabin.

In the cabin scene, Jean is in complete control, systematically deploying the trappings of commodified and fetishized femininity in high heels, a revealing dress, perfume, makeup. She physically draws Hopsie within range of the intoxicating perfume that makes him swoon, instructs him to choose a new pair of high heels and put them on her, and brings his gaze to her legs and breasts. With every little trick, Jean shows that she sees Hopsie clearly as the malleable innocent he is; with every almost-Pavlovian response, Hopsie demonstrates that her perfume literally and figuratively blurs his vision.

But Jean also becomes charmed by Hopsie's innocent sentimentalism, so different from her own cynicism. She likes the honest "good" woman she sees reflected in his lovestruck eyes so much that she decides she will "go straight" and play the role Hopsie has projected onto her. Relieved that she can give up her profession (which is only a Production Code's hairbreadth away from prostitution), she imagines stepping into his paradisiacal world of the wealth she always wanted and the love she barely acknowledged could exist.

Most compelling, though, is the idea of being aboveboard instead of duplicitous. As a con woman, Jean lives on the two levels of her innocent impersonation and her hidden tricky self, splitting herself along the lines of subject and object in her construction of the feminine social self that her marks see; she imagines that marriage to Hopsie will enable her to become whole. With an optimism that sets her up for a big fall, Jean believes that Hopsie will accept her confession of her "bad" past and see that his love has changed her into a "good" woman.

The conversation between Hopsie and Jean after he knows she is a professional con artist (but before she knows he knows) illustrates the poignancy of Jean's situation: for the first time, he doubts her sincerity just when she is being the most honest.

JEAN: You see, Hopsie, you don't know very much about women. The best ones aren't as good as you probably think they are and the bad ones aren't as bad. Not nearly as bad. So I suppose you're right to worry, falling in love with an adventuress on the high seas.
HOPSIE: Are you an adventuress?
JEAN: Of course I am. All women are. They have to be. If you waited for a man to propose to you from natural causes, you'd die of old maidenhood. That's why I let you try my slippers on and I put my cheek against yours and I made you put your arms around me and I, I fell in love with you, which wasn't in the cards.

Hopsie doesn't hear the happiness in her voice or see the hope in her eyes, especially when she says, "the bad ones aren't as bad. Not nearly as bad." When she says that all women "have to be" adventuresses, Hopsie doesn't understand that she is saying that female trickery is necessary to survival. The ironic self-awareness that characterizes Jean's use of language backfires here; her cocksure admission of trickery reinforces his new image of her as a "painted lady" who was conning, not loving him.

Cast out of the garden of goodness she had created in her mind, Jean embodies the role of "bad girl" with renewed vigor. More Satanic (or at least more Lilith-like) than Eve-like, Jean constructs an aristocratic persona out of Hopsie's gender and class ideals. To make things even, this time she makes him believe that his dream of marrying the perfect woman is coming true before she pulls the rug out from under him, toppling the pedestal on which he has put her. Hopsie is unwilling to see either Jean or Eve as a complex human being who is "good" as well as "bad."

When "Eve" interacts with Hopsie (whom she now calls by his real name, Charles, which gives him a new identity, too), she does so from the superior class position of aristocrat. Here director Preston Sturges's class satire is at its most biting, because the wealthy Americans are fawning over con artists. Her impersonation is clinched by the con man posing as her uncle, who tells Hopsie the plot of a "gaslight melodrama": that the coachman, not the duke, was really Eve's father, and that there was a twin sister who stayed with the real father. To Hopsie, Eve is the identical twin of the "adventuress" he met on the ship, but because she has had the class privilege denied to Jean, she can better fulfill his ideal of a good woman. When Hopsie proposes to Eve with the same romantic speech he made to Jean on the ship, it is Jean's turn to see through his duplicity.

Jean gets her revenge by revealing that Hopsie's ideal lady has a promiscuous past. On the train on their wedding night, Eve first tells Hopsie that she was married before and therefore not a virgin; after Hopsie forgives her grudgingly, she goes on to tell him about several more men. In a sequence that cuts between Eve's "confession" and shots of the train hurtling through the stormy night, the tension builds as Eve systematically shatters Hopsie's ideal of femininity. Then we see Hopsie get off the train (and take a pratfall in the mud); but instead of expressing pleasure—or even satisfaction—at her well-executed plan of revenge, we see Jean sadly pull down the window shade. Jean's tragic reaction is in sharp contrast to Hopsie's fall and the farcical elements of Eve's confession (intercut with exterior shots, including a sign along the railroad tracks that issues a silly warning to the audience: "PULL IN YOUR HEAD . . . WE'RE COMING TO A TUNNEL!").

The instant that Jean reacts with regret to her successful trick, we realize that she is no longer a female trickster at heart, reveling in her exertion of power over a mark. Rather, she has been sentimentalized; all she wants is Hopsie, who at this point is a pathetic snob lying covered with mud, surely the least compelling of the heroes of the three films discussed here. Throughout the movie Hopsie is a sap attractive to Jean only because he treats her according to his class-bound notions of romantic sweetness and gentility; once he rejects her on the ship, he forfeits the basis of his charm. Yet even though Jean should be triumphant and Hopsie is covered in the mud he deserves for making her feel dirty and cheap, she is unsatisfied.

In backlash fashion, her trickery only causes her more misery, and her performance of Lady Eve is unnoticed and unappreciated by the hero, unlike the private performances of public women in *Bringing Up Baby* and *The Awful Truth*. Thus, even though *The Lady Eve* expresses a compelling fantasy of female power, that power is limited. Female trickery works, but it works best if kept covert. The movie acknowledges women's emotional and sexual power, but denies any other kind of power (economic, political, intellectual, artistic). In order for female trickery to remain covert, women have to stay in their "place" and perform feminine roles submissively. At the end of *The Lady Eve*, Jean has chosen to define herself by her love for Hopsie and suffers a loss of self unparalleled in screwball comedy.

The ending of *The Lady Eve*, like the endings of *The Awful Truth* and *Bringing Up Baby*, does not resolve the fundamental conflict between the hero and heroine. What will Hopsie do once it finally sinks in that Jean is Eve, that she has been manipulating and tricking him all along? Surrender to her superior tactics of emotional and sexual warfare? Reject her again and hide in the womanless scientific paradise "up the Amazon"? Be able to relate to her as an equal now that she has forced him out of his Edenic innocence and into the deceptive world of sexuality? These questions—and the equivalent ones raised by *The Awful Truth* and *Bringing Up Baby*—are impossible to answer, but that the conclusion of the movie raises them and leaves them unresolved is significant. Ultimately, the embraces suggestive of sex with which these movies end imply that if the men want to have sex (and after his frustrating wedding night, Hopsie really wants to), they have to play the woman's game. And if the women want to have sex (within the "good" confines of marriage), they have to exercise power covertly to trick their men. In this way, *The Lady Eve* reinscribes woman's sphere of influence as the private realm of the emotional and sexual (as opposed to the moral and domestic aspects of the Victorian private sphere).

The movie closes with a sequence that takes us back to where we started, on the cruise ship. When Hopsie trips over Jean, he is happy to see her because, in contrast to Eve, she is a nice girl. Hopsie and Jean run from the dining room of the cruise ship to a cabin; their exhilarating run is used in the film trailer to suggest the wackiness of the screwball comedy and foregrounds the Adam and Eve story that the film alludes to only slightly (Fig. 3.13a–b). With the animated snake in a top hat—suggestive of comedies of the elite—and "Adam" chasing "Eve," the trailer

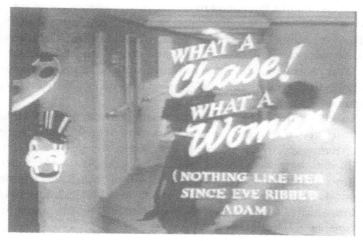

a

b

Figure 3.13. *a,b.* The trailer for *The Lady Eve* (1941) sets up the film's allusion to the Adam and Eve story. Despite the darker aspects of director Preston Sturges's satire, the film is nevertheless cast in a screwball context. Frame enlargements.

treats the ending like farce, and of course it is. However, there are ideological implications to this film, poised as it is on the brink of the backlash. The Eve we see here may seem like Mae West's Eve, but Jean's Eve hinges on the polarization of "good" and "bad" women that West resisted. West's Eve "ribbed" Adam into pleasure and autonomy from the (land)Lord; Stanwyck's Eve "ribs" Hopsie into being the tricked again and again.

The Lady Eve, then, represents the manipulations of the individual female trickster as the only way for women to achieve their desires in a world dominated by men. There is no sense of sex solidarity in the movie; in fact, there are no other women characters who have more than a few lines. Jean's individualism — and isolation from other women — illustrates the lack of female group consciousness that characterized the postsuffrage thirties and forties. As historian Nancy Cott points out in *The Grounding of Modern Feminism*:

For women who imagined the resolution of the woman question in terms of individual advances — as did most women who succeeded in business and the professions, and those who gained influence under the New Deal — the individual line was a way to take intragroup diversities among women into account and to sidestep the pitfalls of conceptualizing women as a gender group. Individualism was a progressive but partial demand for women in the mid-twentieth century. The resort to individualism took the feminist standpoint that women's freedoms and opportunities should be no less than men's, but individualism offered no way to achieve the goal except acting as though it had already been obtained. Although it produced outstanding models of individual accomplishment, it could not engender a program for change in the position of women as a group. (281)

Cott's point suggests the role that representations of female tricksters may have played in the discourses of femininity in the Depression era and war years. By showing individual heroines "acting as though [equality] had already been obtained," screwball comedies were part of an ideological shift in representations of women as equal partners that was not accompanied or caused by a similar shift in the position of women as a group in American society. Because of the disorganized state of the women's movement in the thirties, the challenges to traditional gender roles fostered by the enormous social, political, and economic changes of the Depression decade could not withstand the nation's shift from economic crisis to the war economy.

In general, female trickery symbolizes what is missing in the social relations of the sexes: a female power located in individual women in the private sphere to balance the superior economic and political power to which men have access in the public sphere. In the fantasy world of Depression-era comedy, female trickery blends with the fierce independence and individualism characteristic of women characters in thirties' film. Because Lucy and Susan practice their trickery in front of their men, the men know they are dealing with powerful women who can hold their own in the battle of the sexes, a battle waged by individual couples in the private sphere of relationships. Although Depression-era comedy couched equality in terms of individualism and the private sphere, it represented it nonetheless.

The demands of wartime, however, resulted in a polarization of gender roles, not in an ideology of equality. Women's participation in the war economy called for an ideology that encompassed women's paid work outside the home—and the independence that was its corollary— at the same time that it placed renewed emphasis on women's traditional roles (mother, housewife, consumer). In other words, work was an extension of domestic and patriotic responsibilities; whether at work or at home, women were expected to behave according to the dictates of femininity: submissive not assertive, emotional not rational, nurturing not competitive, sexually attractive but not "loose" (Elaine Tyler May 71).

The Lady Eve illustrates the shift from the Depression-era possibility of equality to the domestic-based femininity and polarized gender roles on which the postwar feminine mystique was based. Dissatisfied with her life as a female trickster, Jean idealizes love and domestic security; she moves toward, not away from, the domesticity that West's Eve called "disgustin'" and the "home on the range" that Lucy found repulsive in the life proffered by Dan. Despite the antisnobbery of the representations of class in the movie, the film reifies dominant notions of the social relations of the sexes. In short, *The Lady Eve* is a "backlash" text that places the blame for women's unhappiness on their independence (here, trickery) and advocates a return to conventional gender roles as the key to female satisfaction. The movie's depiction of female trickery as successful when it is practiced covertly ascribes a power to conventional femininity that is apolitical and individualistic.

In general, postsuffrage (from 1920 on) representations of women's achievement and power pit individual women against individual men in the private sphere, a situation not all that different from Adam and Eve's conflict in the Garden of Eden. The way out of domesticity (articulated by West's Eve) is through female trickery; so is the way into domesticity (Jean's Eve). In the popular culture of the thirties and forties, female trickery is an integral part of female power, whether it is emerging from the cover of submission (in *The Awful Truth* and *Bringing Up Baby*) as evidence of women's agency or taking on the tinges of danger with which female sexuality is represented during World War II and in the postwar period. Like the biblical Eve, female tricksters find trickster tactics powerful weapons in manipulating men, a useful endeavor as long as women are relegated to the private sphere and limited by the dictates of femininity. But as long as female power is defined within a misogynist context, such as the biblical story, it is associated with badness and shame and functions as a scapegoat in discourses of femininity.

The femme fatale is just that scapegoat. Where the female tricksters get what they want in screwball comedy (including *Ball of Fire* and *The Lady Eve*), the dark trickster of film noir finds only betrayal and death. Where *Ball of Fire* and *The Lady Eve* take a dark turn—into the night—that prefigures film noir's preoccupation with female duplicity and impersonation, the femme fatale starts and ends in that night. To state the obvious, what has comic consequences, what is for the rigid hero's own good in the screwball comedies, has tragic, deadly consequences in film noir.

That Stanwyck played both the last of the truly subversive female tricksters in the period of classical Hollywood comedy and the first of the femmes fatales of film noir in Billy Wilder's *Double Indemnity* (1944) is significant. Director Wilder had been one of the screenwriters of *Ball of Fire* and deliberately drew on Stanwyck's morally ambiguous comic roles in casting her as Phyllis. But, as Molly Haskell writes, "Nothing prepared us for the blonde wig and black heart of Phyllis Dietrichson, a dame with no redeeming qualities by Hollywood moral standards" (197).

Nevertheless, the lines between Sugarpuss, Jean/Eve, and Phyllis Dietrichson are not as clear as they may seem. All three are deceptive, all three manipulate men to get what they want. In Hawks's *Ball of Fire*, the most clearly comic of the three movies, Sugarpuss renounces her shady past (but not her ways of speaking and behaving) in favor of true love. Charmed by the awkward prince/professor (and how often do you see those linked together?) and his seven dwarfs, Sugarpuss takes on the persona the men see in her and becomes the romantic princess (Fig. 3.14). Tricky to survive rather than to profit, Sugarpuss is perhaps the most conventionally unconventional romantic comedy heroine portrayed by Stanwyck. Visually, *Ball of Fire*'s night scene in Sugarpuss's bedroom anticipates the style of film noir. Like the 1940 melodrama *The Letter* starring Bette Davis, the low-key lighting and shadows convey the main character's duplicitous use of femininity.

In *The Lady Eve*, Jean also becomes enamored with the image Hopsie has of her before he learns the "truth" about her, so charmed that all she wants is to impersonate his image and let her tricky self recede into the background of her respectable life. Hopsie's rejection makes her inflect that desire to act as if she were his ideal with the fury of a woman scorned. The lighting and music that follows Eve's "confession" on the train also prefigure the visual style of the forties' films of uneasiness and dark trickery.

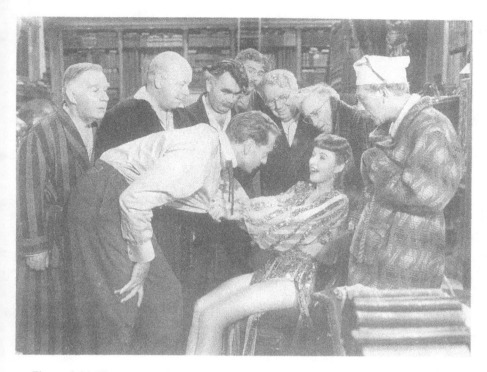

Figure 3.14. The center of male attention and a source for the vitality they lack, Sugarpuss O'Shea (Barbara Stanwyck) shakes up the professors. Publicity still from *Ball of Fire* (1941) courtesy of Museum of Modern Art/Film Stills Archive.

Unlike these prewar films, *Double Indemnity* has no female double, no impersonation other than the cold trickery of Stanwyck's Phyllis Dietrichson (Fig. 3.15). Phyllis dwells in the shadows of this prototypical film noir, hiding behind the men whose falls she precipitates. She is a dark Eve, indeed, whose qualities of shrewdness and beauty are used only for evil. Linked to the private sphere throughout the movie, Phyllis inhabits a confined space both physically and psychologically without the comic possibility of creating a different ending.

The Angel in the War

In sharp contrast to the dark Eve portrayed to varying degrees by Barbara Stanwyck, most wartime popular culture represented femininity as heroic, self-sacrificing, and good. For example, in another form of popular culture, the comics, wartime superheroine Wonder Woman can

Figure 3.15. Femme fatale Phyllis Dietrichson (Stanwyck) is a shadow dweller. Publicity still from *Double Indemnity* (1944) courtesy of Museum of Modern Art/ Film Stills Archive.

be seen as a metaphor of the movement of female tricksters in the Depression era and war years: out of the garden and into the war. Wonder Woman is an Amazon princess who leaves the Edenic herland of Paradise Island to help the Allies fight the war and be near the man she loves.[15]

In America, Wonder Woman masquerades as army nurse Diana Prince, performing a female female impersonation that reinforces the idea that women's power must be contained and exercised covertly, not overtly. In order to participate in society as a woman and war worker (first as an army nurse and then as a lieutenant in military intelligence), she must pretend to be weaker and more submissive than she really is.

Wonder Woman's decision to leave the private sphere of Paradise Island—the garden—and enter the public sphere of war and heterosexuality is an exhortation for women to support the war effort based on obligations of service and love, a twentieth-century revision of the

Victorian "angel in the house"—the angel in the war. Diana's duplicity splits her into two good selves, one Amazon, the other human.

To be sure, Wonder Woman represented women's autonomy and strength as applicable to a range of women's experience, not only war work; the point here, however, is that Wonder Woman emerges to call attention to the price wartime women had to pay for admission to the man-made world: a fractured sense of self and the duplicitous social practices necessary to negotiate the maintenance of submissive femininity while participating in the public sphere of wartime society. Wonder Woman accomplishes this feat not with her considerable Amazon powers, but with female female impersonation, disguise, and deception—the tactics of female trickery. Even the exercise of women's power essential to the enormous economic, social, political, and ideological facets of World War II must remain covert. By the end of the war, any challenges to traditional gender roles that the Depression era may have represented had been co-opted and, like Wonder Woman, integrated as a buttress for the polarized gender roles that served the war economy with a smile.

Trickery in Wartime America

The only trick that mainstream American culture encouraged a woman to perform during wartime was that little trick of looking over her shoulder for the pinup shot (Fig. 3.16). I mean this literally and figuratively—Betty Grable's wartime musical heroines gave up public performance and female trickery for domesticity in films that portrayed the privatization of the showgirl. During the war years, the female trickery central to the screwball heroines of Depression comedies bifurcated into the sharply polarized definitions of "good" and "bad" womanhood—the very contradictions that Mae West brought together in her cultural work. The split, into the dark and self-destructive duplicity of melodrama and film noir and the sunny sentimental girl-next-door heroines of musical comedy, recasts the complexity of the thirties' heroine. The rhetoric of the homefront relies upon the good woman as a faithful, sincere, hardworking participant in the public as well as private spheres, but only inasmuch as her independence and productivity were for the greater good and, as an advertisement from 1942 shows, if her feminine appearance was preserved (Fig. 3.17).

Betty Grable, for example, emerged as an icon of good femininity in the popular culture of World War II. A bridge between the servicemen overseas and the folks at home, Grable's image (in her pinup, movie roles, and star persona) functioned as a stand-in for "real" women in the sex-segregated military and as a symbol for the qualities of American

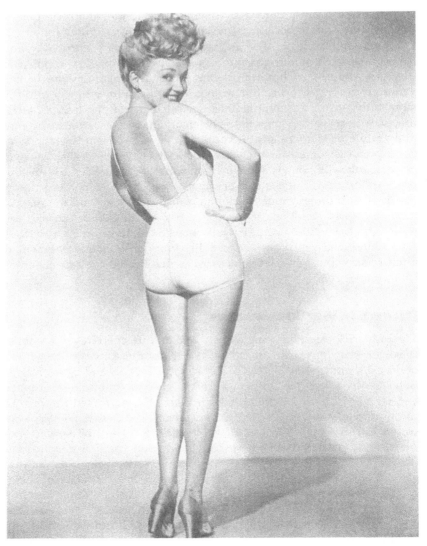

Figure 3.16. The famous Betty Grable pinup shot. Photograph courtesy of Museum of Modern Art/Film Stills Archive.

Figure 3.17. Trousers for women during wartime. *Life*, September 21, 1942.

womanhood that needed defending and protecting. This image proved popular not only among soldiers overseas, but also with women on the homefront, and by the end of the war Grable's salary was the highest earned by an American woman. Further, her popularity soared after she married bandleader Harry James and had a child in 1943; in this way, she prefigures Lucille Ball's immense popularity as wife and mother. Although not as explicitly sexy as Rita Hayworth, Grable was the more popular pinup girl, which, according to Richard Westbrook's excellent article, "'I Want a Girl, Just Like the Girl That Married Harry James': American Women and the Problem of Political Obligation in World War II," suggests that Grable's appeal was that she symbolized the "average" American girl, someone who could be the average serviceman's sweetheart, wife, and the mother of his children.

As icons, the visual representations of Grable, Jane Russell, and Rita Hayworth performed the cultural work of offering private reasons for meeting public obligations. After the war, one serviceman explained Grable's significance to Grable: "There we were out in those damn dirty trenches. Machine guns firing. Bombs dropping all around us. We would be exhausted, frightened, confused and sometimes hopeless about our situation. When suddenly someone would pull your picture out of his wallet. Or we'd see a decal of you on a plane and then we'd *know* what we were fighting for" (quoted in Westbrook, 600).

Pin Up Girl (1944) gives an interesting—and tricky—backstory to the formation of the pinup girl. Bookended by Grable's famous pinup in the opening and closing credits, the movie offers a story that shows that the pinup girl is really the girl next door. Grable plays Lorry Jones, who leaves her life as a local USO Club performer in Missouri and moves to Washington to contribute to the war effort as a stenographer. In the hopes of catching a war hero's eye, she impersonates a glamorous show-girl named "Laura Lorraine." Doesn't that name sound familiar? Despite the similarities of nomenclature, Lorry is Lorelei Lee's opposite; where Loos's Lorelei goes public as a film actress at the end of the novel, for one silent moment at the end of the film, Lorry is able to reconcile her public persona as a showgirl with her private small-town self because they are both in the service of war work.

In this installment of the ongoing saga of how gentlemen prefer blondes, Grable's character learns that her war hero really wants an average girl—her "real" not her "performance" self. (That the "average" girl happens to be a fibber who is engaged to five hundred servicemen remains unresolved in the movie.) When Lorry passes herself off as a famous entertainer to get a good table at a show, Guadalcanal hero Tommy Dooley (played by John Harvey) falls for her, but never calls her. It turns out that Lorry has been assigned to be his stenographer. À la

Wonder Woman, she puts her hair up and glasses on and becomes her own rival, serving as a go-between to smooth over the misunderstandings that have kept Laura and Tommy apart. Lorry lives a double life successfully until Tommy, disgusted with what he perceives as the entertainer's falseness, tells Lorry that he really wants someone like her—honest, unassuming, shy, and private.

In the eloquent words of Richard Westbrook, at the end of the movie Lorry "reveals that Lorry Jones and Laura Lorraine are one and the same woman and accepts herself for the small-town girl who happens to know her way around an elaborate production number" (599). Lorry does this by getting up on stage in her stenographer's outfit and glasses and performing a decidedly subdued routine; in contrast to the private confessions we find at the end of the thirties' screwball comedies, *Pin Up Girl* ends with a public, visible, performed revelation. The schoolteacher number Grable performs in her work clothes moves, with a costume change, into a long marching sequence. Rows of women in uniform and carrying guns follow Lorry's commands and march in and out of complicated military formations with the precision of, well, the chorus line *and* the military regiment on parade. The spectacle does not point our attention to the performers' legs as much as to their rifles, and the whole number is curiously sexless. In the final shots of the film, Grable smiles, looks off-camera, and then into that military middle space of the surveyed serviceman. The last shot is a close-up of her holding a sword so that it divides her face. We fade to black and into Grable's famous pinup photograph; superimposed along with the credits is the information that war bonds are available at the theater.

The difference between how *Pin Up Girl* represents the conflict between public and private, surveyor and surveyed, is that in the context of wartime, the sociosexual display of being a pinup girl whose image represents "what we're fighting for" blurs the line between private "good" girls and public "bad" ones. Like other facets of wartime ideology, movies like *Pin Up Girl* legitimate women's participation in the public sphere as long as it is part of the war effort. Moreover, there is an equality between men and women at the end of the film. With a sidelong glance off-camera and a smiling reaction shot from the hero, the narrative closure of the film rests on wordless exchanges between two people in uniform occupying equal but separate space in the frame.

Consider the differences between *Pin Up Girl* and *The Lady Eve*. Both heroines use female trickery to present two opposing stereotypes to their men—the adventuress and the lady, the showgirl and the stenographer. At the end of each film, the heroine reveals that the two women are really one, but the scenes are significantly different. In *The Lady Eve* we hear only the private moment before Hopsie figures it out; all we see is a kiss and a closed door. In *Pin Up Girl*, however, our information is visual; as the spectator, we too gaze approvingly at Lorry/Grable's performance and we know that both the character and the actress are presenting themselves as spectacles to serve not only an individual man privately, but—in image—the collective publicly. In contrast, Jean/Eve is motivated only by her individual desires.

Like Stanwyck's Sugarpuss O'Shea in *Ball of Fire*, Grable's Laura Lorraine can exist only in an unprotected public arena; to be safe and fulfilled, Lorry must enter the private sphere of marriage and domesticity. And, although the hero was attracted by the public performance of the showgirl, he wants to marry the nice girl. Moreover, Grable's role in *Pin Up Girl* marks the point in American narrative where female tricksters begin to recant in the end. Not only does Grable's role in *Pin Up Girl* anticipate the narrative of *I Love Lucy*, but her public persona as the average, typical wife and mother paves the way for Lucille Ball's star image as "just a housewife." And whether or not Grable actually turned to Marilyn Monroe on the set of *How to Marry a Millionaire* and said, "It's your turn now, kid," this decade's blonde had definitely shifted away from Grable's wartime image of ideal sweetheart, wife, and mother, of "what we're fighting for," and toward "what we're working for," the acquisitive yet innocent sexiness of Marilyn Monroe. Laura Lorraine may have been short-lived, but Monroe's portrayal of Lorelei Lee, like the diamond bracelet desired by Loos's Lorelei, lasts forever.

Chapter 4
Liminal Lucy
Covert Power, Television, and Postwar
Domestic Ideology

"Mrs. Ricardo, what *are* you trying to do to the wives of America?" This question, posed in a May 1952 episode of *I Love Lucy*, is a salient one. The most popular public woman of the 1950s, performer Lucille Ball captured the American imagination with her extraordinary talent as a comedienne and her likable public persona. By the end of the fifties, when the series completed its nine-year run (as a half-hour situation comedy from October 1951 to May 1957 and as thirteen hour-long shows from November 1957 until April 1960), zany, irrepressible, unconventional Lucy Ricardo was an American icon.

Lucy's popularity can be explained in part by her place at the apex of a long tradition of American screwballs, madcaps, and con women that originates in the novels of the late eighteenth and early nineteenth centuries, develops throughout nineteenth-century fiction and theater, emerges in silent film, and shapes the heroine of sound comedy. Because of the specific historical conditions of postwar America, the newness of television situation comedy, and the talents of Lucille Ball, Desi Arnaz, and their collaborators, *I Love Lucy* emerged as a central story cycle in American culture. Trickster Lucy's high jinks captured the contradictions of the gender system, and the series redefined what it meant for a cultural text to be popular. Given this resonance, what cultural work did Lucy perform, or, what *did* she do to the "wives of America?" My discussion of *I Love Lucy* reads the series within the popular representations that legitimized the postwar preoccupation with being, as historian Elaine Tyler May calls it, "homeward bound." In order to establish how female trickery fared in the period, we'll take a brief detour into early fifties' film and focus in on the contrast between two versions of Lorelei Lee and *Gentlemen Prefer Blondes*: the Jazz Age novel discussed in Chapter 2 and the musical comedy film starring Marilyn Monroe and Jane Russell.

Gentlemen Prefer Blondes Revisited: Marilyn Monroe, Brains, and the Female Trickster

When *Gentlemen Prefer Blondes* (1953) opened with Marilyn Monroe as one of the "two little girls from Little Rock," a new and resonant articulation of Lorelei Lee came to life and entered mainstream American (and international) culture, obscuring the Lorelei Lee of Anita Loos's serialized novel *Gentlemen Prefer Blondes* (1925). At that moment, Monroe's star image and the various print, film, and stage incarnations of Lorelei fused, and Lorelei's trickiness was eclipsed by Monroe's embodiment of the "dumb blonde." Loos made Lorelei's "acquisitive intelligence" increasingly visible as she wrote the novel, the sequel *But Gentlemen Marry Brunettes* (the title alone spells out Loos's attempts to revise and recast the cultural phenomenon she spawned), the Broadway musical comedy (1949), and the later Lorelei sketches published into the 1980s. The 1953 movie, however, privileges Monroe's embodiment of the feminine ideal over Lorelei's trickiness. There is only one moment in the movie that seems to me to be in keeping with the Lorelei of Loos's novel, and that is when Lorelei looks at the South African diamond mine owner Piggie Beekman and his head changes into a big diamond (we can only imagine what might appear superimposed over Lorelei from Piggie's point of view). Otherwise, the Lorelei that Monroe and Hawks create has little in common with the 1925 Lorelei, but much in common with postwar ideals of femininity and representations of female power as covert.

Of course, a character as resonant and popular as Lorelei Lee is going to change as she is redrawn and reinterpreted at different historical moments; what is interesting is *how*. As Maureen Turim concludes in her article "Gentlemen Consume Blondes," the gold-digger myth in the movie not only is "renewal and updating into Fifties values, but it also holds on to the layers of meanings circulating in American popular culture for thirty years" (109). As I argued in Chapter 2, Loos's novel only celebrates the blonde inasmuch as she is a female trickster who exploits what "gentlemen" can be fooled by; her dumbness, unrelenting pursuit of material goods, and willingness to turn herself into a commodity are what Loos satirizes. None of the men in the novel will get what they want from Lorelei, including the man she marries at the end because she can manipulate him into aiding her new career as a film actress. Unlike the movie, Loos's novel interrogates the construction of "gentlemen" without which there could be no "blondes."

Perhaps the most expedient way of getting at the differences between the 1925 print and 1953 film texts is to think about how the cultural significance of "diamond" changed from the Jazz Age to the postwar era. Diamonds are just one of the many precious gems the 1925 Lorelei desires, but by the 1950s, the diamond solidified as a signifier of marriage—as the engagement ring judged on the basis of the size of the rock, as the capital the man offers a woman as proof of his ability to provide for her materially. Further, in the novel Lorelei wears the diamond tiara on the back of her head, eager for a "new place to wear diamonds," but in the film, when Lady Beekman puts the tiara on Monroe's head, we see the by then familiar image of the crowned beauty queen. The line from the novel, "kissing your hand may feel very very good, but a diamond and safire [*sic*] bracelet lasts forever" was transformed into the film's lyrics "A kiss on the hand may be quite continental, but diamonds are a girl's best friend." [1]

But a girl's best friend in the movie is not a diamond; her best friend *is* her best friend. In the relationship between Lorelei and Dorothy (Jane Russell), we see director Howard Hawks's career-long interest in the theme of buddies. It is in the friendship, the "intrafeminine fascination" (as Jackie Stacey terms it) between the contrasting characters played by Monroe and Russell (who received top billing in the film), that the emotional center of the film rests.

The difference between the Loreleis of the 1925 serialized novel and the 1953 film is analogous to the difference many scholars have described between Mae West's and Marilyn Monroe's interpretations of the blonde sex goddess. [2] West's deliberate, self-aware display and deployment of her sexuality is in sharp contrast to Monroe's "innocent" lack of awareness of her sexuality; West's perceptive comment "You can be had" (*She Done Him Wrong*) contrasts with Monroe's whispered implication that she can be had. West's hedonistic enjoyment of sex, her reveling in sexual activity despite the condemnation of the moralizing and censoring forces of the twenties and thirties, oppose Monroe's teasing pandering to the male sexualizing gaze. Kathleen Rowe pinpoints the difference between the two blonde icons: "Most important, Monroe, unlike West, derives her sex appeal from weakness rather than strength. That weakness reinforces the ideology of traditional heterosexuality, which eroticizes an imbalance of power based on feminine submissiveness and masculine dominance" (180). Where the Mae West sex goddess retained control over her body, her choice of partners, and her performances, the Marilyn Monroe sex goddess hands over control to the (male) viewer.

Because Monroe's incarnation of female sexuality is passive, she represents not an oppositional figure but a hegemonic model of commodified sexuality in the postwar capitalist sociosexual marketplace. Monroe's Lorelei is only nominally a trickster, or rather, her trickery is restricted to the kinds encouraged by postwar culture as the social practices of femininity in everyday life—makeup, influence over men through the tactics of covert power, manipulation of sexual attractiveness as a survival skill. Think of Monroe's minor part in *All About Eve* (1950).[3] Her sexual allure gets her into parties and auditions (and perhaps bed) with men of power in the theater, but her lack of talent and savvy bar her from attaining the success that the far trickier Eve (Anne Baxter) gets by insinuating herself in Margo Channing's (Bette Davis) life and taking it over from within. The lesson of this postwar drama is that female trickery works best when played in the guise of the sentimental heroine, not the sexual one.

In *Gentlemen Prefer Blondes*, Hawks shifted the female trickster from Lorelei to Dorothy. Jane Russell's performance as Dorothy—a much more prominent role in the film than in the novel (and closer to the Dorothy fleshed out in *But Gentlemen Marry Brunettes*)—becomes the locus of female trickery, a character more like Mae West than Marilyn Monroe.

Indeed, in what may be the most telling scene in the film, Dorothy impersonates Lorelei in court. In a performance reminiscent of Capitola "doing the sentimental" in E. D. E. N. Southworth's novel *The Hidden Hand, or Capitola the Madcap* (1859), Dorothy does the dumb blonde. Clad in her nightclub entertainer costume and a blonde wig, draped in a mink coat and dripping with diamonds, Dorothy distracts the judge and gendarmes by displaying her legs on the witness stand. In a parodic whisper, she tells the judge, "You're so much more intelligent than poor little me. Won't you tell me what I ought to say?" To stall long enough for Lorelei to get the price of the diamond tiara out of Mr. Esmond, Dorothy bursts into a performance of "Diamonds Are a Girl's Best Friend," a reprise markedly different from Monroe's rendition. Where Monroe was wearing an elegant pink gown at the center of a well-dressed (albeit luridly) chorus in a big production number, Russell's fringe-swinging burlesque performance threatens and disrupts the courtroom proceedings (which is her intended goal) (Fig. 4.1). It is a private, explicitly (as opposed to coyly) sexualized entertainment (at least that is how the hand-clapping and smiling gendarmes respond) that also reinforces Lorelei's backstory and present motivation—the only thing a "girl" can count on are the material goods she can get from men now and keep, because "we all lose our charms in the end." What Monroe plays as a flagrant insult to front-row Mr. Esmond (Lorelei flings stage prop diamonds at him and sings, "I don't mean rhinestones"), Russell plays like the scene in the novel when Lorelei gains the judge's preference of her version of why she shot her boss in Little Rock. The staging

Figure 4.1. Jane Russell plays Dorothy, who impersonates the blonde (Lorelei Lee/Marilyn Monroe) in *Gentlemen Prefer Blondes* (1953). Publicity still courtesy of Museum of Modern Art/Film Stills Archive.

of Russell's song and dance also recalls Mae West's courtroom scenes and a famous still of her surrounded by appreciative Bowery policemen. It is indicative of the Production Code and other shifts in morality that Russell's number with the men's Olympic team is about not getting any, rather than the distinctly opposite impression one takes away from an early West number.

Unlike Monroe's exaggerated brainlessness, *this* is the performance of a female trickster who is in full knowledge and control of the effect her machinations have on the men around her. And because of this, Russell's "Lorelei" is indeed a "monster," as Mr. Esmond Sr. calls her. Dorothy is the "bad cat" of Hawks's *Bringing Up Baby*, the flip side of the tame leopard loose in Connecticut.

At the end of *Gentlemen Prefer Blondes*, the double marriage ends the women's participation in the public sphere of performance, whether the mise-en-scène of the final scene celebrates the female couple of Dorothy and Lorelei or not. Fifties' movies do not follow heroines past the "happily ever after" endings, but television situation comedy did. *I Love Lucy* formulates the question: What would happen to a tricky woman, once she attained the goal of marriage that marks the narrative closure of classical Hollywood cinema? This question is raised—but never addressed—at the end of screwball comedies such as *Bringing Up Baby* and *The Lady Eve*. Episodes of *I Love Lucy* play on the marriage and homelife of the Ricardos; most often, the episode begins with Lucy's expression of an unfulfilled desire—to be in "show business" (with Ricky), to have her own money, to appear to be of higher social status in front of other women, to step outside of the private sphere and participate in the public sphere. There is an obstacle to the straightforward satisfaction of her desire, often (but not always) articulated by Ricky's refusal to give Lucy his permission. Because her desire cannot be fulfilled directly, Lucy resorts to the covert tactics of female trickery to create a new context in which she can achieve satisfaction.[4] Lucy's trickery intensifies until the plan backfires—or succeeds—in a comic climax of the episode that showcases Lucille Ball's mastery of physical comedy. After the big laugh to which the episode has been building, the show winds down to end with Lucy's expulsion from the public sphere, leaving her poised to start over with a new plan next time. Think of some of the most famous episodes of *I Love Lucy*: "The Ballet" or "Job Switching," which culminates with the *Modern Times*-inspired scene of Lucy wrapping chocolates on the too-fast conveyor belt.

To enact these escape attempts, Lucy employs an impressive array of female trickster tactics—disguise, impersonation, theft, deception, duplicity, and subversion—in her weekly rejection of the confines of domesticity and the limitations of conventional femininity. By drawing on the three types of female trickery outlined in previous chapters—the madcap, the screwball, and the con woman—Lucy often gets what she wants. Because her trickery transgresses the boundaries between polarized masculine and feminine social roles, separate public and private spheres, and sharply delineated definitions of "good" and shadow femininity, Lucy functions as a trickster figure who converts her position as a woman of domesticity into a one from which to make tactical raids on the public sphere. In other words, Lucy performed the cultural work of embodying the contradictions between female ambition and femininity. She enacted survival strategies that call attention to the possibilities and limitations of the social relations of the sexes within domestic ideology, and articulated anxieties about the breakdown of the traditional separation of public and private. Perhaps most importantly, Lucy provided occasion for laughter and pleasure by creating comedy out of the constraints of the postwar feminine mystique.[5]

In embodying these contradictions, Lucy is liminal. Anthropologist

Victor Turner asserts that the trickster exists "betwixt and between" social categories, behaviors, and spaces; thus, trickster figures are liminal figures who, to use Emily Dickinson's phrase, "dwell in possibility." As Turner explains in *The Anthropology of Performance*, "Just as the subjunctive mood of a verb is used to express supposition, desire, hypothesis, or possibility, rather than stating actual facts, so do liminality and the phenomena of liminality dissolve all factual and commonsense systems into their components and 'play' with them in ways never found in nature or in custom" (101).[6] Liminal Lucy always sees opportunity in ordinary, everyday situations; despite Ricky's dictates and any other rules or restrictions, she creates new roles for herself that bend and warp the social institutions she subverts. No social space is off-limits to her; just as she moves freely between social spaces, she performs impersonations that cross the boundaries demarcating gender, race, age, and class. Thinking through the ways that Lucy embodies a subjunctive mood within a postwar American culture obsessed with consumption, conformity, and containment moves us closer to an understanding of the cultural work that a trickster figure performs.[7]

The series articulates an ambivalent attitude toward female trickery; that Lucy's trickery both works and backfires reflects cultural anxieties about woman's place and women's power in the cold war era. The contradictions between social concerns (humanity and femininity, public and private spheres, male and female social roles, egalitarian and male-dominant ideals of marriage, women's labor in and out of the home) combine with textual tensions (representations of "real life" and fiction, and the traditionally antithetical dichotomy between comedy and femininity) to form the conflicts from which the comedy of *I Love Lucy* emerged and point to an answer to the question, "Mrs. Ricardo, what *are* you trying to do to the wives of America?"

Time and Again

"Lucy's Schedule" (episode 33, broadcast May 26, 1952) is an example of how *I Love Lucy* portrays female trickery as successful and necessary for women's autonomy in the home. It shows how Lucy embodies the contradictions of women's social practices in the private sphere, where female power has traditionally been covert. The episode begins with Lucy's attempt to trick herself into being dressed on time for dinner at the house of Ricky's boss, a situation that parodies the time required for the "masquerade" of feminine appearance. Lucy's reaction to Ricky's criticism about her tardiness is an excellent example of her liminality—she decides to move the clock ahead so she will think she has less time than she has (an irrational but possibly effective manipulation of the construct of time), but she ineptly sets the clock *back* one hour. By the time the Ricardos get to the Littlefields', dinner is over. Not only has Lucy's lateness reflected negatively on Ricky, but she continues to embarrass him: having gone without dinner, she gobbles down an entire bowl of mints while her hostess's back is turned and tries to eat wax fruit. Instead of exhibiting the appropriately feminine self-abnegation and self-restraint, Lucy is primarily concerned with her own hunger. Here is Lucy as trickster: a self-involved liminal character whose mode of interaction in society is characterized by nonconforming behavior and subversion (Fig. 4.2a).

As a female trickster, Lucy enacts the shadow role of the good wife in companionate marriage; instead of enhancing Ricky's image in front of his boss, her lateness, excessive hunger, and strange behavior make Ricky appear as a husband who is not in control of his wife (an accurate depiction). By embarrassing him in front of his boss, Lucy calls the audience's attention to the construct of the ideal companionate wife, as it was inflected by the demands of an increasingly corporate society; wives were expected to assist their husbands' careers in social interactions outside of the workplace, functioning as extensions of the husband.

Displeased with Lucy's failure to perform this role, Ricky decides that he will take control and puts Lucy on a schedule that allots so many minutes for each domestic task she should perform. Although Lucy's inability to manage time is the excuse for this regimentation, the issue is really control over the domestic sphere. Because she failed to perform the proper role—of wife—Lucy becomes a slave to the schedule Ricky has posted on a big placard in the living room. In sharp contrast to her behavior at the Littlefields', Lucy gamely follows the schedule.

That Lucy attempts to manipulate time is telling, both of her function as a trickster in American culture and of the importance of time in television. As Mary Ann Doane states, "The major category of television is time" (222). Television sells time, fills time, keeps time, and distorts time. Interestingly, Ricky's schedule looks like a page from *TV Guide*. He *programs* Lucy's domestic time, insisting that the imposition of linear time from without the home will correct for the nonlinearity and irrationality of "women's time" from within.[8] Nevertheless, Lucy resists Ricky's attempt at discipline and regiment through the "logic" of the subjunctive mood: she adds extra time to the bottom of the daily schedule.

Lucy's willingness to go along with the schedule, albeit in a screwball fashion, poses a problem for the other two women in the episode, Lucy's best friend, Ethel, (played by Vivian Vance) and Mr. Littlefield's wife, Phoebe. Both women are concerned that Lucy's "good" behavior will cause their husbands to put them on schedules. This is what prompts Phoebe's question, "Mrs. Ricardo, what *are* you trying to do to the wives of America?" Phoebe tells Lucy that when Ricky invited Mr. Littlefield to dinner to watch Lucy "perform," he bragged, "I've got her jumping around like a trained seal."[9] Furious at Ricky's representation of his control over her, Lucy proposes a scheme to undermine the schedule as well as male authority over the rhythm of their lives. Before the "performance" begins, Lucy and Ethel appear to be obedient, but they have plotted resistance (Fig. 4.2b).

Lucy, Ethel, and Phoebe enter into a cross-class effort to regain their autonomy. They concoct a trick that parodies the schedule by serving and removing the dinner courses so fast that the men don't get a chance to eat; this scene culminates with Ethel throwing the dinner rolls from the kitchen to Lucy, who catches them in a catcher's mitt and passes them off to Phoebe, who puts them in the basket on the table (Figs. 4.2c–d). Order and power relations have been disrupted and, for the moment, suspended by the women's organized assault on their husbands' authority. Despite the class differences between Lucy and Phoebe, they can unite as women to combat their husbands' attempts at controlling their activities in the home. The episode ends with everyone calling Ricky a monster for his treatment of his wife; the twist is, as the boss declares, "Being a slave driver is no way to run a home, but it's the only way to run a nightclub . . . Mr. Manager!"

By being tricky rather than submissive, Lucy defends not only her own autonomy but that of other women as well. When Lucy is a dutiful wife who obeys her husband's dictates, she presents a model that is damaging to "the wives of America." But when she rebels against his attempted coup of the domestic sphere, when she participates in the conventional battle of the sexes, she is successful both in preserving women's autonomy in the private sphere and helping Ricky get his promotion. In this episode, the success of female trickery in preserving women's power in "woman's place," the home, articulates cultural justifications for polarized gender roles based in separate spheres. In the ideology of the feminine mystique (which insisted that there was a proper balance between public and private, male and female), women's autonomy in the home compensates for their lack of power in society at large. In a passage from the feminist classic *Man's World, Woman's Place*, Elizabeth Janeway explains how female autonomy in the private sphere is part of a "bargain" between men and women:

So when women cling to their traditional role, it is not primarily because they find masochistic pleasure in being dominated (though no doubt some do) but because this role offers them power too: private power in return for public submission. This is the regular, orthodox bargain by which men rule the world and allow women to rule their own place. Sometimes it is a better bargain than at others. When women's activities are publicly acknowledged to have social and

a

b

c

d

Figure 4.2. Frame enlargements from "Lucy's Schedule": *a.* No tricky Eve here: Lucy can't get the wax apple out of her mouth. *b.* The sexual division of labor is depicted in this frame, but with the comic twist of dramatic irony. Smug Ricky (Desi Arnaz) and Fred (William Frawley) don't know that their obedient-seeming wives have "cooked up" a scheme to regain their autonomy. Note the images of containment: the women are framed within the frame, Lucy's time is captured by the schedule. Note also that the audience is aware that the women are about to go wild. *c.* In performing dinner, Ethel (Vivian Vance) breaks out of the frame when she lobs dinner rolls. *d.* To the delight of Mrs. Littlefield and the distress of Ricky, Lucy catches the rolls with a catcher's mitt.

economic value, when within their place they can control the work to be done and order its processes, when they do not feel themselves isolated and cut off from man's world by a barrier of incomprehension, then the bargain will be accepted unquestioningly by a great majority of women. Enough authority within their traditional place balances an external subordination that is not too wounding. (56)

"Lucy's Schedule" uses a comic expression of female covert power to restore the "balance" between male and female control over their spheres. As other episodes dramatize, the tactics of covert power that work in the private sphere backfire when Lucy deploys them in the public sphere.

As my reading of "Lucy's Schedule" suggests, Lucy's use of female trickery is a metaphor for the contradictions of postwar domestic ideology, which on the one hand represents marriage as an equal partnership based on the "companionate ideal" and "togetherness," but on the other hand insists on polarized gender roles and a separation of the public and private spheres. This sexual doctrine, which could be termed "separate but together," was as riddled with tension as the racial segregation implied in "separate but equal." This ideology of the "domestic mystique" —an idealization of marriage, family, and the home prescribed to both men and women[10]—was an inherently unstable one (like the other postwar ideologies of containment), one that tried to legitimize traditional definitions of gender and the separation of spheres at a time in which those divisions were breaking down. At the core of the ideological construct of femininity in the postwar era was woman's role as a housewife.

Liminal at Heart

A cover story from *Cosmopolitan* magazine's series of articles on "America's top saleswomen," quotes Lucille Ball as saying, "I'm just a typical housewife at heart" (Morehead 19). The quotation appears next to a photograph of Ball wearing a dress reminiscent of Carmen Miranda, complete with a basket of fruit in her hat, with the caption: "An ex-dancer, today she is established at the top of the entertainment world." Does this describe the typical American housewife? The irreconcilable tensions on this page of *Cosmopolitan* alone—Ball as top saleswoman, top entertainer, and "at heart" a housewife—are echoed by many other articles in popular magazines such as *Time, Life, Look, Newsweek,* and *TV Guide.* Taken together, they suggest the contradictions of the feminine mystique at the "heart" of the *I Love Lucy* phenomenon as they emerged in the popular press.

Ball's claim to ordinary femininity (as opposed to the freakish unfemininity of the career woman) demonstrates that no matter what women did inside or outside the home, they were defined as housewives. Although the enormous structural changes in women's domestic and public work begun in the Depression and war years were evident in the postwar period, traditional values were not so quick to change. As historian William Chafe summarizes, "The poll data showed that most citizens preferred to retain traditional definitions of masculine and feminine spheres, even while modifying the content of those spheres in practice" (171). In other words, the gap between dominant domestic ideology and social experience was yet another example of the contradictions of postwar life. Such a denial of change characterized mainstream American culture. Historian Sara Evans explains, "Domestic ideology redefined a new reality—female labor force participation—to remove the potential threat of female power and autonomy by making women's work legitimate only as an extension of traditional family responsibilities" (262). Lucille Ball's public self-definition as a housewife "at heart" was typical, indeed.

Ball's public image of typicality extended Betty Grable's iconic model of a wholesome, all-American wife and mother. A February 10, 1953, *Look* article lauding Ava Gardner's star image asks, "Now that it's 1953, should movie stars be 'normal human beings?' Or should they live up to the oldtime legends?" The text above six photographs of legendary actresses bemoans the loss of female stars who were larger than life:

In the old days, a real movie star was a fairy princess of fantasy, a sublime being who was never caught doing the dishes. Theda Bara, Barbara La Marr and Gloria Swanson portrayed slinky "vamps"; Clara Bow, Jean Harlow and Carole Lombard were "madcap" comediennes. Whatever the subtle differences of sex appeal, personality and changing standards that make up a movie star, these women had one thing in common: They symbolized the same kind of dream girl off screen as well as on. The public was never confused by seeing Theda Bara or Jean Harlow attired in an apron, copying that overrated "girl next door." (54)

Although the star persona of Betty Grable was just as fabricated and as much of a fantasy figure as those who came before her, it was not one that she created or controlled, as Mae West did to a large extent. It is telling that World War II marked the move away from images of powerful, mysterious, extraordinary women and toward images of ordinary women. If not for Grable's public persona and other representations such as the article quoted above, we might assume that Ball's status as a television, and therefore domestic, star was the issue.

Whatever Ball is, she is it "at heart" and a "natural," just as it was considered natural for a woman to be in the "love economy," where being a housewife was to be a properly feminine woman. Such circular reasoning is at the heart of what influential feminist author Betty Friedan termed the "feminine mystique," which "says that the highest value and the only commitment for women is the fulfillment of their own femininity" (43).[11] It is within this web of socially sanctioned female female impersonation that *I Love Lucy* became not only the most popular show on television but also a cultural phenomenon. Significantly, the "housewife at heart" played by Ball was a housewife who didn't want to be "just a housewife," a character who exceeded the boundaries of conventional femininity.

In order to appreciate Lucy's transgressions of cultural ideals of femininity, we can glance at an example of dominant discourses of feminine power and marriage: "Making Marriage Work," a monthly feature published in *Ladies' Home Journal* ("The Magazine Women Believe In") during the postwar period. Written by Pennsylvania State College psychologist Clifford R. Adams, Ph.D., the one-page feature exemplifies the therapeutic approach to problems which characterizes mass consumer culture: individual personal adjustment rather than social institutional change.[12] Every month, Adams prescribed ways by which women could better adjust to marriage at the same time that he presented an ideal marriage based on partnership.

The headline "Co-operation is the rock, selfishness the sand, upon which marriage is built. Which do you choose?" (*Ladies' Home Journal* July 1953, 14) suggests Adams's emphasis on partnership. In an item titled "Don't Dominate Your Partner," Adams explains that, unfortunately, one spouse may abandon cooperation and attempt to control the relationship. Men employ "tangible and obvious methods," such as physical dominance, including violence, and financial control "to enforce submission rather than to win co-operation." Women also practice "techniques of control," which are "more subtle, [but] are no less deplorable and destructive." This article is interesting not only for its clear delineation of how "feminine wiles" can be transformed into weapons, but also in its equation of women's covert tactics with men's overt ones.

In contrast to Adams's prescriptive warnings about how love and tactics of exerting power are oppositional, historian Carolyn Johnston explains that covert power and love have gone hand in hand for women in America:

Excluded from most forms of public power until recently, women have primarily operated in the "love economy" of motherhood, housework, and voluntarism; although millions of women have been employed, they have still exercised power only covertly in their homes through emotional and sexual influence. Such covert sexual power relies on persuasion, manipulation, giving and withholding sex; it may be exerted in the nurturing of children and in making men dependent on women for daily needs of all kinds. Sexual power may be used to acquire material possessions, to influence family decisions, and generally get one's way. Covert sexual power works only when it is unseen and undetected, like any subversiveness. (ix)

The "love economy," then, fosters women's use of covert tactics, reinforcing woman's place in the private sphere.

As an influential representation of the "love economy," *I Love Lucy* made this self-perpetuating circle of domesticity and female trickery seem cute, essential, and, well, lovable. The title of the series, the name "Desilu," the heart that closes each episode, the mise-en-scène that creates such a desirable image of "home"—everything about the series reinscribes the centrality of the couple, the irreducible place of the "love" that motivates Lucy's trickery and Ricky's forgiveness of her covert tactics.

Moreover, the series dramatizes how the covert tactics that work so well in "Lucy's Schedule" backfire in the public sphere and only return her to domesticity. In the episode "The Moustache" (no. 23, March 17, 1952), for example, Lucy successfully uses female trickery to get her way in the marriage, but then her trick backfires on her when she tries to move beyond the private sphere. The conflict is over Ricky's new mustache; she does not like kissing a man with a mustache. At first, she demands that he shave it and pouts when he refuses, choosing to stay home and sulk while Fred and Ricky go to the movies. Her sulking soon gives way to an idea: she will put on false whiskers and see how *he* likes kissing someone with a mustache. When Ricky comes home to find a bearded wife, he concedes this battle and shaves. But when Lucy tries to remove her whiskers, she can't: rather than spirit gum, she has used a glue that is no longer manufactured.[13] At this point, Lucy's whiskers are the result of her trickery; she has become, and may have to remain, a bearded lady, unable to return to her female appearance because of her attempt to dominate her partner and withhold sexual activity until he capitulates. Although her use of sameness and equality (a mustache for a mustache) successfully demonstrates her point that maintaining their mutual sexual attraction is more important than either spouse's individual autonomy, it is not as easy to reverse her status from repulsive to alluring (Fig. 4.3a).

However, the stakes shift from the private power struggle of the Ricardos' marriage to the arena from which Lucy is barred by the situation of the situation comedy: public performance. When Ricky brings home a movie producer who is considering Ricky as the lead in *Moon Over Baghdad*, Lucy wants to audition for a part as well, despite her distinctly unfeminine facial hair. Here, again, is Lucy the trickster: Faced with what seems like an insurmountable obstacle, she embodies the sub-

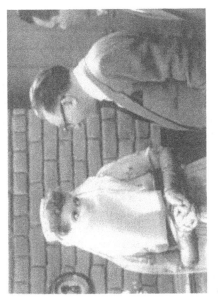

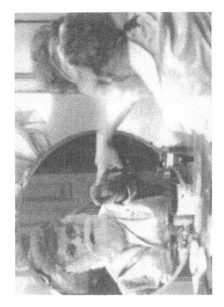

b

a

c

d

Figure 4.3. Frame enlargements from "The Moustache": *a*. Liminal Lucy points to the image of her boundary-crossing. Compare this mirror image to Figures 2.8 and 3.1. *b*. Cleverly, Lucy hides her facial hair behind a veil, *c*. until Ricky unmasks her, *d*. horrifying the producer (John Brown).

junctive mood and creates possibility. Cleverly deploying a harem-girl veil to cover her face (Fig. 4.3b), Lucy performs an impressive dance routine that charms the producer—until he removes her veil and is horrified by the bearded lady (Fig. 4.3c). Lucy's trick may have succeeded in manipulating Ricky, but the price she has to pay for that effective trick is being seen as unfeminine not only in a funny way (in her home dressed as a man), but in a horrifying way that prevents her from being in show business. When Lucy crosses the line between private and public, between feminine and masculine, her trickery fails.

Significantly, Lucy's female female impersonation of a non-Western exotic harem girl implies and denies the sexual willingness that she exploited when she, too, wore a mustache. Although we know that the veil hides the unfeminine whiskers, the producer sees the veil as the traditional symbol of female submission and a device with which to negotiate the gap between the private sphere of the harem where women belong and the public sphere where they must be covered to avoid the male gaze. That the producer can't see Lucy's face drives him to insist that she remove the veil; despite her protestations, he chases her and, with Ricky's help, succeeds only in being repulsed by the antithesis of the attractive woman he expected (Fig. 4.3d). A harem girl represents on the one hand the relative autonomy of women within the severely limited female sphere of the harem and on the other a formidable female power that can only be expressed to arouse and satisfy male sexual desire. Lucy's beard, first used as an offensive weapon in the battle of the sexes, now offends with its implication of Lucy's unwillingness to please men. The parodoxical juxtaposition of the sexy harem outfit—suggestive of Oriental indulgence and polygamy—and Lucy's parodically excessive facial hair—which plays on the cultural ideal of feminine hairlessness codified by film and television images and commodified by the beauty industry's marketing of body hair removal products—evokes women's anxieties about the equation of women's value with sexual allure. By meeting Ricky on equal ground, mustache against mustache, Lucy eventually causes her inability to fit into the role of "pretty girl," a term repeatedly used in the series to describe women's place in show business. Ultimately, her lack of submission in the private sphere protects her against the sexual slavery and exploitation represented by the film producer; her mustachioed self saves her from self-objectification.

This episode also comments slyly on how women's work is often portrayed as maintaining an attractive feminine appearance. By ridiculing Lucy's attempt to cover up an exaggerated physical flaw, it shows how the hedonic power promised by advertisements for the beauty industry takes the form of the social practice of female trickery in everyday life. Women, encouraged to manipulate their appearance and sublimate assertive impulses behind a mask of feminine behavior, are necessarily involved in duplicitous practices in everyday life. The emotional, sexual, and social machinations of the dating and marriage market, the self-objectification that presents an appealing facade, are achieved by employing the trickster tactics of deception, impersonation, disguise, duplicity, and subversion. Because the social practice of femininity is a form of trickery, characters in cultural texts who are female tricksters resonate with and expose a fundamental tenet of the social relations of the sexes in American culture: The only way for women to survive, given their subordinate position and limited opportunities for exercising overt power, is to use the covert power of female trickery.

That Lucy is not in complete control of her trickery shows how postwar culture depicted women's power as ineffectual, a force that no one has to fear. Unlike Scheherazade's successful manipulation of Shahryar's narrative and erotic desire, Lucy's harem girl is unable to prevent the producer from removing her veil. In contrast to wartime images of female sexual power as potent and dangerous (think of Jean's sardonic sexual and emotional power, which Hopsie cannot resist, or even detect, in *The Lady Eve*, or the femmes fatales of early film noir), postwar representations of women's sexuality tended to be nonthreatening. That sexy women in the war years were called "bombshells" suggests the connections between female sexuality and other forces that threatened postwar society—communists at home and abroad, the bomb, atomic power. And like these other forces, women's sexual and economic autonomy had to be contained and, in this case, channeled into the family and the home. "Outside the home (or even inside the home without a strong male authority), they would become a dangerous, destructive force" (Elaine Tyler May 109). Lucy's subversive energy—illustrative of a destructive force—repeatedly exceeds the boundaries her husband and society draw around her, a comic representation of the fragility of domestic containment in the wake of female ambition.

Danger—Woman at Work

I Love Lucy also shows how Lucy's incompetence undercuts her subversiveness, reinforcing the home and the social role of the housewife as the only option for women. When Lucy attempts to earn her own money by working outside the home, expected calamity and hilarity transpire. With this in mind, think back to the 1953 swimsuit ad with the headline "danger . . . woman at work" (see Fig. I.2, discussed in the Introduction). The words in the ad play on the implied contradiction between the familiar sign that alerts passersby to construction or roadwork being done by men and the idea of women's work. The warning "danger" refers to the idea that a woman's work is to attract men, by then an established tenet of advertising. The warning also has connections with popular discourses of women's incompetence—from widespread notions of women drivers to numerous representations of women's dependence on men for income and protection. The drawing of a woman standing with her head tilted back, eyes closed, and mouth slightly open reinforces the paradox of a passive working woman, as if a woman's best use of her labor time is the deployment of "curvallure" to attract men. The visual and verbal bisociations of the ad work because they articulate the irreconcilable contradictions at the heart of early 1950s' discourses of women and work.

Like the swimsuit ad, *I Love Lucy* plays on men's and women's beliefs and anxieties about women's work outside the home. For example, the episode "Job Switching" (no. 39, September 15, 1952) dramatizes the difficulty of housewives finding paid work without "experience." This episode echoes the scene in *Mildred Pierce* in which Mildred searches for work. In "Job Switching," the Ricardos and Mertzes demonstrate the chaos that results from transgressing the spheres, labor, and roles considered appropriate to their gender. The episode culminates in what may be the most famous *I Love Lucy* scene: Lucy and Ethel are not fast enough to keep up with the conveyor belt at the candy factory.

In this hilarious scene, Lucy and Ethel's lack of job experience and incompetence at various tasks at the candy factory land them the assignment of wrapping the chocolate candies that move past them on a conveyor belt. As dictated by the tradition of comic representations of a human at the mercy of a machine (theorized by Henri Bergson and best exemplified by Chaplin in *Modern Times*), Lucy and Ethel cannot keep up with the increasing speed of the conveyor belt. As the chocolates zoom past them, they stuff them in their mouths, down their shirts, in their hats so they can deceive the supervisor. Instead of being efficient workers, Lucy and Ethel break the social taboo against female gluttony and, like mythical tricksters, gorge themselves.

This scene and the one of the men in the kitchen are typical of the comic climaxes to which episodes of *I Love Lucy* build, hilarious moments when the situation is beyond human control, yet the person continues to react as best he or she can, forced to behave in sillier and sillier ways. These moments showcase Lucille Ball's talent as a physical comedienne (and in this case, Desi Arnaz's slapstick) and demonstrate Ball's mastery of *sprezzatura,* "the art that conceals art, the supremely artificial that strikes us as supremely natural" (Mast, *The Comic Mind* 26). The illusion of spontaneity was created by careful writing, Ball's talent working with props, and a strong streak of perfectionism among the show's collaborators. Producer Jess Oppenheimer explained the comic structure of *I Love Lucy*: "I always insisted that everything in an 'I Love Lucy' story have a logical foundation. I wanted there to be a sound reason for everything in the script, because I knew from experience that if you take viewers one step at a time, and they know *why* they're being taken there, you can go to the heights of slapstick comedy and outlandish situations. . . . Don't forget, we didn't always *try* to get the laugh. We took time to develop a situation that would eventually pay off with a bigger laugh" (quoted in Bart Andrews 142–44). It is during the setup that ideological discourses come to the forefront; this is where the writers (Oppenheimer, Bob Carroll Jr. and Madelyn Pugh) had to negotiate the gap between the comic climax and the situation of ordinary, domestic life.

The way "Job Switching" bridges that gap is particularly revealing of dominant definitions of the sexual division of labor in mass consumer culture. Fired from their jobs at the candy factory and sick to their stomachs from eating so many chocolates, the women stagger into the apartment, defeated. The men are nowhere to be found, but on the kitchen door is a note asking Lucy and Ethel to stay out of the kitchen until their husbands can explain. Lucy collapses on the couch next to Ethel after seeing the kitchen. When Ricky and Fred return, the men and women confess their respective failures. "What say we go back to the way we were," Ricky concedes. "We'll make the money and you'll spend it." The men admit that housework is harder than they had thought, and to show their appreciation for their wives, they bought each of them a gift—a five-pound box of chocolates!

The ironic twist of the truce in this installment of the battle of the sexes is that the men have brought the women the one thing that they do not want. Chocolates, a commodity signifying luxury and the pleasures of consumption as well as the love implied by the heart-shaped boxes, represent what women can hope to gain from their labor. It is much more pleasant (and less messy) to have treats handed to you by an appreciative husband than to go out into the public sphere where the chocolates speed by on the conveyor belt, either out of reach or stuffed in your mouth.

The contrast between the rewards of paid labor in the public sphere and unpaid—but autonomous and appreciated—housework in this backlash representation shows how domestic ideology obfuscates the material terms of marriage. Housework, according to philosopher Carole Pateman's analysis of the sexual contract of marriage, "is the work of a sexually subject being who lacks jurisdiction over the property in her person, which includes labour power. . . . A (house)wife does not contract out her labour power of her husband. She is not paid a wage—there is no token of free exchange—because her husband has command over the use of her labour by virtue of the fact that he is a man" (135–36).

"Job Switching" does not represent that reality, however, but rather obscures the inequalities inherent in traditional marriage by substituting consumption as compensation for the lack of "free exchange" in marriage. Specifically, the episode concludes by recasting women's domestic labor in terms of the gendered roles in mass consumer society, which reify consumption as the goal of labor. When the men and women gratefully agree to switch back to their "normal" roles, they are defined as earners and spenders, not as public and private or paid and unpaid workers.[14] This reinforcement of mass consumer culture is typical of situation comedies, in which consumerism was dramatized as the center of American domestic life.

By representing daily life as commodified, television functioned as "an instrument of legitimation for transformations in values initiated by the new economic imperatives" (Lipsitz 44). As historian George Lipsitz goes on to explain, "Commercial network television emerged as the primary discursive medium in American society at the precise historical moment when the isolated nuclear family and its concerns eclipsed previous ethnic, class and political forces as the crucible of personal identity. Television programs both reflected and shaped that transition, defining the good life in family-centric, asocial, and commodity-oriented ways" (55). The "good life" that *I Love Lucy* portrayed was relentlessly commodified. Not only are people's roles defined in terms of their relationship to consumption, as we saw in "Job Switching," but many episodes concern the lengths to which Lucy goes to secure a consumer item or make the money to buy things. The series seems to offer consumption as the solution to Lucy's dissatisfaction, an example of the consumerist-therapeutic ethos that presented private solutions to public problems. Week after week, *I Love Lucy* endorsed the processes of mass consumer culture. From Lucille Ball and Desi Arnaz clothing, furniture, and nursery items to Lucy and Ricky dolls, record albums, and comic books, *I Love Lucy* spawned a widening circle of commodification, with the series' complementary values of domesticity and consumerism at its center.[15]

At the same time that Desilu vigorously participated in the mass consumer economy, the show's comedy played on conflicts about the pleasures of consumption and the comforts of domesticity. For example, although Lucy's trickery is often motivated by her acquisitive zeal, the consumer goods she gets obviously do not quell her yearning for satisfaction. By portraying consumption as a site of struggle between husband and wife, the series undercuts its central tenet that love is the most valuable facet of privatized family-oriented life. In depicting the transformations of values to those Lipsitz identifies, television texts like *I Love Lucy* portrayed a "good life" characterized by unresolved tensions and multiple meanings.

Reel Life and Real Life

The immediacy of *I Love Lucy*'s representation of the "good life" created and was created by the public's perceived knowledge about Ball and Arnaz. The story of the Ball-Arnaz marriage disseminated by Desilu is akin to a parable of marriage in the forties and fifties. Married in 1940, the couple spent years separated by the demands of their careers (analogous to separations during the war years); because they were apart, they almost divorced twice (evocative of the strains on marriage immediately after the war), but their marriage survived because they channeled their careers into a situation that guaranteed togetherness. In a *Newsweek* article, *I Love Lucy* is credited with preserving the marriage: "Both the Arnazes love their TV show because it saved their marriage" ("Desilu Formula" 57). Opposite this comment is a photograph of Ball and Arnaz in front of the ranch they named Desilu captioned "Lucille, Desi, and the home that television kept together" (Fig. 4.4).

Because television was broadcast into people's homes at a time when domesticity was a central tenet of the dominant value system, the more the Ricardos mirrored ordinary people (and Ball and Arnaz were represented as typical, not glamorous stars), the more appealing they were; the more enticing they were, the more they reinforced domestic ideology. In order to transform the popularity of the show's characters into a cultural phenomenon (on which the sale of commodities and continued success of the series could be based), Ball and Arnaz had to be perceived to be as personable as the Ricardos. Further, Ball and Arnaz could increase their popularity by calling attention to the ways that their television characters were based on themselves. For example, a June 3, 1952, *Look* article, titled "Laughing Lucille," claimed, "There has never been a divorce between the public and private lives of the Arnazes, and their TV comedy is no exception" (Silvian 7). Or as "a friend" of Ball's explained in the same article, "The trouble with Lucy is that her real life is so much like her reel life" (7).

Lucille Ball's description of the appeal of *I Love Lucy* further demonstrates the importance of appearing typical and obscuring the line between "real life" and fiction:

We had a great identification with millions of people. They could identify with my problems, my zaniness, my wanting to do everything, my scheming and plotting, the way I cajoled Ricky. People identified with the Ricardos because we had the same problems they had. Desi and I weren't your ordinary Hollywood

Figure 4.4. Television saves domesticity: Lucille Ball and Desi Arnaz pose on their ranch, Desilu. This uncredited photograph accompanied an article about the Ball-Arnaz marriage and television show published in *Newsweek*, January 19, 1953. Used with permission of *Newsweek*.

couple on TV. We lived in a brownstone apartment somewhere in Manhattan, and paying the rent, getting a new dress, getting a stale fur collar on an old cloth coat, or buying a piece of furniture were all worth a story.

People could identify with those basic things—baby-sitters, traveling, wanting to be entertained, wanting to be loved in a certain way—the two couples on the show were constantly doing things that people all over the country were doing. We just took ordinary situations and exaggerated them. (quoted in Bart Andrews 225–26)

In her explanation, Ball puts Lucy's trickery—her "scheming and plotting, the way I cajoled Ricky"—into the context of everyday life. To be sure, the Ricardos embodied an ideal, but it was an ideal that encompassed the frictions and tensions of a middle-class domestic ideal, and represented those problems as endurable because of love. As producer and writer Jess Oppenheimer summarized, "The things that happen to the Ricardos happen to everyone in the audience. We call it 'holding up the mirror.' Whatever happens, they love each other" (Oppenheimer 23).

The only way to make sense of Oppenheimer's explanation that the series holds up a mirror to everyday life is if we recognize that it is a distorted mirror. There are many levels of refraction at work in the construction of the cultural phenomenon surrounding *I Love Lucy*: the individual episode, the series as a whole, the commercials and other facets that constitute television "flow," the secondary texts that offer extratextual information that viewers might use in their interpretations of the text (like *TV Guide* and other magazines), and viewers' social experience. Because of television's place in the home and the domestic subject matter of the series, *I Love Lucy* speaks in and to the homelife of its viewers. Further, the visual style creates a sense of intimacy between the viewer and the stars. Cinematographer Karl Freund (who was also the cinematographer of Fritz Lang's stunning silent film *Metropolis* [1926]) used three thirty-five millimeter cameras that captured wide, medium, and close-up shots (the system was developed by Al Smith). The editors (Dan Cahn in the first and second seasons, Bud Molin thereafter) chose a series of shots that preserved the sense of continuity central to classical Hollywood style and created an intimacy between the viewers and the stars, especially through alternating medium shots and close-ups. The off-camera sound of the studio audience reminds us that the stars are performing live, so the viewer is placed in privileged space.

Probably the most important factor in equating real life and reel life was the marriage of Ball and Arnaz. Like the "fictional" marriage of the Ricardos, the "real-life" marriage of Ball and Arnaz also highlights the "love" of a companionate marriage, but one between equals in the joint enterprise of Desilu. When Ball and Arnaz take their bows and their names appear on the trademark heart, the episode is framed by "real-life" as well as "fictional" love. Yet, the "reality" of the stars' marriage not only frames the episode but erupts from within it, disrupting the suspension of belief of the "fiction."

A detail from "The Ballet" (no. 19, February 18, 1952) illustrates how the "real-life" marriage does not remain external to the "fictional" marriage of the Ricardos. In the scene in which Lucy gets a private lesson from a demanding ballet teacher, Ball performs some of the funniest physical comedy in the entire series. Lucy cannot make her body obey the teacher's or her own commands; she barks at her leg, which will not budge from the ballet barre and ends up dangling from the barre (Figs. 4.5a–b). Ricky, of course, does not know about the lesson and would disapprove if he did. But the soundtrack catches Arnaz's distinctive laughter coming from offstage, which has the potential to draw the audience's attention to the artifice of Lucy's performance. Although Lucy is a bumbling dancer, we know that Lucille Ball is a consummate entertainer who is in control of her body. And, more importantly, we

a

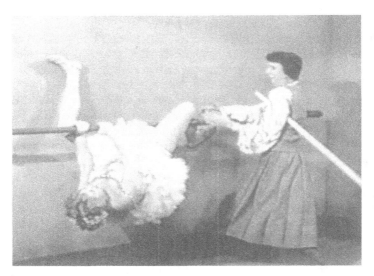

b

Figure 4.5. Frame enlargements from "The Ballet": *a.* At the ballet lesson, Lucy's body does not obey her will; *b.* she gets caught in her pursuit of femininity.

know that although in the fiction Ricky refuses to allow his wife to perform, the actor Desi Arnaz delights in his wife's/partner's antics. This interweaves another comedic level, an in-joke predicated upon the bisociation of the series' representation of "reality" and "fictionality." How seriously can we take Ricky's injunctions that his wife can't be on television when Ball and Arnaz *are* a husband and wife on television? On one level, the show does what on another level it says shouldn't happen. This contradiction illustrates the gap between the social experience of women who were working in the public sphere and the ideology that attempted to contain them within domesticity. The series itself is a kind of trick that encourages the audience to participate in the attractive image of the stars' happy marriage, a fiction representative of postwar behavior and attitudes that obscures asymmetry in the sex-gender system.

The series' depiction of the "real-life" marriage of Ball and Arnaz was constructed by Desilu and disseminated in the media, but with various emphases. The secondary texts of *I Love Lucy*—the hype surrounding the series that gave the audience the impression that they "knew" Ball and Arnaz—provided "insider" information about the stars' marriage, family, and house as well as about the production of the series. To generalize, like the *Cosmopolitan* cover story quoted earlier, articles in *Time, Newsweek, Look,* and *Life* portray Ball in terms of being or wanting to be a housewife. The Desilu strategy seems to have been to highlight the typicality of Ball and Arnaz. Ball's gender role, therefore, is defined by the prevailing feminine mystique. For example, the May 26, 1952, *Time* cover story takes Ball's statement, "I look like everybody's idea of an actress, but I feel like a housewife" (62) and assumes that the role of Lucy lets "Lucille fulfill her lifelong ambition of playing a housewife" ("Sassafrassa" 67). At the bottom of seven photographs of Lucy's more outrageous escapades, the caption echoes the *Cosmopolitan* cover story discussed earlier: "At heart, she's a housewife" (63). Thus, the article ascribes the desire to be a housewife to Ball, who clearly isn't a housewife and doesn't even *play* a character who wants to be a housewife.

Another layer of contradictions about Ball's enactment of her gender role comes at the end of the article: "In reaching the TV top, Lucille's telegenic good looks may be almost as important as her talent for comedy. She is sultry-voiced, sexy, and wears chic clothes with all the aplomb of a trained model and showgirl. Letters from her feminine fans show as much interest in Lucille's fashions as her slapstick. . . . Lucille belongs to a rare comic aristocracy: the clown with glamour" (68). Here Ball is reinscribed within a value system that privileges female attractiveness over other qualities such as talent and intelligence. The short article in *Life*, which precedes stills from "The Ballet," also contrasts Ball's glamour with her comedy. Evocatively titled "Beauty into Buffoon," the article comments: "[Her] figure has been obscured by baggy-pants costumes; her adeptness at comedy has been translated into slapstick pratfalls, and her versatility has been almost completely ignored. Such use of beauty and talent might seem wasteful but for the fact that *I Love Lucy* now ranks [first in popularity]. . . . Miss Ball is deliriously happy with TV" (93). The commentary that frames the photo essay of "The Ballet" makes Ball's work sound not quite understandable; there's obviously something a little odd about a beautiful woman who finds the unfeminine world of slapstick comedy fun. Moreover, the article describes "Miss" Ball's work not as a career, but as a job that does not threaten the primacy of marriage and family: she works "only" four days a week—in togetherness with her husband—and the couple owns their own show in the same way that other couples aspire to own their own home or business.

The photographs in the *Life* article foreground Lucy's negotiation of gendered performance. Ballet is feminine, traditional clown comedy is masculine, and liminal Lucy is caught somewhere in between, as she was in "The Moustache." Repeatedly in the series, Lucy aspires to be the "pretty girl" in the act who will "advertise the sponsor's product. She eats it, or drinks it, or waxes the floor with it, or cuts potatoes with it, or drives off in it . . . or smokes it!" This line from the episode based on the March 1951 pilot, "The Audition" (no. 6, November 19, 1951), shows how women in performance are valued primarily for their appearance and makes a joke based on the audience's extratextual knowledge that Ball smokes the cigarettes of the show's sponsor, Philip Morris. In-jokes like this one, bisociate inept housewife Lucy Ricardo and TV star Lucille Ball, calling attention to how she both is and is not the "pretty girl" in the various narrative frames of the *I Love Lucy* phenomenon (the episode, the advertisements during the episode, knowledge about the series and its stars from secondary texts, the cultural contexts that inflect the combinations of private housewife/public pretty girl and femininity/comedy with contradictions, and the ideology of the feminine mystique). As Lucy says when Ricky refuses to give her a part in his new nightclub act, "Here I am with all this talent bottled up inside of me and you're always sitting on the cork!"

In "The Ballet," Lucy uses trickery to get around this cork-sitting obstacle to her participation in the sphere of public performance. The episodes that concern Lucy tricking her way into Ricky's act are often skewed by the series' premise that Lucy doesn't have the talent she thinks she has, but the comic climax of this episode does not hinge on Lucy's lack of talent. In fact, the episode shows her ability to improvise as both a ballet dancer and a burlesque comic to create a synthesis of agonic and hedonic entertainment. However, the two distinctly gendered types of performance—feminine ballet and masculine comedy—

suggest an underlying theme of the series as a whole—that there is no tradition of the female comic, and that Lucy/Ball spontaneously creates that possibility week after week. Further, the secondary texts, such as the *Life* article that circulated in advance of the show's broadcast, called attention to the paradox of the female comic.

In "The Ballet," both the ballet and the comedy lessons highlight Lucy's liminal gender status as a funny woman. In the ballet scene, Lucy's comportment and actions do not fit the rigid classical ideals of ballet. Unlike the "real" dancers, she is dressed in the tutu she wore in a ballet recital in her youth, and from the moment she tries to pull her skirt down to better cover her legs in front of the male dancers to the hilarious moment when she gets caught on the barre, she is obviously no ballerina (see Figs. 4.5a and 4.5b).

When the feminine performance of the ballerina is revealed to be too much hard work, Lucy decides she will try comedy. Just as the part of the ballet dancer exemplifies conventional feminine appearance and behavior, the burlesque comic lampoons masculinity. Dressed in baggy pants and armed with comic "weapons," the performer comes over to the Ricardo apartment to teach Lucy a routine (Fig. 4.6a).

In order to be a comic, Lucy must impersonate a man—the straight man. She is the dupe here, the one who suffers the physical humiliation of the butt of the joke. The burlesque comic tells the second man (Lucy) the story of why he is so sad: his wife Martha left him for another man. The gag is that every time the comic hears the name Martha, he reenacts the moment when he saw his wife with another man and flew into a blind rage, saying, "Slowly I turned, step by step, inch by inch," moving closer to his victim (now Lucy), and attacking until Lucy snaps him out of the flashback. Lucy, of course, repeatedly says "Martha." As the comic takes menacing steps toward her, he mutters the tag line, "Slowly I turned, step by step" and smacks her with a bladder, sprays her with seltzer water, and finishes with a pie in her face. When the comic asks if she wants to try the routine again, she agrees only if this time he's the straight man. In the burlesque act, aggression is at the center, whereas in the ballet scene she is at odds with her own body, which stubbornly refuses to enact the commands she gives it. As the subordinate man in the routine, she is in no more control than she was as a ballet dancer.

So here we have thesis—Lucy should be in the feminine ballet act—and antithesis—Lucy will try the burlesque act. Next comes the synthesis of the two, which Ball does metaphorically all the time. We pick up the plot on opening night, when Lucy sits home alone, sulking because she is not in the show. Although she was successful in the comedy routine, by the time she had finished her lesson Ricky had hired a comic.

a

b

Figure 4.6. Frame enlargements from "The Ballet": *a.* Lucy tries masculine comedy; *b.* Lucy (dressed as a male comic) breaks into the act and takes aim at the heart of feminine performance.

To play a trick on Ricky, Fred and Ethel call Lucy to stand in for one of the dancers. In the kind of misunderstanding that constitutes comedy, Lucy thinks she is replacing the male comic, not the ballet dancer. "You mean 'Slowly I Turned?'" she asks Ethel, who replies, "Yeah, all that turning stuff."

The scene at the nightclub is a comic climax that highlights Lucy's liminality, her embodiment of the state of being "betwixt and between" gender roles as a female comic. Much to the surprise of the ballet dancers and Ricky (who is singing a love song about a woman named, of course, Martha), Lucy bursts onto the stage dressed as a burlesque comic, armed with bladder, seltzer, and pie. While Ricky sings his romantic song in the background, Lucy gamely does the ballet routine in her baggy man's suit; here Lucy's appearance is masculine, but her behavior is feminine. But when Ricky sings the name "Martha," Lucy launches into the comedy routine, hitting her male dance partner; now her behavior is aggressive and violent. Then she returns to her feminine role in the dance routine, until Ricky sings the fateful name again, and she squirts the female ballet dancer in the face with the seltzer. Here Lucy takes revenge on the female dancer who successfully performs the female female impersonation of ballet dancer and brings agonic aggression to the hedonic display of feminine beauty (Fig. 4.6b). Oscillating once more between the hedonic and agonic modes of entertainment, Lucy slams a pie into Ricky's face as the male dancers whisk her offstage.

In this comic synthesis, Lucy disrupts and subverts the performance by transgressing the boundaries between gendered appearance and behavior. Physically, she conflates masculine appearance with female performance. Narratively, she brings the comic's tale of burlesque cuckolding into collision with Ricky's ballad of idealized romance. She publicly upstages the dancers, as well as her husband and his authority at his job, humiliating him with the pie in his face as he is singing. Her disruption puts her not only at the center of attention, but (unlike the scenes in which she learns the ballet and comedy routines) also in full control for the first time in the episode. By escaping domesticity and participating in the public sphere of show business, Lucy has quelled her dissatisfaction and isolation. The transgressive practice of cross-dressing further enabled her to enact a carnivalesque reversal of the power relationship in her marriage as well as to act in ways prohibited to women, using behavior that is a crucial part of the conventionally male tradition of physical comedy. Lucy also successfully circumvents her husband's authority by stepping outside the boundaries of woman's sphere and the role of housewife. Her tricky manipulations of gender and genre call attention to the limitations of women's roles in the public and private spheres.

The episode ends with Lucy returning, literally and figuratively, to the home, and to Ricky's trickery. She hovers at the door, still dressed in a suit, until Ricky assures her he is not angry about her performance. She opens the door all the way and is hit by a stream of water (Fig. 4.7a), prompting Ricky's laughter at his successful deployment of the classic bucket of water atop the door trick. "Well, I guess I had it coming," Lucy admits, and the Ricardos embrace, kissing several times as the music swells. Lucy says, "Now we're even," Ricky agrees, and the audience applauds as the two halves of the heart-shaped *I Love Lucy* logo close like stage curtains over the image of the couple kissing (Figs. 4.7b–d). The names Lucille Ball and Desi Arnaz appear side by side on the heart, and the credits roll.

The resolution of this episode is typical of many others that end with a balance of egalitarianism within the Ricardo marriage, which is reinforced by the frame of the actors' real-life marriage. In the tradition of the screwball comedy, the couple demonstrates the strength and appropriateness of their union through mutual trickery. However, although they are "even" for the moment, the image of two people dressed as men embracing is hardly conventional, and it undercuts the typicality of the Ricardos. The image of equality sits uneasily here in the closing image alongside irreconcilable differences between egalitarian and companionate marriage, private and public, gender and performance.

The multiple meanings represented in this ending illustrate my point that narrative closure is not necessarily ideological closure. The concluding kiss is both conventional (symbolic of the happy ending) and emblematic of the primacy of "love" in the series.[16] No matter what zany thing Lucy does, Ricky loves her; the husband's love (the most important aspect of marriage expressed, for example, in the *Ladies' Home Journal* feature "Making Marriage Work") incorporates her rebellious refusal to play only one social role in the "love economy." Nevertheless, even an idealized marriage like the Ricardos' is a battle between husband and wife in which "love" is only indicative of a temporary truce; the asymmetry between Lucy and Ricky remains to prompt another episode. Like Scheherazade's tales, the episodes of *I Love Lucy* break off where they do to keep us coming back for another chance to peer into the inner workings of the Ricardo marriage. And like the trickster she is, after temporarily "going wild," Lucy returns to the social situation she started in. As anthropologist Robert Pelton writes,

The trickster violates boundaries to humanize them, but the "new" shape that the world assumes is its present one. This is one of the points of the trickster's irony: all that wheeling and dealing, that endless juggling, simply keeps new balls flying through the air in the same order and at the same speed. Even where his only ritual is the telling of his stories, his work is, above all, synchronous. His transforming power has worked in the past to create the present, and it works

in the present to make the future reflect the past. He moves past society's cir-
cumference to ensure the permanent rediscovery of its center. (248)

That center was the home and the family. The conflation of Ball and
Arnaz with the characters they portrayed was intensified by the virtually simultaneous births of Ball and Arnaz's and Ricky and Lucy's sons
in January 1953. When Ball and Arnaz revealed her pregnancy to the
show's producer, they transformed what could have been the end of the
top-rated series into a new arena for comedy; not only had television
"saved" their marriage, but it enabled Ball to maintain her career and
have a family.

Moreover, Ball performed the cultural work of a trickster in mainstream America by being the first openly pregnant woman to perform
on television, which challenged accepted ideas about the impropriety
of public representations of pregnancy. For example, even though the
censors would not allow anyone to say the word "pregnant" on the show
(the French "enceinte" was used instead), Arnaz drew the line when
Philip Morris wanted Lucy's pregnant body hidden behind furniture
(Bart Andrews 93–94). *I Love Lucy* met the challenge of giving pregnancy
comic treatment with bits about cravings, Ricky's sympathetic morning
sickness, and cute maternity clothes (the inspiration for a line of Lucy
and Desi commodities that allowed the parents of the baby boomers to
model themselves after Lucy and Ricky, or Ball and Arnaz). The conflation of fictionality and "reality" in the pregnancy shows resulted in
an emotional intensity that allowed the viewer to participate in a highly
mediated but nevertheless moving enactment of expecting a baby. At
moments such as when Lucy tells Ricky that they are going to have a
baby (Ball and Arnaz were understandably emotional as they filmed the
scene), the audience is privy to a reenactment of personal events, or
rather, Ball and Arnaz turned their private experience into a public representation that reflected and shaped the popular pursuit of marriage
and family. As *New York Times* critic Jack Gould wrote in his January 16,
1953, column, "Far from ridiculing motherhood, 'I Love Lucy' has made
it appear one of the most natural things in the world."

The convergence of Lucy/Ricky and Ball/Arnaz in media representations of the births of their babies drew considerable public attention in
baby boom America. The January 19, 1953, *Newsweek* cover story, "Desilu
Formula for Top TV: Brains, Beauty, Now a Baby," describes the blessed
events: "If all goes well, newspaper readers all over the country will be
treated on Jan. 20 to the story of Mrs. Arnaz having a baby—the morning after they see Mrs. Ricardo go to the hospital on TV. All this may
come under the heading of how duplicated in life and television *can*
you get" (56). That the baby was part of the "Desilu formula" suggests

a

b

Figure 4.7. Frame enlargements from "The Ballet": *a.* Ricky uses the old bucket-of-water-over-the-door trick to get back at Lucy for disrupting his show; *b,c.* the camera dollies in on the couple as they laugh, and Lucy acknowledges, "Now we're even"; *d.* the heart closes over the kissing couple like stage curtains, framing the husband and wife team at the "heart" of American culture.

c

d

the recognition of the pregnancy as not only "true" but a gimmick, a trick, as well. *Lucy* producer and writer Jess Oppenheimer made a sales pitch to the readers of *Look* in an April 21, 1953, article titled, "Lucy's Two Babies": "The audience will see Lucy and Ricky struggling through the exasperating, wonderful problems experienced by parents everywhere—from pacing the floor with the crying child, getting up for the two o'clock feeding, through teething, first steps, first words and on and on until, one day, maybe we'll see little Ricky marching off to school" (24). By cleverly redefining pregnancy, birth, and parenting, subjects previously deemed indecent, as comic fodder for television, *I Love Lucy* helped bring television into the home and the home into television. And when more people tuned in to watch the birth episode of *I Love Lucy* than watched the Eisenhower inauguration the next day, they participated in the cultural primacy of domesticity and family that characterized the postwar era.

Because *I Love Lucy* centered on Lucy's tricksterism, Lucy became a tricky mother, unrelenting in her pursuit of self-satisfaction. For example, a few months after Little Ricky's birth, the episode "The Indian Show" (no. 59, May 4, 1953) concerned Lucy's desire to be in show business. Although Ricky thinks Lucy should be satisfied in her role as wife and mother, Lucy goes behind Ricky's back and wangles her way onto the show. When the shocked Ricky demands to know who is taking care of the baby, Lucy reveals that she has had the baby strapped to her back as a papoose during her performance. The contradictions between woman's place in the home in the role of housewife and female ambitions to participate in the public sphere were intensified, not erased, by Lucy's entrance into motherhood.

In blurring the line between reality and artifice with the synchronous "real-life" and "fictional" births, *I Love Lucy* exemplified what television as an institution and apparatus was doing—making more permeable the traditional boundaries between public and private, truth and artifice, and representation and social experience.[17] Moreover, *I Love Lucy* was a bizarre public fantasy that recreated the Ball-Arnaz marriage along more traditional lines; not only is Ricky the star and Lucy the ordinary housewife who wants to be a star (in contrast to "real life" in which Ball's career was more successful than Arnaz's), but each week the happy ending implied that the love between Lucy and Ricky was ideal and unchanging. In "real life," however, Ball and Arnaz's marriage was rife with problems (the demands of their careers, the strain of "togetherness," drinking, and infidelity).[18] When Ball and Arnaz divorced in 1960, the layer of fiction that *I Love Lucy* and Desilu provided was stripped away, ironically revealing married life to be a "nightmare," the "last five years [of the series and the marriage] were sheer, unadulterated hell"

(Ball, quoted in Bart Andrews 216–17). The public breakup of America's favorite couple is symbolic of the social turmoil that pulled back the deceptive cover story of domestic bliss to reveal the inequality and unhappiness within. Even for stars, "reel life" is better than "real life."

Lucy's Legacy

Lucy employs the tactics of female trickery to circumvent her husband's authority and the limitations society puts on her as a woman who is expected to be a housewife. Lucy's ambition and dissatisfaction result in hilarious machinations that propel her outside domesticity into the public world; in the process, she orients herself so her focus expands from, rather than contracts into, domesticity. The qualities she embodies are antithetical to conventional definitions of femininity: self-absorption, inability to conform, lack of bodily control, disruptive activity. When Lucy embodies these qualities, she enacts an individualism and self-development that constantly lead her to challenge the boundaries surrounding her.

These characteristics are also those of the trickster. To reiterate, in his synthesis of trickster scholarship, William Hynes delineates six qualities that define trickster figures: "At the heart of this cluster of manifest trickster traits is (1) the fundamentally ambiguous and anomalous personality of the trickster. Flowing from this are other such features as (2) deceiver/trick-player, (3) shapeshifter, (4) situation-invertor, (5) messenger/imitator of the gods, and (6) sacred/lewd bricoleur" (in Hynes and Doty 34). Lucy demonstrates these character traits. First, she is "fundamentally ambiguous" in her unfulfilled housewife role. Second, she constantly uses tricks and deceptions. Third, she shapeshifts by using the tactics of female trickery (makeup, costume, comportment, behavior) in her impersonations. Fourth, she subverts situations to her advantage, most recognizably when she disrupts a performance. The fifth characteristic Hynes names, "messenger/imitator of the gods," refers to the trickster figure's transgression of the boundaries between humans and gods; the division between masculine and feminine is as central to postwar "ideology" as the line between human and divine is to the belief systems of the pre- and early-modern cultures on which most trickster scholarship focuses. Lucy fulfills this fifth criterion, then, by crossing the line between masculine and feminine, most obviously in her male impersonations. In the male-dominated world of performance, Lucy imitates forms of comedy associated with men (for example, the burlesque comic in "The Ballet"). She also ventures into other male behaviors and activities. Finally, Lucy cleverly transforms elements of the situation at hand in her creative and resourceful schemes to get what she wants; she conflates definitions of good and shadow femininity: she is a wife and mother (as sacred a role as there is in the cold war era) who desperately wants to be in the lewd sphere of performance.

Most importantly, Lucy functioned as a trickster figure in postwar American culture because, as "paradox personified" (Babcock-Abrahams 148), she embodied the quagmire of the feminine mystique—the representation of women's power as both potent and benign. Elizabeth Janeway explains: "The double myth of female weakness and female power is not a contradiction, or a mask over reality, but two streams of feeling which commingle and feed each other. Not only does one aspect support the other, so that the weak are able to dream they have power, and the powerful find they can retreat into irresponsibility. There is an ambiguity at the heart of the psychic situation producing both myths which links the two, so that one can become the other, so that each implies the other" (57). Lucy is a nexus at which these two "streams of feeling" intersect in a comic bisociation of women's covert power. At a historical moment when women's public participation challenged the traditional division between public and private spheres based on polarized gender roles, female trickery—women's covert power—was an issue at the crossroads of reactionary and liberated definitions of femininity. In the postwar era, women as a group were moving away from covert power based on emotional and sexual manipulations in the private realm of family and marriage and toward overt exercises of power in the economic, social, and political arenas of the public sphere.

I began this chapter with a question about the cultural work that Lucy performed: "Mrs. Ricardo, what *are* you trying to do to the wives of America?" In order to answer this question clearly, it is necessary to consider what roles a character in a popular text *can* do and what functions trickster figures tend to play. Perhaps Jane Tompkins's explanation of the role of stereotyped characters in popular fiction can illuminate the first issue:

Stereotypes are instantly recognizable representations of overlapping racial, sexual, national, ethnic, economic, social, political, and religious categories; they convey enormous amounts of cultural information in an extremely condensed form. As the telegraphic expression of complex clusters of value, stereotyped characters are *essential* to popularly successful narrative . . . [they] operate as a cultural shorthand, and because of their multilayered representative function are the carriers of strong emotional associations. Their familiarity and typicality, rather than making them bankrupt or stale, are the basis of their effectiveness as integers in a social quotation. (*Sensational Designs* xvi)

Although Lucy is not as much a stereotype as a synthesis of the types of heroines I have categorized as madcaps, screwballs, and con women, she nevertheless plays on the sexist stereotype of the incompetent woman. By both drawing upon and subverting that stereotype, Lucy articulated anxieties about women's abilities—covert and overt power—in the private and public spheres.

Trickster figures do not change the social structure that they temporarily subvert and ridicule; embodiments of a sometimes socially threatening individualism, they recognize the inconsistencies and exploit them for their own satisfaction. Tricksters articulate the uncertainty of life, the perverse irony that seems to characterize much of human existence. When they attempt to control the situation around them through trickery, they only succeed up to the point that they, too, are enmeshed in the beliefs and practices of their culture; at that point, they become the tricked, victims of their own greediness and self-absorption.

As a trickster figure in the story cycle of *I Love Lucy*, Lucy showed where the boundary lines of gender roles and public/private were drawn. The points at which her escape attempts fail reveal the barriers to women's emancipation, providing a map of the contested terrain on which the battle of the sexes takes place. Through the bisociation of comedy, *I Love Lucy* reflected and shaped the clash between prescriptions of femininity and the wholesale mass redefinition of those ideals in the women's movement of the 1960s and 1970s.

Lucy in *I Love Lucy* clearly fits the characteristics and functions of the trickster figure that scholars in the fields of folklore, religious studies, and anthropology have delineated. There is, of course, a leap I am making between pre- and early-modern cultures and modern, mass communications analogues. When Lucy, like her tricky predecessors, looks around in search of the opening in the system that seems to enclose her, she presents a model of female ambition that is relentless in its craving for freedom, participation, and equality. This is the kind of prefeminist scrutiny of the sex-gender system that resulted in the second wave of feminism in America.

Early in this chapter, I raised the question of what cultural work the series performed in the postwar years—what *was* Lucy trying to do to the wives of America? Similar questions end this chapter: What cultural work does *I Love Lucy* perform today? What *has* Lucy done to the wives (and others) of America? What does she do to them now?

The answers revolve around what George Lipsitz terms "memory as misappropriation" in his fine book *Time Passages: Collective Memory and American Popular Culture*. In his discussion of one of *I Love Lucy*'s predecessors, *I Remember Mama* (1949–56), Lipsitz explains that *Mama*'s appeal to viewers might rest not with the show's accurate depiction of the past (the series was set in the turn of the century), but with its representation of the past as people wished it had been. This line of argument supports the allegations of some media critics who view popular culture as a source of compensatory fantasy, but Lipsitz points out some of the liberatory aspects of memory as misappropriation as well. It enables us to see beyond our own experience, rendering the oppressions of the past as contingent and unnecessary while modeling an alternate past, one as responsive to human wishes and desires as to the accidents of history. "If our own personal pasts cannot be venerated as moral guides for the present, we must choose another from history or art and embrace it as our own. But such leaps cannot be fashioned purely from the imagination; the past has more informative power and more relevance to the present if we believe that it is what actually happened, because what people have done before they can do again, while what they imagine may never be realized" (Lipsitz 80). Seen in this light, contemporary audiences' enjoyment of *I Love Lucy* may very well be linked to the series' portrayal of the fifties. Seen from the perspective of the 1990s, Lucy's protofeminism is probably clearer than from a vantage point immersed in the "feminine mystique"; such a perspective, of course, is inescapably the point of view of this study. *I Love Lucy* recasts the domestic prison of the fifties into the easily escapable terrain of the female trickster; in doing so, it offers contemporary audiences a version of the past that is a fitting precursor to the changes caused by the second wave women's movement. Lucy's daring pursuit of her desires and her irrepressible insistence that Ricky—and everyone else—acknowledge her as a talented individual provide a model that may be radically different from our impressions of our mothers and grandmothers during that time. *I Love Lucy*'s representations of the battle between the sexes makes the development of the second wave women's movement seem logical, and in turn legitimizes feminism in a way that makes more sense to us in the misnamed "postfeminist" era than it could have during the height of the women's liberation movement.

And it's *funny*. Of course Lucy doesn't want to stay in the home, of course she doesn't want to be financially dependent on Ricky, of course she wants to take action to satisfy her considerable desires. Ball's physical comedy is still unparalleled by other actresses. The more Lucy's antics are recast as in the past, the funnier her trickery becomes because the social conditions that necessitated her trickery have changed. Or rather, some of those conditions have changed and others, such as Lucy's concern with her attractiveness, her desire to be treated as an equal, persist. Like Coyote, Brer Rabbit, the con man, and other American incarnations of the trickster, Lucy can withstand historical and cultural changes and remain a central figure in the culture's mythos. Further, the global syndication of *I Love Lucy* means that Lucy may be the trickster figure whose stories have touched more people around the world than any other.

I Love Lucy not only persists but reigns in what the cable television network Nickelodeon calls "TV land." More than other modes of syndication, Nick at Nite's self-conscious programming of "classic TV" creates collective memories of American life since the postwar era, misappropriated images of how family life never really was, but, in our collective memory, the way we see it represented over and over again.

Coda: Think of Lucy

In a 1996 episode of the situation comedy *Ellen*, created by and starring stand-up comedienne Ellen DeGeneres, Lucy's comedy is transformed into a survival strategy. Ellen meets a cool new friend (played by guest star Janeane Garafolo) while they are waiting for mammograms. Both women are apprehensive, and Garafolo tells Ellen her secret for getting through stressful situations: think of *I Love Lucy* episodes. Thus, while Ellen reacts comically to her fear of the procedure, to the pinch of the mammogram, she recites a list of zany Lucy situations: Lucy in the freezer, Lucy makes a TV commercial, Lucy works in the candy factory, Lucy and the handcuffs, Lucy crushes grapes. Thinking of Lucy distracts Ellen with the fantasy world of Lucy where everything turns out all right. The rest of the episode concerns Ellen's (platonic) crush on her new friend, their inability to start up a lasting friendship, and it ends when they meet again at the doctor's waiting room, where Ellen has gone to sign the form she forgot, but her friend has been called back for a second mammogram. That a situation comedy would dramatize a specifically female medical procedure like a mammogram—and end with information about the risks of breast cancer and the importance of testing—shows the changes that have occurred since the days when the word "pregnant" could not be spoken on *I Love Lucy*.

Some of the energy in Ellen's "crush" on her new hip new friend foreshadowed a collision of real life and reel life that rivals the birth of the Ball-Arnaz baby: the character Ellen, like actress DeGeneres, came out in April 1997. Two hype-filled weeks after DeGeneres was on the cover of *Newsweek* with the headline, "Yep, I'm gay," a special one-hour episode of *Ellen* aired in which Oprah Winfrey played the therapist who helped Ellen recognize her sexual preference. When Ellen said "I'm gay" to guest star Laura Dern—and into the airport microphone so her statement came over the loudspeaker—the possible melodrama yielded to the comic bisociation of public and private that played on the viewer's knowledge that new ground was being broken, that there had never been a heroine of situation comedy who was not heterosexual before, that a famous star had never come out on television like that before. A certain kind of trickery ended with this intersection of real life and reel life: no longer would DeGeneres play the trick of portraying a heterosexual character. And 45 million viewers "shared" the moment.

Coming out is a rejection of the duplicity that keeps a gay person acting as if he or she were straight. Refusing to live a lie means going against the grain of heterosexual society, having to create a new identity that is outside the mainstream system of representations. Depending on how DeGeneres and her collaborators on the series make comedy out of the character's sexuality, Ellen may very well emerge as a trickster in the "new country" of fin-de-siècle television. Like Ball refusing to hide while she was pregnant, DeGeneres has the opportunity to create a new context in which a hitherto unrepresented aspect of life is treated in situation comedy. It is unlikely that *Ellen* will be radical, but it does signal the continued entrance of homosexuality into mainstream hegemonic culture. Once again the boundaries are redrawn.

Although DeGeneres's comic style is closer to the linguistic comedy of Gracie Allen, her homage to Lucy in the mammogram episode demonstrates her understanding of her position in Lucy's legacy. When *Ellen* represents thinking of Lucy as a survival strategy, it is a telling testament to Lucy's function as a trickster. Lucy's antics, her ability to create possibility where others would only recognize restraint, and her untiring optimism that this time her scheme will succeed, above all, keep Lucy, and the trickster, alive and at the center of our popular culture. To paraphrase Pelton, Lucy's ever-present past creates our past and, as it makes sense of our present, it works to make the future reflect that past.

Chapter 5
You Can't Go Home Again
Feminism and the Female Trickster
in Contemporary American Culture

The women's liberation movement of the sixties and seventies envisioned women's participation in the private and public spheres as overt, not covert. By attacking sexist ideology, representations, and institutions, feminists sought to eliminate the necessity of impersonating little women, or using sexual allure for survival. Instead of trying to "influence" their husbands and sons so their point of view would be expressed, second wavers would articulate and act on their own beliefs. Two well-publicized protests exemplify second wave unwillingness to remain in the "love economy": the protest at the 1968 Miss America pageant, which attacked the image of women as objects of "beauty" whose value was judged by men,[1] and the 1970 Women's Strike for Equality, a nationwide event that called attention to the crucial role that women's work played in everyday life.

By withholding their domestic work, protesters called attention to the invisible work that women perform. A facade of cheerful ease concealed women's work from the mid-nineteenth-century ideology of true womanhood to the mid-twentieth-century's feminine mystique—and the backlash trope of the superwoman that followed it. Protesters in the Women's Strike for Equality shattered the image of service with a smile and, in its place, demanded recognition of the importance of women's work and their ability to bargain with it.

This kind of second wave rhetoric is clearly antithetical to the submission necessary for the exercise of covert power. Another example of how second wave ideas attacked the basis for the influence strategy of women's power is the campaign for women to keep their own names when married and for the use of "Ms." These forays into the power relations signified by language and nomenclature replace the division between feme covert and feme sole, insisting that every woman is feme sole.

Second wave rejection of covert tactics prompted Anita Loos to quip, "I'm furious about the Women's Liberationists. They keep getting up on soapboxes and proclaiming that women are brighter than men. That's true, but it should be kept very quiet or it ruins the whole racket" (*The Observer*, "Sayings of the Year," December 30, 1973). Loos's comment shows how the "racket" of female trickery and covert power depends on exploiting—not confronting and dismantling—sexist asymmetry. Second wave feminists did not want to keep women's abilities "very quiet" any longer. That it was Loos who said such a thing is noteworthy; after all, her use of irony in *Gentlemen Prefer Blondes* backfired. Rather than exposing the machinations of the blonde to undercut her "power," Loos's creation of Lorelei Lee embodied and reified the materialistic ethos symbolized by the association of the blonde as an ideal of commodified femininity. As Nancy Walker comments, *Gentlemen Prefer Blondes* "did more to establish the stereotype of the 'dumb blonde' . . . than did any other single work" (*A Very Serious Thing* 92).

Loos perpetuated her characterization of the blonde because Lorelei brought her fame and fortune. She emerged as a media star of sorts, building on her participation in the silent film industry and the New York literary and cultural elite. Her public persona was the "flapper-novelist," the "world's leading expert on blondes." A 1927 *Cosmopolitan* article titled "Little—But" featured a drawing of Loos by Ralph Barton (who illustrated *Gentlemen Prefer Blondes* in *Harper's*) that portrayed her size (she was four feet, eleven inches tall) and cute appearance dwarfed by chair and typewriter (Fig. 5.1). Although Loos's irony and wit were clearly part of her public persona, her ambivalent stance toward the mass consumer culture that made her famous resulted in her playing the part of the "little woman."

In his excellent book on comedy, scholar Harry Levin remarks, "Irony is so ambiguous a device—not to say two-edged—that it is more than ordinarily susceptible to miscarriage, since it aims at levels of perception beyond the ironist's control" (202). Despite her increasingly explicit attempts to characterize Lorelei as a con woman and thief, her satire did not counteract the celebratory tone of the international phenomenon of *Gentlemen Prefer Blondes*.

As Loos expanded the original sketch into what became the novel *Gentlemen Prefer Blondes*, she made Lorelei's trickery more explicit, so that what seemed like natural behavior at the beginning (sending Mr. Eisman away on her birthday) emerges as self-conscious, constructed duplicity. For example, on the boat trip back to New York Lorelei discovers that there is a diamond dealer on board: "So I met the gentle-

❡ *Anita Loos according*
to Ralph Barton, the artist.

Figure 5.1. Caricature of Loos, drawn by Ralph Barton, the artist who illustrated *Gentlemen Prefer Blondes*. *Cosmopolitan*, February 1927. Reproduced with permission of *Cosmopolitan*.

man, and we went around together quite a lot, but we had quite a quarrel the night before we landed, so I did not even bother to look at him when I came down the gangplank, and I put the unset diamonds in my handbag so I did not have to declare them at customs" (176–77).

Loos conveyed her original satiric motives in a 1927 *Cosmopolitan* article, several of the Lorelei Lee pieces that Loos wrote throughout her career, and the essay "The Biography of a Book" (1979), which relates the genesis of *Gentlemen Prefer Blondes*. In the essay (which is reprinted as the introduction to the 1989 Penguin edition of *Gentlemen Prefer Blondes*), Loos suggests that she meant the original piece as a satire that would expose the covert power women exerted over men, blowing the scam and making the world safer for women like herself who were trying to achieve success through intelligence, wit, assertiveness, and hard work rather than by luring a man to do it for her. The *Cosmopolitan* article, published at the height of the international *Gentlemen Prefer Blondes* craze, indicates the anger and resentment Loos meant to convey in her representation of Lorelei but concealed too cleverly with comedy:

> Not one reader in a thousand sensed the real meaning of the book. They read of the gold-digging diversions of the beautiful and dumb Lorelei and Dorothy and cried, "Aren't they cute?"
> They did not know that Anita Loos had discovered what many silver-haired Romeos have never learned, that beneath the simpering smile and baby lisp of the immature Broadway gold-digger was the dangerously calculating tigress — a potential Borgia. I confess I did not grasp this myself. It was Miss Loos who told me.
> She was writing tragedy under the thin veneer of humor and let it go at that.
> (McIntyre 65)

Loos continued to make this point in many of the Lorelei Lee pieces she wrote throughout her career. For example, as a "letter" from Lorelei Lee to Anita Loos in a 1953 *New York Times Magazine* article indicates, when the book was published, "Lorelei" thought that revealing her manipulative tricks would cause "we blondes" to "be left severally alone." The piece continues: "But I soon begun to note that gentlemen were reading that book in droves and then laying it down and going right over to pick up the telephone and make another date with a blonde. And when a book of the same ilk was written by Mr. Hitler, who called it 'My Kampf,' where he, himself, told everything he was up to, his admirers went right on associating with him" ("History of the Preferred Blonde," in *Fate* 30). Of course, Loos's tone is less than, or more than, serious here as it is in all of her writing, but, even in her covert way, her words draw attention to the connections between the book and men's behavior and more than suggest that the men are dupes.

In this and other pieces, Loos's continued use of her popular character's voice shows her ambivalence toward Lorelei. On the one hand, people loved Loos's wit, but on the other hand, they celebrated what she satirized. Lorelei was funny to Loos, sitting on that train or wherever she first wrote the sketch, in a way different from how her readers understood it. To use cultural studies scholar Stuart Hall's distinctions between the "dominant," "negotiated," and "oppositional" readings that the audience can create, Loos's satire conflates the "dominant" and "oppositional" readings, offering only the position of a "negotiated" reading as readers decide the extent to which they can believe the unreliable narrator. The statement "Gentlemen prefer blondes" seems to state a fact that men like blondes best, that "blonde" equals "attractive," but as I explained in Chapter 2, Loos raises questions about the category "gentlemen."

Gentlemen Prefer Blondes is an example of how and why covert power is so easily co-opted. By reinforcing and extending existing stereotypes of femininity, "tricks," like Loos's critique of the "love economy," and the social practices of female trickery, like impersonating a "little woman," may seem tactically useful at the moment, but they fail to challenge the structure, institutions, and ideology of the sexist limitations that originally prompted the tricks. It is ironic, therefore, for Loos to complain about how women's liberation undermines the "racket" from which she could not extricate herself.

By putting the blame on feminism, Loos's quotation expresses a "backlash" idea. "Backlash," as theorized by political scientists Seymour Martin Lipset and Earl Raab and popularized by Susan Faludi in her bestselling book *Backlash: The Undeclared War on American Women* (1991), is the reaction by groups who feel that they are losing power to previously subordinate groups. Backlashes—and there have been many recurrences against women, African Americans, the working class, lesbians and gays, and a range of ethnic groups—are amplified in cultural discourses to seem as if they describe the social reality of the majority, but they are distortions that reflect the opinions of a small group of people who realize that they have already lost. There is always some expression of backlash, but when it reaches critical mass, it emerges as a system of representation that inflects every aspect of mass consumer culture.

We can understand the increased attention paid to polarized gender roles in the postwar era as a backlash against the increased independence of women and the destabilization of gender roles during wartime. During the war, film and magazine images of women stressed their strength, but only in the context of serving the war economy. The wave of a mass women's movement (as opposed to the always present feminist activists, writers, and thinkers) in the 1970s was a reaction to the backlash culture of the feminine mystique—a domestic ideology that was in sharp contrast to women's social experience.

In the previous chapter, I argued that, in the postwar trickster cycle *I Love Lucy*, Lucy's desire to move beyond the domestic sphere was a metaphor for the gap between the ideology of the feminine mystique and people's social experiences of women working outside the home. Dealing with the rift between, on the one hand, cold war images of consensus and conformity and, on the other, people's subjective experiences that deviated from the social norm was a main function of ideology in the postwar period. The fear of being singled out as un-American which fed McCarthyism created a system of representations of idealized domesticity and, in backlash fashion, portrayed the unhappiness as the result of not conforming to the ideal. In contrast to the nostalgic view of the fifties as the end of traditional family life, the decade ushered in a new era of emphasis on how the home could fulfill all the personal needs of each family member (Elaine Tyler May 17).

In fact, women left the home to work and participate in the public sphere in increasing numbers during the twentieth century. Although the numbers of women working in the professions decreased in the twenties and thirties, women, mostly single, participated in the workforce. During the Depression, women—still mostly single—continued to work, although the notion that married women shouldn't work persisted. By 1940, 30 percent of all women were employed, but only 15 percent of married women were employed. Despite the 3.25 million women who lost their industrial jobs after World War II ended, 2.75 million went into the workforce in lower-paid "pink-collar" jobs, and by 1952—when *I Love Lucy* was depicting Lucy's bungled attempts to work outside the home—the number of women working exceeded the largest female workforce during the war. By the mid-1950s, the average married woman worked until her first baby was born and then returned to work outside the home after her children reached school age. By 1960, the number of women who were employed had tripled, and ten million of them were married.[2]

However, many jobs were part time and very few were in the professions. Overall, in the postwar period, women's work outside the home was low paid, offered little status, and did not lead to a "career." Married women were expected to put their husband's career and their family first, and to define themselves, like Lucille Ball's public persona, as a housewife. The "love economy" was still the one in which women participated most.

As historian Elaine Tyler May evokes brilliantly in her book *Homeward Bound: American Families in the Cold War Era*, America developed not an egalitarian family structure with two equal, working parents but a family structure bifurcated by polarized gender roles. This kind of power structure encourages the exercise of covert power and female trickery within the love economy. Popular culture reinforced the idea that a woman's work was to deploy "curvallure" and other feminine wiles to get her husband (or intended husband) to give her what she wants. For example, in the Sandra Dee movie *If a Man Answers* (1962), the newly married heroine successfully uses a dog training manual to "train" her husband. This farce, like *Sex and the Single Girl* (1964), reinforces the idea that women can only find fulfillment in the private sphere. Similarly, in *Breakfast at Tiffany's* (1961), Audrey Hepburn portrays female trickster Holly Golightly, "a phony, but a *real* phony" with buoyant grace, but the romantic ending undercuts her independence and mobility.

In the early sixties and into the seventies, the domestic medium of television continued to represent women as belonging in the home in situation comedies, but with an important difference. After the end of *I Love Lucy* and the *Lucy-Desi Comedy Hour*, Lucille Ball continued to make Americans laugh in *The Lucy Show* (1962–68) and *Here's Lucy* (1968–74) — as a widow, not a divorced woman. Although the restrictive function of Ricky the husband could be taken up by the banker/boss figure played by Gale Gordon (in seasons 1963–74), Lucy couldn't continue without an Ethel, and so Vivian Vance played Viv, Lucy's friend, roommate, and partner in high jinks from 1962 to 1965, with occasional visits after Mary Jane Croft became Lucy's cohort from 1965–74. In these shows, the domestic sphere was clearly (although not always smoothly) under the control of women.

With *Bewitched* (1964–72), the representation of women in the private sphere shifted from the incompetent albeit subversive scheming of Lucy (in black and white and then in color) to the superhuman power of Samantha the witch. In contrast to Lucy, Samantha wants to live the unmagical ordinary life of a housewife in suburbia. As in *I Love Lucy*, the pleasure of the series lies in Samantha's slips in living like an average housewife. Although Samantha is no trickster figure, Elizabeth Montgomery sometimes donned a brunette wig and played Sam's look-alike cousin Serena, who did function as a trickster figure with her links to the hippie counterculture and willingness to impersonate the sentimental heroine Samantha and cause trouble. Once again the trickster surfaces as the shadow of good femininity.

In *The Mary Tyler Moore Show* (1970–77), which reflected many of the ideas of the women's movement, the female trickster is the "Happy Homemaker" Sue Ann Nivens (Betty White). Although she plays a super-efficient domestically oriented woman on her own television show, off the set Sue Ann is self-involved, sexually aggressive, and she constantly attempts to manipulate and trick those around her for self-satisfaction. White played her with a sweet, feminine voice, and her outrageous and unladylike utterances benefit from aural as well as conceptual bisociation. In a different system of cultural representations, Sue Ann might have been the protagonist whose on-screen masquerade and off-screen (yet still on-screen) deflation of traditional femininity the audience cheered, but in 1970s' American television, she is the foil to Mary's sentimental heroine. Unlike Mary and Rhoda, "dumb blonde" Georgette, and even the "feminist" Phyllis, Sue Ann had an edge that went against the grain of conventional femininity. In the few episodes that did foreground her character, though, Sue Ann was revealed to be an unhappy and lonely woman who just wanted love, although White always managed to undercut any sympathy that might be directed her way. A perpetuator of the "racket" of female covert power, Sue Ann's split between public and private personas called attention to the masquerade of domesticity and femininity and to the role that television played in creating that artifice.

The successes of the women's movement that created the context for *The Mary Tyler Moore Show* paved the way for popular representations of rebellious women characters who do not hide behind cultural stereotypes of femininity. Roseanne exemplifies a refusal to feign the submission necessary to perpetuate the "racket" Loos endorsed. Although the character she plays on the popular sitcom *Roseanne* does not lose control or become inept when she attempts to get what she wants, she is nevertheless an inheritor of the typical yet funny housewife role codified by Lucy. However, where Lucy's rebellion was covert—embedded within her comic machinations—Roseanne's refusal to try to live up to social standards of femininity is explicit. Both the character and the comedienne's public persona violate taboos about women's appearance and personality and transgress the boundaries of acceptable feminine behavior. No one's "little woman" in appearance, personality, or behavior, Roseanne plays on the gap between a working-class woman's social experience and the myth buttressed by middle-class fantasies like *I Love Lucy*. Her attitude toward housework can be summed up in a one-liner from her stand-up comedy act: "I don't even care about that cleaning stuff anyway—the day I worry about cleaning my house is the day Sears comes out with a riding vacuum cleaner" (quoted in Mile 41). As this joke illustrates, Roseanne's humor plays on her unwillingness to happily and spritely perform the duties of the housewife. In *Roseanne,* we glimpse what might *really* be lurking behind the TV mom's smile.[3]

Moreover, the character Roseanne is not a female trickster who plays the feminine, sentimental woman for all its worth—although Roseanne the icon may very well perform cultural work similar to Mae West's. As Kathleen Rowe points out, Roseanne is an "unruly woman" who is connected to representations of "pig women" rather than to the feline or foxy tropes that inflect portrayals of the female trickster. Although Roseanne's antisentimentalism, working-class allegiances, and frustration with the roles of housewife, worker, wife, and mother may give her much in common with women's social experiences of everyday life, in the world represented by television situation comedy, Roseanne is not an insider gone awry but an outsider who has taken over.

Although neither *Ellen* nor *Cybill* can match the popularity or the centrality of *I Love Lucy*, these are the shows that I think are the inheritors of Lucy's legacy. I discussed *Ellen* at the end of the previous chapter, so suffice it to say here that, depending on the direction Ellen DeGeneres and ABC go with her character's sexuality, Ellen may very well emerge as a female trickster in American culture if the series makes comedy out of the paradoxes of coming out as a lesbian in a representational system that renders homosexuality and bisexuality invisible.

Cybill, however, is full of female tricksters: the title character, her best friend Maryann, and Cybill's youngest daughter Zoey. *Cybill* plays on some of the same intertextual levels that *I Love Lucy* did. Cybill Shepherd—movie star, cover girl, advertising spokesperson, television star, singer—plays Cybill Sheridan, a not quite successful actress and singer. Each episode opens with another rotten, dehumanizing, often sexist and always comical job—singing the part of a chicken in a commercial, playing the part of a clown in a children's television show, being the voice of a singing potty training toilet.

All the characters deflate traditional images of gender and domesticity. Cybill has two daughters by two different ex-husbands, all of whom spend much time in her house. But her closest, most important relationship is with her best friend, Maryann, who spent the first few seasons enacting complicated covert vengeance on her ex-husband "Dr. Dick." Maryann is a self-involved, wealthy woman whose economic and erotic power is considerable, almost akin to magic in the culture of consumption of Los Angeles at the end of the twentieth century. Together, Cybill and Maryann concoct schemes and get into zany situations in the tradition of Lucy and Ethel, some of which, as when Maryann and Cybill go to Japan and dress as geishas, are direct homages to *I Love Lucy*. Like Lucy, Maryann and Cybill are represented as grotesque as well as glamorous, and many episodes climax with food fights or other messy and unfeminine activities.

In this comedy, feminism and female trickery not only are compatible, they may be inseparable. Although Cybill balks when a woman gives her daughter Zoey the advice that making the man think he is smarter than you is the best strategy for relationships between men and women, the trickster tactics of impersonation, deception, theft, disguise, and pranks abound in the series. For example, in a recent episode, Cybill is on a ride-along with a cop as research for an audition; when the cop leaves Cybill alone in the car while his wife has a baby, Cybill puts on his hat and drives off to rescue Maryann, who, dressed in army camouflage, is on a revenge mission. By impersonating a police officer and, with impunity, racing through the streets of Los Angeles to satisfy her whims, Cybill disregards society's conventions in true madcap style.

Overall, situation comedies, as part of the domestic medium of television, center on the home. In *Cybill*'s case, it is an unconventional female-controlled home rather than the traditional one Lucy escaped from and returned to. In a cluster of films made in the late 1980s and early 1990s, however, the heroines leave and choose not to return "home" to domesticity and femininity. Instead they forge onward into the "new territory" of an American society influenced by the recession of the second wave of the women's movement and the emerging current of the third wave. Movie heroines Roberta in *Desperately Seeking Susan* (1985), Margaret in *House of Games* (1987), Tess in *Working Girl* (1988), the dual protagonists of *Thelma and Louise* (1991), Deloris in *Sister Act* (1992), Selina in *Batman Returns* (1992), and Bridget in *The Last Seduction* (1994) are female tricksters who use impersonation and other trickster tactics like theft, duplicity, and "feminine" wiles to escape limited and limiting circumstances and create new possibilities on both sides of the ironic tightrope poised between comedy and tragedy, between the screwball heroine and the femme fatale. These films also walk a fine line between feminism and female trickery. Significantly, all the heroines have doubles or are split themselves.

Thelma and Louise is the central text chronologically in this group, and the most ambivalently comic and tragic. As Thelma (Geena Davis) and Louise (Susan Sarandon) go on the road as outlaws in the beautifully photographed landscape of the American Southwest, they, like the Native American female trickster "Yellow Woman," participate in a freedom from society and constraint that is as truly mythic as it must be temporary. Callie Khouri's screenplay and Ridley Scott's mise-en-scène form a response to the backlash of the eighties in their refusal to yield narratively or visually to the idea that feminism and female desire for equality, mobility, and liberty are the cause of women's unhappiness.

Thelma and Louise confronts the question that lurks in all stories of female tricksters: what if men are not gentlemen? The answer in the film is that some men are dangerous, and no feminine wiles or covert power can stop Harlan (Timothy Carhart) from attempted rape or J.D. (Brad Pitt) from stealing the money they needed to escape to Mexico. When men are not gentlemen, the kind of female trickery based on covert power must be replaced by the trickery of the outlaw and the survivor.

At the opening of the movie, director Ridley Scott's deft imagery delineates the major differences between the two characters. In particular, two details stand out: the water glass Louise washes and leaves upside down in her tidy, self-contained apartment; and the way that Thelma eats a candy bar—she repeatedly takes it out of the freezer, takes a bite, puts it back, and then takes it out again. The glass shows how Louise has built an orderly, controlled, independent life for herself; Scott brings our attention to it in lingering shots and reinforces its importance when the detective (Harvey Keitel) seems to recognize its significance. In contrast, the candy bar shows Thelma's indulgent nature, her attempts to live by the rules that she immediately and blithely transgresses. Louise, who is older, works outside the home as a waitress and is independent and in control. Thelma is married and financially dependent on her husband. She gathers everything she can think of—including the fateful gun—as she packs for the weekend trip. Louise is purposeful and savvy; Thelma is random and naive.

In the course of the movie, we see how their characters have been shaped by their experiences of rape. Louise responded to being raped by moving away and creating an orderly, controlled, independent life. She repressed what happened to her in Texas so deeply that she cannot speak of it even with Thelma when she knows they may not be able to make it to freedom, and it is this repressed rage that explodes in violence when Harlan refuses to apologize for attacking and attempting to rape Thelma. Although Louise does not think of herself as a victim, she is a grim survivor, rooted to material security and marked forever by her experience. When she sees Thelma in the same situation she was in years ago, it triggers anger and a desire to make someone pay for the crimes, and she pulls the trigger. And when J.D. steals her life savings—the sum total of her years of self-control and thinking of the future—she is divested of the frame she has created for her life.

Thelma, on the other hand, goes blank and then goes wild. Where Louise has to confront the physical and material, Thelma is faced with the inaccuracy of her belief in emotional and social rules of gentility. Her idea that she can depend on the kindness of strangers is shattered. First the attack and the shooting, then the betrayal by her husband Darryl, her sexual awakening with J.D., and J.D.'s betrayal: these events shake her loose from the structures of society. The soundtrack as well as the film's mise en scène call our attention to Thelma's transformation; for example, in the sex scene, the seductive strains of Peter Conway's harmonica on Chris Whitley's song "Kick the Stones" coax us into the feeling of liberation that prompts Thelma to go wild. She becomes an outlaw, a criminal, a trickster, bringing Louise along with her.

Their most liberatory—and comic—moment is when Thelma and Louise blow up a truck driver's rig. In the metaphor of the road, the truck signifies physical size and strength, the sexualizing of women, and sexist intimidation; the women's use of the power of the guns (one stolen from a police officer who pulled them over), after they use the promise of sex to trick the disgusting and stupid trucker off the road, is a triumph in the symbol systems of film. In this moment and throughout the breathtaking cinematography of their journey, the film represents women as full and equal participants in the mythic space of American liminality—the road—and signifies the collapse of the public/private split as a demarcation of gender in America. In *Thelma and Louise*, the women do not become female tricksters as much as they become American film tricksters. When Thelma says "Something's crossed over in me, and I can't go back," she articulates the spatial and social boundary crossing typical of the male trickster/outlaw in film.

Thelma and Louise shares much with *It Happened One Night* (1934), the quintessential screwball comedy/road movie: the escape from the constraints of society, the freedom of the road, role-playing, and the creation of a new identity based on the experiences of the journey.[4] Louise may pull a naive Thelma into being an outlaw, but the new Thelma that emerges is a screwball heroine who pulls Louise out of her seriousness and into the mode of play.

When the male critics who complained about *Thelma and Louise*'s "toxic feminism" became upset by the screen representation of the pair robbing a store, putting a police officer in the trunk of his car, or blowing up the truck, they failed to see it as comedy. That truck, like the dinosaur in *Bringing Up Baby*, has to come down, and it is played for laughs, as long as the spectator shares the point of view of the heroines. As Geena Davis said in an interview, "If you're threatened by this movie, you're identifying with the wrong person."[5] Or, as classic Hollywood comedy teaches us, if you don't get the joke, then you are socially inflexible and the joke is on you.

The film's use of play as a response to a violent and alienating society parallels the role ascribed to play by feminist philosophers such as Sarah Hoagland and Linda A. Bell. In her book, *Rethinking Ethics in the Midst of Violence: A Feminist Approach to Freedom*, Bell argues, "A spirit of play, coupled with a critical and political awareness, can be used by those who are oppressed to expunge from themselves internalized aspects of oppression and to open a space in which they may begin to relate nonoppressively to themselves and to one another" (47). The spirit of play in *Thelma and Louise*, linked as it is with the women's feelings of being "awake" and Thelma's realization that, if Harlan had succeeded in raping her, "My life would have been ruined a whole lot worse than it is now," is analogous to what Bell describes. *Thelma and Louise* opens a space of possibility—in film representation and in the mind of the viewer who sees that women can be tricksters and outlaws too. After seeing the movie, my friend Phyllis and I decided to drive across America, inspired by the film's images of open and sacred space and portrayal of female mobility. That sacred and symbolic space of the road, formerly the province of men, could be ours, too.

But the ending of *Thelma and Louise* is not comic; it is tragic, or at best transcendent. Can so little have changed since the 1899 publication of Kate Chopin's novel *The Awakening*? The temporary role of the female trickster that Thelma and Louise take on during their spree comes to an abrupt end—or does it?—at the brink of the Grand Canyon, the place in the Hopi Indian tales where the first people came out of the last world and into this one, and also the place in the Hopi prophecies that connects this world to the next. Like Yellow Woman, the characters participate in the mythic experience of going wild and living sideways, but unlike the case of Yellow Woman, there is no home to go back to because the culture will not accommodate women's needs and experiences.

If the movie is a fantasy, and it certainly isn't reality, why can't the heroines escape, like Matty in *Body Heat*, Margaret in *House of Games*, and even the evil Bridget in *The Last Seduction*? The film does not offer any answers to this question, although the ambiguities of the ending certainly do raise it and encourage a reading that gives the heroines a mythic escape. The freeze-frame and fade to white of the image of the glorious green car—so symbolic of consumer freedom and mobility—at the top of its flight arc suggest a mythic moment of transcendence and denies the deaths of the heroines by flashing back to their lives. Perhaps their decision to keep going, into the unknown, keeps *Thelma and Louise* in the subjunctive mood of possibility.

The subjunctive mood of possibility is expressed fully in the comedies of this period. In *Desperately Seeking Susan*, *Working Girl*, and *Sister Act*, the heroines take on new identities out of confusion, ambition, and survival, respectively. Roberta (Rosanna Arquette) leads a dull life as a suburban wife who fantasizes about the excitement suggested by the personal ads to and from someone named Susan. When an accident causes her amnesia, she takes on the identity of "Susan," along with a job as a magician's assistant and a new lover (Aidan Quinn), moving out of middle-class dullness and into an exciting world of adventure and romance. In *Working Girl*, Tess (Melanie Griffith), a secretary, seizes the opportunity to take credit for an idea her boss (Sigourney Weaver) stole from her; she impersonates an executive to gain corporate success and her boss's boyfriend, Jack Trainer (Harrison Ford), moving from working-class drudgery to a professional middle-class life. In *Sister Act*, Deloris (Whoopi Goldberg) is a Reno lounge singer who witnesses a mob hit and goes undercover as a nun, metamorphosing from a secular sinner to a spiritual savior who connects the nuns' parish to its urban community.

In the three movies, female trickery works in both the public and private spheres and provides a way to create a new, better identity. However, feminism and female trickery have at best an uneasy relationship, and all three movies imagine female success in terms of mass consumer culture. The female trickster's use of impersonation works where explicit action could not. Their plots revolve around a "logic of the absurd" similar to the screwball comedies of the thirties. But unlike those Depression-era comedies, these movies are interested in the heroine's relationships with other women as much as, if not more than, her romance with a man.

In *Working Girl*, the only strategy that works is female trickery. Tess's boss, Katherine Parker, pays lip service to feminism when she tells Tess she thinks of them as a team, but she betrays that sisterhood when she takes credit for Tess's idea. In this movie, it is every woman for herself. Susan Faludi notes that *Working Girl* is an example of a backlash film: "Only the woman who buries her intelligence under a baby-doll exterior is granted a measure of professional success without having to forsake [male] companionship. . . . She succeeds in love Sleeping Beauty-style, by passing out in a man's arms" (128). Director Mike Nichols's contemporary fairy tale ends with the evil queen deposed and the prince and the princess sharing a quick and egalitarian cup of coffee before they both go off to their corporate jobs. Unlike Melanie Griffith's character Lulu in *Something Wild* (1986), Tess is never dangerous, never anything more than meek; she is the most conservative of all the female tricksters discussed in this book.

In sharp contrast to the agonic, competitive struggle in which Tess destroys Katherine, takes her boyfriend, and is rewarded with a better job, *Desperately Seeking Susan* and *Sister Act* portray female friendships as cooperative and sustaining. In Susan Seidelman's film, Roberta's (Rosanna Arquette's) fascination with what she imagines the unconventional, nomadic, independent Susan (Madonna) to be like shows her readiness to fantasize about possibilities outside of her conventional wife life. In this film, that willingness to imagine leads Roberta's identity to become entangled with Susan's. Susan is a female trickster—a thief who is highly mobile, crafty, and who uses costume, makeup, and comportment to attain her desires. Roberta follows Susan and buys the jacket (with the plot-necessary key and other clues) that Susan trades for a funky pair of shoes; in putting on Susan's clothes, Roberta takes on a willingness to go wild. When Roberta loses her memory in an accident and is mistaken for Susan, in part because she is wearing the jacket, the synchronicities that rule the comic world grant her desire to be Susan.[6]

Involuntarily at first and then more willfully, Roberta creates a new identity that befits a screwball heroine. By the end of the movie, when the mix-up and mystery about Nefertiti's earring (which Susan took and left in the locker to which Roberta found the key) is finally resolved, Roberta chooses not to go home again, but to keep going in the new life that she stumbled into, led by the possibilities she knew existed outside of her traditional life.

Similarly, in *Sister Act*, the heroine finds herself with a new identity based on an impersonation, although this heroine's transformation runs counter to Roberta's: she changes from streetwise lounge singer and mob boss girlfriend to nun in a convent where she hides out until she can testify about the mob murder she witnessed. Whoopi Goldberg's performance of "bad girl" Deloris plays on visual and thematic paradoxes—"bad girl" in nun's habit, secular and sexual woman who has to stay within the confines of the convent, black woman in an all-white order, white women in black nun's habits, black woman in white nun's headgear. The film is a fantasy of integration—racial and social—that hinges on how Deloris enlivens and energizes the nuns' choir with revisions of the black girl-group songs that made up her Reno act. The film presents a marriage between the church and female popular culture designed to appeal to baby boomer nostalgia, and it does so within a community of women, a sisterhood. Finally, visually and narratively, the film appropriates African-American culture, using it as an infusion of life into a soulless, dying white culture. Deloris is the trickster who brings the fire of music and chutzpa into the order, disrupting it for its own good.

As we see in the opening scene, Deloris as a young girl resisted the structure of Catholic school. In response to Deloris's misbehavior, the schoolteacher nun remarks, "You are the most unruly, disobedient girl in this school . . . Mark my words, Deloris, if you continue on this disruptive track, it will lead straight to the devil. Have you any idea what girls like you become?" The smile on the girl's face that dissolves into Goldberg doing her Reno lounge act lets us know that Deloris has an excellent idea of what bad girls become, and she can't wait. However, the adult reality that Deloris experiences as an unappreciated performer and mob boss girlfriend is not as great as the little girl thought it would be.

Strange as it may seem at first, *Sister Act* is a revision of *Ball of Fire* (1941). In the Howard Hawks movie, Barbara Stanwyck was Sugarpuss O'Shea, a nightclub performer and gangster's moll who hides out among a group of bachelor professors who are writing an encyclopedia (see Fig. 3.14). She brings slang—the living language—into Professor Potts's (Gary Cooper) research on the English language and a strongly sexual female presence into the mausoleum where the professors live and work. Although Sugarpuss deliberately uses the professors to evade the police's questions about her lover Joe Lilac, she comes to realize that Potts can offer her happiness where Joe cannot.

Sister Act revises *Ball of Fire* by substituting the convent for the single-sex (male) mausoleum, and Deloris's race for Sugarpuss's gender. *Sister Act* also rejects the mutual recognition of the romance plot at the center of *Ball of Fire* and the screwball comedy in general, and replaces it with a mutual recognition between the mother superior (Maggie Smith) and Deloris. In contrast to *Ball of Fire*'s creation of a couple that reconciles polarized class and gender differences, *Sister Act* reconciles race and class differences by bringing the nuns into the urban community around them.

The bridge between the nuns and their wider community is the black girl-group music that Deloris adapts from her Reno act to the nuns' choir. In her engaging book *Where the Girls Are: Growing Up Female with the Mass Media*, Susan J. Douglas argues that girl-oriented songs were used by white baby boomer girls to express their protofeminist resistance to a male-dominated society:

> The Shirelles and the other girl groups mattered because they helped cultivate inside us a desire to rebel. The main purpose of pop music is to make us feel a kind of euphoria that convinces us that we can transcend the shackles of conventional life and rise above the hordes of others who do get trapped. It is the euphoria of commercialism, designed to get us to buy. But this music did more than that; it generated another kind of euphoria as well. For when tens of millions of young girls started feeling, at the same time, that they, as a generation, would not be trapped, there was planted the tiniest seed of a social movement. (98)

In both her guises—Reno singer and nun—Deloris interprets the girl-group songs to suit her purposes. In the beginning of the film, she changes "I Will Follow Him" into a double-time version, à la Sid Vicious and "My Way," in order to speed up the act that no one pays attention to or appreciates; here Deloris uses the song to express her disgust at the situation she is in. Later, in the nuns' choir concert for the pope (!), the lyrics change from "No one can keep me away from my guy" to "my God." The strength and female solidarity that Douglas reads in songs like "My Guy" and "I Will Follow Him" become explicit in the choir performances, as these songs are ripped out of their heterosexual and secular context and inserted into a homosocial and spiritual one.

So Deloris the trickster, with her clever readings and revisions of popular culture, brings the convent to life. And when the mother superior stands up for Deloris at the end, we see how the trickster reshapes the dominant society so that she is included in it; the new, up-to-date mother superior recognizes Deloris as a "good girl," unlike the nun in Deloris's youth. Moreover, the end credits indicate Deloris's secular reward of fame and success with a device for narrative closure popular in recent comedies: mock-ups of magazine covers (from *Newsweek* to *Rolling Stone*). By removing herself from the hell of Reno and putting the needs of the group before her own, Deloris finds community, acceptance, and material success.

There is a curious yet familiar appropriation of blackness by white culture at work in *Sister Act*: in the same way that white girls found agency in the music of the Shirelles in Douglas's cultural history, so too do the nuns. Moreover, the convent literally takes in and remakes Deloris, whose disruptive presence is summarized when the mother superior takes one look at her and calls her "a conspicuous person designed to stick out." As a conspicuous and public woman, Deloris is the antithesis of a nun, and because of this difference, she becomes their culture hero.

Perhaps more than any other actress in mainstream American popular culture, Whoopi Goldberg signifies "blackness" within a dominant white culture, and her persona is characterized by paradox. Her name and sense of shtick places her at the intersection of African-American and Jewish performance that has held a curious place in American popular entertainment from *The Jazz Singer* on. Her endorsement of Comic Relief (along with Robin Williams and Billy Crystal) is just one of the very public ways she continues to speak her own mind and call attention to issues such as homelessness which received (and continue to receive) short shrift in the Reagan years and since. Her stand-up routines can be as bawdy as any man's, and her compelling but short-lived nighttime talk show contrasted an informality and homelike environment with the production values of *The Tonight Show* and *Letterman*. Guinan, her character on *Star Trek: The Next Generation*, is a liminal figure whose relationship to linear time, like her relationship with Captain Picard, is ambiguous. Goldberg's rejection of good girl behavior in favor of the brazen critique of the status quo has caused her to be a figure of ridicule and insult, yet she remains well-known and popular. Her roles in successful movies like *The Color Purple* and *Ghost*, and in unsuccessful ones like *Boys on the Side* and *Made in America*, always bring the Whoopi persona into conflict with the ordinary and the normal. And recently, in the movie *The Associate*, she pulled a disappearing act by impersonating a white man to gain access to privileges and connections inaccessible to a black woman.

The ending of *Sister Act* defies the conventions of the romantic clinch as closure and offers instead the successful independent woman. The other films I discuss here present similar endings; and by defying cinematic as well as social expectations, their heroines, like Deloris, function as trickster figures in the worlds of the films and in popular discourse. Although *House of Games*, *The Last Seduction*, and *Batman Returns* are not comedies, their heroines learn to use trickery in order to escape and survive.

Margaret (Lindsay Crouse) in David Mamet's *House of Games* is poised between two con games: the one she runs as a psychiatrist and the one in which she is the dupe in the shady underworld of Mike (Joe Mantegna). Mike sets her up in an elaborate scheme to con her out of $80,000, and she falls for it. But in the end, she disengages herself from the twinned social structures of psychoanalysis and patriarchy and emerges as a female trickster. The end of the movie finds her dressed in a brightly colored dress (in sharp contrast to the grays and neutrals she has worn up to this point) and stealing a bright gold lighter she has coveted throughout the movie. This final image, attained after she rejects the guilt that made her vulnerable as a con artist's mark, and the guilt of killing Mike (before he can murder her), suggests that she has realized that social interactions are cons and games run by people playing roles, and now she will exploit that knowledge for her own benefit and pleasure. A dark and flattened out character throughout the film who analyzes life rather than living it becomes a bright and tricky character; the death of the conman marks the birth of the female trickster.[7]

In *The Last Seduction*, Bridget (Linda Fiorentino) starts where Margaret ends—fully cognizant of the noir principle that in a world of cons and frames, the only person who survives is the one who ruthlessly exploits his or her mark and sees the biggest frame. Bridget takes off with the $700,000 from a drug deal she and her husband Clay (Bill Pullman) have pulled off, leaving Clay to the mob. She runs out of gas in a little town in New York State and creates herself a new persona. She inveigles Mike (Peter Berg) into her schemes and, after an array of tricks and lies, sets him up to take the fall for killing her husband. When she gets away with it at the end, Bridget is the most successful femme fatale in film. Her careful deployment of a specifically female trickery (based on sex, emotions, and appearances) gets her what she desires. Like Margaret, Bridget does not allow her "feminine" emotions to turn her trickery against herself, and she survives. Bridget is morally reprehensible and possibly the meanest con woman in film, but the final scenes that show that she won't be punished never suggest that she should be. Like other neo-noir films such as *The Usual Suspects* and *Heat*, *The Last Seduction* separates the Production Code equation of crime and punishment and represents an amoral society in which crime does pay. The film encourages a reading based on admiration for Bridget's skill and guts.

The irony that figures prominently in both *House of Games* and *The Last Seduction* is fully expressed in the fantasy figure of Catwoman in *Batman Returns* (1992), perhaps the best example of a female trickster who embodies the legacy of second wave feminism.[8] A revision of the working-girl-marries-rich-boss plot articulated in the silent movie *It*, the Catwoman narrative substitutes a nightmare of crime, murder, and revenge for the fairy tale of commodification and romance that *It* perpetuates by conflating the economic and erotic in the marriage plot.

When Selina staggers back to her apartment after her boss Max Shreck pushed her out of a window to her "death," she hears a message on her answering machine: a computer-voiced advertisement for perfume that claims, "One whiff of this at the office and your boss will be asking you to stay after work for a candlelight staff meeting for two." Here the marriage plot collides with a symbolic rendering of women's subordination in the workplace. This advertisement, encapsulating as it does the commodification of sexual allure and the insidious myth that women's real work is to attract and please men—the message of the 1950s' "Danger . . . woman at work" swimsuit ad (see Fig. I.2)—sends Selina into a fit of destructive rage. Her "murder" by Shreck points out that when men are not rich *gentle*men but violent power seekers, it is useless to act like a genteel little woman or an alluring sex kitten. Therefore, the targets of her fury are the trappings of girlish femininity—cute stuffed animals spread around her pink apartment, a doll house, a nightgown decorated with pictures of kittens. Her rejection of submissive femininity is summed up when she transforms a neon sign from "HELLO THERE" (Fig. 5.2a) to "HELL HERE" by casually knocking out the appropriate letters.

The joke that the cheery greeting "hello there" contains the stark assessment "hell here" exemplifies an awareness of the absurd that characterizes Catwoman's sense of humor, which is informed by feminism. "I am Catwoman; hear me roar," declares Selina Kyle after her transformation from a mousy secretary into an icon of female empowerment and antisentimentalism; this line, a play on Helen Reddy's popular 1970s' song "I Am Woman," incorporates a familiar second wave slogan with an anger absent from the original.

In her keen awareness of the absurd, Catwoman illustrates philosopher Sandra Bartky's insight that "[s]ince many things [in sexist society] are not what they seem to be and since many apparently harmless sorts of things can suddenly exhibit a sinister dimension, social reality is revealed as *deceptive*" (17). The "things" to which Bartky refers—"[i]nnocent chatter, the currency of ordinary life, or a compliment ('You don't think like a woman'), the well-intentioned advice of psychologists, the news item, the joke, the cosmetics advertisement" (17)—are the aspects of life that *Batman Returns* director Tim Burton highlights in the details of the film; we see them as deceptive when Catwoman reveals that "hello there" masks "hell here."[9] This, of course, is the knowledge that con women such as Jean Muir and Lorelei Lee understand and exploit in their attempts to get the "goods" of mass consumer culture. Catwoman, however, does not buy into that acquisitive ethos and therefore refuses to play the role of the "little woman." Her grasp of social reality as a deceptive construct enables her to act on her desires for vengeance with a smile—not the smile of accommodation, but of power. Catwoman's sense of humor is located in the liminal territory between feminine cheer and female rage;[10] her forays into violent behavior begin and end on that bisociation of comedy and anger. In other words, she is the "bad cat" who lurks in the background of the screwball world of *Bringing Up Baby*; what is threatening but contained in the madcap Susan is out of the cage and on the loose in *Batman Returns*.

a

b

Figure 5.2. Frame enlargements from *Batman Returns* (1992): *a.* The neon sign in Selina Kyle's apartment that Catwoman modifies to "HELL HERE"; *b.* the shadow of femininity.

Catwoman's jokes demonstrate the radical rejection of societal conventions that accompany her transformation into an outlaw. Remember: in the movie, Catwoman is a villain, albeit a sympathetically portrayed one. She plots to bring about Batman's downfall because he is the one who saved the helpless Selina when she was attacked during the riot at the beginning of the movie. After her transformation, after she has crossed over the line and is outside of society, she wants to destroy anything connected with the system of rules that failed her. Although she redirects her anger away from Batman (after realizing that the Bruce Wayne Selina has been dating is the Batman Catwoman has been fighting), she does not accept the happy-ending marriage to the rich man because she refuses to buttress the structure of society the way Batman does.

Unwilling to pay the price of submission to be the female counterpart to the superhero, as Wonder Woman does, Catwoman maintains her independence from Batman and the culture he defends. Significantly for this discussion of shadow figures of culturally sanctioned femininity, one of the last images we see of Catwoman is her shadow against the alley walls, present but elusive (Fig. 5.2b).

The shot of Catwoman's shadow informs us that she survived mortal combat with her boss Shreck; his death is her revenge: "A die for a die." As a survivor, Catwoman illustrates how female tricksters can be "creative nonvictims." [11] Catwoman refuses to participate in her own victimization and recreates herself beyond the victim/survivor dichotomy. Like all the female tricksters discussed here, Catwoman is a fantasy figure who transcends her culture's restrictions on feminine appearance, comportment, and behavior. By playing on cultural images of female power as feline, Catwoman subverts and reverses the sexist limitations imposed on women and emerges as a mythical trickster figure.

Catwoman can't go home again. The home, workplace, and self Selina knew are shattered, just as the gender-demarcating boundaries between the public and private, between subject and object, have become permeable in the twentieth century. Unlike nineteenth-century female tricksters who are defined in relation to their sentimental doubles, twentieth-century modern figures who create and impersonate their own doubles before returning to their original selves, or postmodern Lucy who shifts between a myriad of personas, fin de millennium Catwoman is the permanent replacement for the duplicitous conventional feminine subject who remains subservient in the love economy. The "good" woman changes into the shadow; what will the shadow become? As an explicitly feminist mythical figure, Catwoman may prefigure the female tricksters of the twenty-first century who provide models of resistance to the continued mutations of sexism in society. Teetering on the brink of the next millennium as she slinks through the liminal terrain of the city streets of the American imagination, Catwoman can remind us of Abigail Adams's 1776 warning to her husband John: "If perticular [*sic*] care and attention is not paid to the Laidies [*sic*] we are determined to foment a Rebellion, and will not hold ourselves bound by any Laws in which we have no voice, or Representation" (quoted in Ravitch 31). By articulating the possibilities of becoming creative nonvictims, female tricksters — whether madcap, screwball, con woman, or catwoman — perform a part of the cultural work of transforming the feminine into the human.

Notes

Introduction

1. Turner, *Forest of Symbols*, 98. Turner's discussion of liminality, frame analysis (based on the work of Gregory Bateson and Erving Goffman), and performance has been a central influence on my understanding and approach to the trickster. See Turner, *Ritual Process*; *Dramas, Fields, and Metaphors*; and *From Ritual to Theatre*. See also Schechner.

2. Pelton's review of the scholarship on the trickster can be supplemented by Basso, 4–8.

3. Henry Louis Gates Jr. is a notable exception. Although he does not discuss tricksters who are specifically female, he remarks, "Despite the fact that I have referred to him in the masculine, Esu is also genderless, or of dual gender" (29). Karen Ruth King Keim mentions a female trickster in postcolonial Cameroon novelist Mongo Beti's *La Ruine presque cocasse d'un polichinelle* (Paris: Peuples Noirs, 1979); see Keim, 13. An issue of the journal *Semeia* (Exum and Bos, eds.) is devoted to the topic of the female trickster. Jurich discusses the prevalence of witty and wily heroines in American folktales.

4. The public/private dichotomy has received considerable attention in political philosophy and feminist theory. For an overview, see Sharistanian, *Gender, Ideology, and Action*, especially 1–10. Also important are Rosaldo and Lamphere, and Elshtain's discussion on public/private in the Western philosophical tradition. Okin presents a perceptive argument that philosophical definitions of public citizen are based on the unexamined assumption of women's labor in the private sphere.

5. By the time of universal suffrage (in theory albeit not in practice), the locus of power in the public sphere has shifted from primarily political (in the classic sense of the term *polis*) to economic. On the issue of power in mass culture, see Jürgen Habermas, "The Public Sphere: An Encyclopedia Article" in Bronner and Kellner, 136–42; and *Transformation of the Public Sphere*.

6. On the shift to consumer-hedonist values, see Ewen, *Captains of Consciousness*, Marchand, Lipsitz, and Fox and Lears. On the commodification of women's beauty and the cosmetics industry, see Banner and Freedman. On Victorian-sentimental ideas about makeup, see Halttunen. For an insightful discussion of women's appearance and subjectivity, see Bartky, especially the chapters "Phenomenology of Feminist Consciousness" and "Foucault, Femininity, and the Modernization of Patriarchal Power."

7. See Stacey for an excellent critical overview of the theories of Laura Mulvey,

Raymond Bellour, Mary Ann Doane, and Teresa de Laurentis. I agree with Stacey's resistance to psychoanalytic models that conflate gender identity and sexuality, and deny difference between desire and identification.

8. See especially Babcock-Abrahams.

9. This categorization is from a syllabus created during the 1977 Modern Language Association-National Endowment for the Humanities Summer Seminar on American Indian Literature, published in *Studies in American Indian Literature,* ed. Paula Gunn Allen (New York: MLA, 1983), 50.

10. See Babcock-Abrahams, Turner, and Makarius.

11. See Holmes, Patricia Clark Smith with Paula Gunn Allen, Miller, Vizenor, and Babcock and Cox.

12. See Ekkehart Malotki and Michael Lomatuway'ma, *Hopi Coyote Tales,* American Tribal Religions Series, no. 9, gen. ed. Karl Luckert (Lincoln: University of Nebraska Press, 1987).

13. In *The Signifying Monkey,* Gates interprets the figure of the animal trickster as symbolic of signifyin(g) "the black trope of tropes," which in turn he uses as the foundation for his theory of the African-American literary tradition. His work is less applicable to my project than Levine's, although his tracing of the African-American trickster figure to African antecedents is an interesting counterpart to Robert Pelton's work on African tricksters and Roberts's insightful exploration of a continuum of black trickster heroes.

14. See William L. Andrews, 205–14, for a discussion of *Narrative of the Life of J. D. Green,* an obscure slave narrative that casts Green as a trickster.

15. Roberts's discussion of the relationship between the "bad nigger" and the "badman" figures raises intriguing issues about the relationship between female tricksters and "bad women," especially the con woman and the femme fatale of detective fiction and film noir. Significantly, representations of con women and femmes fatales recur after women's suffrage; perhaps this is analogous to the changing role of the law in the experiences of enslaved Africans and black freedmen.

16. William L. Andrews, 240–43. See also Ginsberg, 12–13; and Weinauer.

17. In Carl Van Vechten's infamous novel *Nigger Heaven* (1926), Lasca Sartoris has much in common with the female trickster, but she is a destructive character and articulates Van Vechten's belief that African-Americans were essentially primitive. Langston Hughes's novel *Not Without Laughter* (1930) grapples with the contradictions between female and male rebellion in its portrayals of Jimboy and Harriet. Countee Cullen's novel *One Way to Heaven* (1932) depicts Constancia as an unconventional heroine. I intend to continue exploring the trickster in the literature of the Harlem Renaissance in the future.

18. Social scientists have been the members of the academic community who have studied African-Americans and Native Americans. In Vizenor's essay "Trickster Discourse," he contrasts the tragic story that sociologists have told about Native Americans with the comic trickster discourse that is at the center of their culture.

19. Lenz's study is the most comprehensive of the scholarship on the confidence man and Southwest vernacular hero. See also Blair, Lindberg, Justus, and Wadlington.

20. What is useful about these approaches is Haltunnen's location of the issue of confidence in American ideology; her approach places a cultural figure in its ideological context with specific attention to gender demarcations. An examination of the scholarship on the humor of the Old Southwest highlights issues

of the contested space of the frontier, monetary gains, and narrative strategies (juxtaposing vernacular and gentlemanly characters) which show the conflict between two ideals of masculinity.

21. Although Huggins is referring to masculinity and primitivism, the issue of the gender and tricksterism is analogous.

22. Turner discusses the "subjunctive mood" in several places in the essays collected in *The Anthropology of Performance*, including 25, 41, 101–2, 105–6, 169.

23. I am using the term "transfer point" in a way similar to Janet Staiger's discussion of "the productive aspect of discursive constructions of woman as a cultural sign. I shall use Foucault's notion of a 'transfer point' to describe this. Foucault conceives of discursive nodes as places for generating a resurgence of power and pleasure; I shall also consider the intersections as sites of potential transformations from one form of meaning to another. A transfer point, like any generator in a revolution, is a valuable site to control. Images that disrupt norms, that display current norms, also set agendas for changes" (xvii).

Chapter 1. Running Mad, Taking Cover

1. A delineation of the tradition of female tricksters in British literature is beyond the scope of this book. Suffice it to say here that unconventional, antisentimental heroines who subvert existing power structures through rebellion and trickery include many of Shakespeare's comic heroines and Becky Sharp in Thackeray's *Vanity Fair*.

2. For exemplary discussions of subversive and antisentimental heroines in nineteenth-century fiction by American women, see Ammons, Baym, Dobson, "The Hidden Hand," Kelley, Morris, *Women Vernacular Humorists*, and Walker, "Wit, Sentimentality, and the Image of Women."

3. From pioneering delineations of a woman's tradition of literature such as Ellen Moers's *Literary Women* (1976), Elaine Showalter's *A Literature of Their Own* (1977), and Gilbert and Gubar's *The Madwoman in the Attic* (1979) to influential feminist interpretations of American cultural history in Mary Kelley's *Private Woman, Public Stage* (1984), Jane Tompkins's *Sensational Designs* (1985), and Carroll Smith-Rosenberg's *Disorderly Conduct* (1985), literary and cultural critics have illuminated women's use of covert (literary as well as social) strategies to reject conventions of cultural ideals of womanhood. The public/private demarcation has been central to discussions of gender in nineteenth-century America from Smith-Rosenberg's essay "The Female World of Love and Ritual: Relations between Women in Nineteenth-Century America" in Cott and Pleck, eds., and Nancy F. Cott's *The Bonds of Womanhood* (1977) to more recent studies including Glenna Matthews's *The Rise of Public Woman* (1992) and Carolyn Johnston's *Sexual Power* (1992).

4. *Behind a Mask*, like many of Alcott's other thrillers, was published pseudonymously under the name A. M. Barnard. See Stern and Elbert for the relationship between Alcott's thrillers and the rest of her work.

5. See L. Moody Simms Jr.'s entry on McGinley in *The Encyclopedia of American Humorists* (303).

6. The attribution of feminist rebellion and protest to women's comic writing made here by Walker and Dresner and echoed by Barreca and Morris is in sharp contrast to the other major body of scholarship on women and comedy: studies of twentieth-century popular culture. Patricia Mellencamp's essay

"Situation Comedy, Feminism, and Freud: Discourses of Gracie and Lucy" is an example of the argument that the comedy of female figures like Lucy in the television series *I Love Lucy* (played by Lucille Ball) was conciliatory and reinforced women's containment in domesticity.

7. Walker, Dresner, Barreca, and Morris are motivated by the invisibility of women's humor. Walker and Morris are specifically interested in the canon of American literary humor; Walker's book *A Very Serious Thing* documents that women have used comedy in their writing from the beginning of what is considered American literature (Anne Bradstreet). Morris's dissertation on Ann Stephens, Frances Whitcher, and Marietta Holley focuses on their participation in the tradition of vernacular humor popular in the nineteenth-century. In her book, *Women's Humor in the Age of Gentility,* she reads Whitcher's writing in the context of biography; her argument views gentility as the target of women's humor in the nineteenth-century. *American Women Humorists: Critical Essays,* edited by Morris, brings together key essays which are indispensable to those interested in the field.

Barreca's interest also encompasses British women's humor in her book *Untamed and Unabashed*; the two collections of essays she edited, *Last Laughs* and *New Perspectives,* argue for a uniquely female tradition of humor and tend to characterize that tradition as subversive and women's comedy and laughter as dangerous. Sochen takes the more cultural approach exemplified by Walker.

8. See Cott, *Bonds of Womanhood*; the essays in Cott and Pleck; Baker; DuBois and Gordon; DuBois, Buhle, et al.; Smith-Rosenberg, *Disorderly Conduct*; Kelley; Evans; Elaine Tyler May; and Matthews, *The Rise of Public Woman.* The degree of separation of woman's sphere is a topic of debate in these works and many others. See Evans's bibliography for more sources.

9. See Henry Nash Smith's analysis of the ritual of taking tea in *The Wide, Wide World.*

10. See Johanna M. Smith, "Feeling Right: Christianity and Women's Influence in *Uncle Tom's Cabin.*"

11. See *The Hidden Hand: A Drama in Five Acts,* adapted by Robert Jones. There was also a three-act version performed in London called *Capitola, or The Masked Mother and the Hidden Hand: A Drama in Three Acts,* adapted by C. H. Hazelwood.

12. A side note: The Jones script omits the line, "It means that you have been outwitted by a girl."

13. See Joanne Dobson's introduction to the Rutgers reprint of *The Hidden Hand* for a discussion of the significance of the names.

14. Jean's success can be read as a revision of Thackeray's trickster heroine Becky Sharp in *Vanity Fair;* Jean accomplishes the transformation from governess to lady that Becky does not. Another example of a con woman along the lines of Jean Muir is Undine in Edith Wharton's novel *The Custom of the Country* (1913). Undine's impersonation of a good society woman masks the tactics she employs in the sociosexual marketplace: deception, duplicity, costume and (like Jean Muir) expression, and the emotional and sexual manipulations of others. Wharton's portrayal of Undine's insatiable material desire exposes the shallowness of the goals of the con woman: wealth, jewels, and status whose worth is measured in the eyes of others. Undine embodies a restless unfulfillment characteristic of the emerging society of consumption; at the end of the novel, "She had everything she wanted, but she still felt, at times, that there were other things she might want if she knew about them" (591).

15. Reynolds describes another novel, *Southwold* (1859) by the suffragist Lillie

Devereux Blake, with a heroine whose manipulations and deceptions rival those of Jean Muir. According to Reynolds, the intelligent and creative Medora Fielding "repeatedly outsmarts male characters in philosophical dialogues and dreams of a society in which women are granted full equality with men, but her own experience testifies to the tragic reality that, in a world of devalued males, women are driven to sexual manipulation and constant posing" (402).

Reynolds also mentions several pamphlet novels in which heroines of the type he calls the "adventure feminist" either disguise themselves as men to live as sailors and soldiers, or become female outlaws, bandits, pirates, and spies (347).

16. Quoted in Bendixen, xx. Details about the creation of *The Whole Family* are from Bendixen's introduction and editor Elizabeth Jordan's autobiography. Bendixen's scholarship on the letters between the participants shows that Jordan's account is not always accurate.

17. Freeman was the most successful but not the only author to inflict an individual vision on the novel. Most of the writers, especially Henry James and Elizabeth Stuart Phelps, entered the fray, each not only telling the story of their character, but also trying to force the other characters into their mold.

Chapter 2. Economics and Erotics

1. The term "masquerade" is from Joan Riviere, "Womanliness as Masquerade" (1929); see Gilbert and Gubar, *No Man's Land*, vol. 3, esp. 57–60, and Butler, *Gender Trouble*, 50–54, for discussions of this important essay. I chose the term "public self" because it highlights the tactics women use to negotiate the public sphere, formerly the province of men. It blends the awareness of woman as "surveyed" because she is in public with the term "social self," from 1920's social psychology. The consciousness of social selves emerges in the early twentieth century because of mass culture; for women, it concerns sexual objectification, and the mask is literally manifest in makeup and manipulations of style. For African Americans, the mask is submissive and objectified behavior; see, for example, Paul Lawrence Dunbar's poem "We Wear the Mask" and W.E.B. DuBois's discussion of double consciousness in *The Souls of Black Folk*.

2. The quandary of self-representation expressed in *Portrait of Myself* and "Occasionally" is an issue with which Stettheimer continued to grapple. Over the course of her career, she put herself into many of her paintings as the artist or observer. For example, in *Beauty Contest: to the Memory of P. T. Barnum* (1924), Stettheimer portrays herself as surveyor of the circus-like scene, looking on calmly from her vantage point in the upper, left corner. See Nochlin for a discussion of Stettheimer's work.

3. See Marchand for a discussion of how, although researchers cannot ascertain how people perceived the ads, if they had an impact on how people perceived themselves or society, or whether they succeeded in performing the cultural work they intended, we can explore the rhetorical and visual patterns that advertising as a whole created and circulated.

4. Women's role as the consumers of male production is a given in the world Lorelei Lee inhabits. Loos's novel *Gentlemen Prefer Blondes* casts the sociosexual relationship between men and women as an economic one.

5. Loos accomplishes this by several techniques, the most striking of which is the use of Lorelei's friend and foil Dorothy, who, although along for the ride as Lorelei's companion, has no illusions about what the men want, and, much to

Lorelei's disgust, acts to satisfy her erotic desires, not economic ones. Dorothy's quips provide a running commentary that counters Lorelei's highly subjective and untrustworthy narrative.

6. The term "acquisitive intelligence" comes from Nella Larsen's novel *Passing* (1929). It refers to Irene's assessment of her friend/rival/double Clare's ability to get what she wants. As women who "pass" for white in order to be included in the privileges of whiteness (and judged as attractive and therefore valuable by cultural standards of female beauty based on whiteness), Clare and Irene carry out impersonations of white women that mark them as liminal figures, "betwixt and between" racial categories.

7. Loos also uses Dorothy's earthy quips as a device for registering surprise at Lorelei's resourcefulness: "So when I got through telling Dorothy what I thought up, Dorothy looked at me and looked at me and she really said she thought my brains were a miracle. I mean she said my brains reminded her of a radio because you listen to it for days and days and you get discouradged [*sic*] and just when you are getting ready to smash it, something comes out that is a masterpiece" (116). In this passage, and throughout the novel, Dorothy gives the reader a point of view more trustworthy than Lorelei's willful distortion, and as Loos herself explained, "my brunette's true inner self was inspired by girls I could laugh *with* and not *at*. . . . For in affairs of the heart I was Dorothy's most accurate prototype" (*A Girl Like I* 275). In a letter of "envious congratulations on Dorothy," William Faulkner admired specifically "the way you did her through the (intelligence?) of that elegant moron of a cornflower" (quoted in "A Girl Can't Go On Laughing All the Time," *Fate Keeps on Happening* 63). As a stand-in for the author and a welcome counterpoint to Lorelei's subjective narration, the character of Dorothy is an impressive achievement, indeed. In the companion volume to *Gentlemen Prefer Blondes*, called *But Gentlemen Marry Brunettes* (1927), Loos uses Dorothy to relate a semiautobiographical tale, which includes among its highlights a description of the wits of the Algonquin Round Table.

8. Banner notes that in antebellum discourses of attractiveness, blonde hair was associated with sentimental, insipid heroines and with innocence; dark hair was associated with passion, a notion popularized by romantic writers such as Byron and Scott (62–63). Of course, creating "fashionable," sensual, secular heroines was not Stowe's goal in *Uncle Tom's Cabin*. See also Banner, 121–25.

9. Locating the origin of the popularity of blonde hair in burlesque sheds light on Mae West's choice of hairstyle. See the beginning of Chapter 4 for a discussion of Marilyn Monroe's—and Jane Russell's—incarnation of Lorelei Lee in the 1953 film *Gentlemen Prefer Blondes*. Blondeness continued to move along the axis of innocence and sexuality in response to cultural definitions of femininity.

10. French theorist Louis Althusser argues that society "hails" people as subjects that are already defined in some way. He uses the example of a policeman saying, "Hey, you" to someone, and that person interpreting that "you" as specifically him or her, rather than the generic mass "you" that it is.

11. This dualistic structure of modes of power is replicated in mass consumer culture as, concurrently, women enter the public sphere and the public sphere is redefined as increasingly economic rather than political.

12. See Wilson, 108–14.

13. Incidentally, Anita Loos claims that when Santayana was asked to name his favorite book of American philosophy, he replied, *Gentlemen Prefer Blondes*. (Loos, *A Girl Like I* 274).

14. Jean Franco, "The Incorporation of Women: A Comparison of North

American and Mexican Popular Narrative," in Modleski, 128. Franco bases her discussion of popular romance narratives on Fredric Jameson's discussion of modern romance.

15. By the middle of the twenties, Clara Bow had come to represent the working girl flapper in silent films including *The Plastic Age* (1925), *Dancing Mothers, Mantrap, Kid Boots*, (1926), and, most evocatively for this discussion, *It* (1927). Bow portrayed flirtatious, charismatic, active flapper heroines in fourteen movies in 1925, eight in 1926, and six in 1927. In 1929, Bow starred in *The Wild Party*, a surprisingly sentimental talkie about a college girl who gets involved with her professor; the facial expressions and mannerisms that were so cute in the silent films did not transfer well in this sound film.

16. Interestingly, Betty resists the "trap" of sex without marriage that Jessie Fauset's heroine Angela falls into in *Plum Bun*.

Chapter 3. Out of the Garden and into the War

1. Arch Oboler, "Adam and Eve Sketch," *Chase and Sanborn Hour*, December 12, 1937, audiotape, National Recording Company, 1981. All quotations are from my transcription of Oboler.

2. The word "dispossession" was a popular Depression-era term for the evictions and losses suffered by so many. That Oboler uses this word to describe the expulsion from the Garden shows how the sketch reinterprets the biblical story in terms of Depression domesticity.

3. From the vantage point of the moralists who interpreted expulsion from the Garden as tragic, the comic treatment of the Bible story by the famously "immoral" Mae West was no joke. As the following excerpt from a newspaper editorial conveys, the moralists' reaction was censorship: "the radio has brought to many a fuller life, carrying the culture of the world into the homes of America. The home is our last bulwark against the modern over-emphasis on sensuality, and we cannot see why Miss West and other of her ilk should be permitted to pollute its sacred precincts with shady stories, foul obscenity, smutty suggestiveness, and horrible blasphemy" (quoted in Wertheim 364–65). This editorial is indicative of the rhetoric used by the social purity crusaders in the 1930s to wage war against the forces of lewdness.

4. See Susman, esp. chaps. 9, "The Culture of the Thirties," and 10, "Culture and Commitment," for discussions of shame and fear as prevalent psychological responses to the Depression. See also my discussion of *Bringing Up Baby* later in this chapter.

5. "Camp" is a playful way "of seeing the world as an aesthetic phenomenon . . . in terms of the degree of artifice, of stylization" (Sontag 106). According to Sontag, camp is an ironic sensibility that often plays on androgyny as a way of exposing the artifice of gender and the construction of a social self.

6. Kendall refers to Frank Capra, the director of the genre-defining screwball comedy *It Happened One Night* (1934). Other important directors include those of the three movies I discuss in this chapter: Howard Hawks (*Bringing Up Baby, Twentieth Century, His Girl Friday*, and *Ball of Fire*); Leo McCarey (*The Awful Truth, Belle of the Nineties* starring Mae West, *Love Affair*, and *Ruggles of Red Gap*); and Preston Sturges (*The Lady Eve, The Palm Beach Story, Sullivan's Travels*, and *The Beautiful Blonde from Bashful Bend*).

For discussions of the definition of the genre of screwball comedy, see Kendall; Gehring; Cavell; Sennett; Mast, *Comic Mind*; Schatz; Haskell; and Cawelti. The following list of exemplary screwball comedies is drawn from a synthesis of these works: *Design for Living* (1933), *It Happened One Night* (1934), *The Thin Man* (1934), *Twentieth Century* (1934), *Ruggles of Red Gap* (1935), *The Whole Town's Talking* (1935), *The Libeled Lady* (1936), *My Man Godfrey* (1936), *Theodora Goes Wild* (1936), *The Awful Truth* (1937), *Nothing Sacred* (1937), *Easy Living* (1937), *Topper* (1937), *Bluebeard's Eighth Wife* (1938), *Bringing Up Baby* (1938), *Holiday* (1938), *Joy of Living* (1938), *The Philadelphia Story* (1940), *His Girl Friday* (1940), *My Favorite Wife* (1940), *Too Many Husbands* (1940), *Ball of Fire* (1941), *The Lady Eve* (1941), *Mr. and Mrs. Smith* (1941), *I Married a Witch* (1942), *The Palm Beach Story* (1942), *Heaven Can Wait* (1943), *The Miracle of Morgan's Creek* (1944).

7. The heroines of screwball comedy were portrayed as equal participants in the battle of the sexes (which symbolized both conflict and cooperation between the sexes) partly because of their verbal prowess. As Haskell writes, "The more a heroine could talk, the more autonomous and idiosyncratic she became, and the more she seemed to define herself by her own lights. Conversation was an index not only of intelligence, but of confidence, of self-possession" (139).

8. For an excellent discussion of the historical and cinematic meanings of the couple and romantic love, see Wexman esp. part 1.

9. See Ann Douglas.

10. Neither Lucy nor Jerry seems to work; they live a life of leisure. For a fuller discussion of class in *The Awful Truth*, see Kendall 186–209.

11. The term "love impulse" comes from the character Dr. Lehman, a psychiatrist who is also dining in the club. After David tells Susan to "go away," and goes to find Mr. Peabody, Susan follows him, pausing at the psychiatrist's table to snag more olives for her trick, and decides to ask him his opinion about a man who "follows me around and fights with me." Lehman replies, "Well, the love impulse in man very frequently reveals itself in terms of conflict" (53). As critic Gerald Mast explains, "His psychiatric cliche turns out to be another of the film's verbal predictions which appears to be totally false but will prove to be perfectly true" ("Bringing Up Baby," 301). Like all the characters in the movie, Lehman is portrayed as a screwball for comic effect; after his line to Susan, "All people who behave strangely are not insane," the script gives the following direction, "Lehman suddenly and inexplicably twitches and blinks both eyes grotesquely" (52). Actor Fritz Feld's eyebrow manipulations here undercut any authority that might be in his German-accented pronouncements.

12. See Frye, "The Argument of Comedy," and Gehring.

13. See Haskell 189–230.

14. The plot of *The Lady Eve* is basically a revision of the plot of the silent movie *It* (1927, discussed in Chapter 2); like Betty Lou, Jean performs a cross-class female female impersonation to get the hero to propose marriage so she can reject him as payback for his rejection of her, which she considers to have been based on false moral standards. Further, both heroines regret scorning the hero almost immediately and win him back by being the lively working-class woman with whom he first fell in love.

To be sure, *The Awful Truth* and *Bringing Up Baby* also follow the model set by *It*, but the higher economic class of those heroines puts a different spin on the plot. Nevertheless, in all four movies, the heroine uses a cross-class trick to achieve her goals.

15. Created by William Moulton Marston, a psychologist and inventor of a lie

detector machine, the Wonder Woman comic book series began in December 1941 and continues today. Marston's obituary in *Time* (May 12, 1947) said that Marston "averred that in 1000 years women would be running the US."

Chapter 4. Liminal Lucy

1. Anita Loos collaborated on the earlier film, the stage play, and then the Broadway musical comedy starring Carol Channing on which the film was based.

2. See Curry and esp. Rowe, 179–80.

3. *All About Eve* is another film based on "intrafeminine fascination"; see Chapter 2 and Stacey.

4. Female trickery highlights the issue of women's exercise of covert power, which necessitates that practitioners maintain positions of submission. Covert manipulations may not increase self-esteem or self-worth and certainly do not challenge sexist ideology; instead, as historian Carolyn Johnston puts it, "covert power without public power led to a loss of self-esteem and to physical and economic vulnerability" and perpetuates women's private, feme covert status (243).

5. Critic Patricia Mellencamp makes the important point that the audience wants Lucy's schemes to fail, and that Lucy's failures are actually Ball's triumphs: "if Lucy's plots for ambition and fame *narratively* failed . . . *performatively* they succeeded" (88). Mellencamp uses this insight to support her contention that *I Love Lucy* exemplifies comedy as containment for women, a reading that neither puts the series in its sociocultural context nor steps outside of the limitations of Freudian models of discussing comedy. In contrast, my point is that although the comedy of *Lucy* may be (in media scholar Douglas Kellner's terms) "conciliatory," it is also "emancipatory"; further, I see comedy as more subversive than Mellencamp. Finally, and most importantly, I disagree with Mellencamp's interpretation of how popular culture functions in the construction of ideology; I do not look to a text like *I Love Lucy* to provide an exhortation for women to remain or leave the home. My focus is on how a popular culture text articulates and calls attention to the contradictions of dominant ideology, enacting in a pleasurable way the absurdities and frustrations of daily life.

See Alexander Doty for a reading of the series that foregrounds the clash between talentless housewife Lucy and successful movie star Ball. Doty's argument supports mine; he explains, "The resulting tensions between 'Lucy Ricardo' and 'Lucille Ball' in Ball's televisual star image often threatens to disrupt the series' sitcom characterizations and narrative development, thereby opening a space for more complex, if not always progressive, readings of Lucy Ricardo and the series" (4).

6. Turner termed the "successor of the liminal in complex large-scale societies, where individuality and optation in art have in theory supplanted collective and obligatory ritual performances" the *liminoid* (Turner, *Anthropology of Performance* 29). Of course *I Love Lucy* is liminoid, a commodity, but I am using "liminal" here to describe Lucy because I want to stress that the cultural centrality of the *I Love Lucy* phenomenon is like the "collective representations" that unite a community.

7. See especially Elaine Tyler May. May's important contribution to the social history of the postwar era is her demonstration of how discourses about domesticity (usually thought of as private) shared the cold war preoccupation with

containing atomic power and communism (usually thought of as public concerns); in other words, May's book shows the interpenetration of public and private discourses.

8. See Julia Kristeva for an interesting perspective on the connections between time and female subjectivity.

9. This is one of the ironic moments that fuse the "real life" of Ball and Arnaz with their fictional characters. In the vaudeville act on which the pilot for *I Love Lucy* drew heavily, Ball played a character who (dressed as a man) impersonated a trained seal. See episode 6, "The Audition," which recycles the pilot material.

10. In his history of gender roles, Peter Filene uses the term "domestic mystique" to extend Betty Friedan's ideas about the "feminine mystique" so that the ideology encompasses both genders. See *Him/Her/Self* 169.

11. The *Cosmopolitan* article supports Friedan's contention that "When you wrote about an actress for a woman's magazine, you wrote about her as a housewife" (53).

12. In an item titled "Wives Who Compete Lose Out," Adams advises that the competitive wife (because of her own inadequacies) "can cultivate self-respect, not by competing with Phil but by pursuing her own talents and skills independently. Perfecting her needlework, becoming an expert gardener, establishing a reputation for impromptu entertaining—these are just a few of her opportunities to demonstrate her worth" ("Making Marriage Work," *Ladies' Home Journal*, January 1952, 14). Adams also advises an unhappy wife to examine her priorities: "unless she wanted to build her life around her husband, why did she marry him?" (*Ladies' Home Journal*, September 1953, 32).

Titles of selected items in the "Making Marriage Work" feature include "Wives Who Compete Lose Out," "Don't Dominate Your Partner," "Naggers Take the Joy Out of Marriage," "Be Easy to Live With and Avoid Friction," titles of the monthly quizzes, "Do Men Drop You?" "Does He Lack Self-Confidence?" "How Irritable Are You?" "Are You a Restless Wife?"

13. The whiskers and glue came from Fred's old vaudeville trunk, a virtual cornucopia of faulty props for Lucy's antics. In another episode, "The Handcuffs" (no. 37, October 6, 1952), Lucy wants Ricky to stay home with her instead of going to rehearsal and playfully handcuffs herself to him while he sleeps. But the handcuffs are not the trick ones Fred showed her earlier, but Civil War handcuffs with no key. Before the locksmith can separate them, Lucy and Ricky have to spend a day and night fastened together, an interesting metaphor of the "togetherness" touted in the popular media. Ricky performs a song on a live television program while Lucy stands behind the curtain, literally as well as figuratively operating as her husband's right hand.

14. There is another incongruity in "Job Switching": neither Ricky nor Fred makes money by the kind of regimented wage labor Lucy and Ethel attempt; Ricky is a bandleader and Fred is a landlord.

15. *I Love Lucy* was a commodity in itself as well as an advertisement for Philip Morris cigarettes, the show's sponsor. The series' popularity also sparked a plethora of consumer goods (of which Desilu, the Ball-Arnaz production company, received 5 percent of the gross earnings of the products the stars endorsed); beginning in October 1952, there were 2,800 retail outlets for Lucille Ball dresses, blouses, sweaters, and aprons as well as Desi Arnaz smoking jackets and robes. There were pajamas for men and women like the ones Lucy and Ricky wore and a line of dolls. In one month, 30,000 dresses, 32,000 aprons, and 35,000 dolls were sold. The pajamas sold out in two weeks, and the Christmas

rush sold 85,000 dolls. In January 1953, the first month of selling a line of bed-room suites, $500,000 in sales in two days was reported. In the works in January 1953 were layettes and nursery furniture, Desi sport shirts and denims, Lucy lin-gerie and costume jewelry, and desk and chair sets ("Desilu Formula" 58). There were also *I Love Lucy* albums, sheet music, coloring books, and comic books.

16. Over sixty films out of a random sample of one hundred Hollywood films from the studio era ended with kisses or other displays of the couple's romantic union (Wexman 19). See Wexman for detailed discussions of the centrality of the couple and the romance plot in Hollywood film narrative.

17. See Spigel, *Make Room for TV,* for an intriguing exploration of the cultural discourses of installing the television set in the home physically as well as in-sightful commentary on the self-reflexivity of early television.

18. See Bart Andrews 217 ff.

Chapter 5. You Can't Go Home Again

1. This was the famous "bra-burning" event disseminated in the media; al-though no bras were burned, the protesters did have a trash can to collect re-strictive objects of femininity. This protest was organized by a group called Radi-cal Women in New York to make the point that "all women were hurt by beauty competition" (Hole and Levine 123). Although the national press and television coverage was hardly flattering, it did publicize the presence of the movement. The Radical Women group started the "rapping" that would develop into "con-sciousness raising"; some of the women split off into the group called WITCH that performed the trick of "hexing" the New York Stock Exchange later in 1968.

2. See Evans, Faludi, and E. T. May.

3. *That Girl* (starring Marlo Thomas) portrays a single woman who must be resourceful and wily in her negotiation of independence (living alone in an apartment, having a career, relating to her boyfriend); the wink that ended the title/theme song sequence at the beginning of the show indicates the joke, the trick, of everyday life.

4. See Peter N. Chumo II, "Thelma and Louise as Screwball Comedy" in "The Many Faces of *Thelma and Louise*," 24.

5. Quoted in Carol J. Clover, "Crossing Over," in "The Many Faces of *Thelma and Louise*, 22.

6. See Stacey for an analysis of how the female spectator is invited to look at the two women who are defined by their differences (112–29). Also see my dis-cussion of *Passing* in Chapter 2.

7. See Wexman for an analysis of how *House of Games* offers an alternative to the couple (201–14).

8. In addition to the characters discussed in this chapter, other contemporary film heroines who are female tricksters include Judy Maxwell (Barbra Streisand) in *What's Up, Doc?* (1972), a movie that self-consciously draws on the Depression-era screwball comedies, especially *Bringing Up Baby*; Linda Marolla (Liza Min-nelli) in *Arthur* (1981), the working girl who breathes life into the boring exis-tence of the wealthy hero; Victor/Victoria (Julie Andrews) in *Victor/Victoria* (1982), a gender-bending tale of impersonation; the cross-dressing and ambi-tious heroine (Barbra Streisand) of *Yentl* (1983); Joan (Kathleen Turner), who becomes the kind of adventurous heroine she writes about in *Romancing the Stone* (1984); Edwina Cutwater (Lily Tomlin) in *All of Me* (1984), who sends her soul

into the body of Roger Cobb (Steve Martin); Meg (Jessica Lange) in *Crimes of the Heart* (1986); Sandy (Bette Midler) and Lauren (Shelley Long) in *Outrageous Fortune* (1987); Barbara Rose (Kathleen Turner) in the blackest of all screwball comedies, *The War of the Roses* (1989); Tina (Andie MacDowell) in the decadent *Object of Beauty* (1991); escape artist Lucy (Rosanna Arquette) in *The Linguini Incident* (1992); Amy Archer (Jennifer Jason Leigh), the tough-talking woman reporter undercover as a "Muncie girl" in *The Hudsucker Proxy* (1994). Dual heroines who team up for female trickery include Abby (Janeane Garofalo) and Noelle (Uma Thurman) in *The Truth About Cats and Dogs* (1996), and Corky (Gina Gershon) and Violet (Jennifer Tilly) in *Bound* (1996).

9. Exposure of the deceptive nature of social reality runs through *Batman Returns*. The Penguin was born into a wealthy family who dumped him into the river near the zoo when he was a baby, rather than confronting the freakish and possibly evil nature of their offspring. He is raised by penguins and finds the truth about Max Shreck's irresponsible toxic waste disposal and slum lord activity; Gotham City's wealthiest and most respected citizen is, underneath, a criminal. Selina incurs Shreck's murderous wrath when she reveals that she knows that his plan to build a power generator masks his real plot—to construct a power capacitor to drain and collect Gotham City's power, giving him a monopoly on the valuable commodity, which he will sell back at exorbitant prices. In other words, Shreck appears to be generating power but is really stealing it and selling it back. Further, the movie contrasts the daytime personas of Bruce Wayne and Selina Kyle with their nighttime counterparts; daytime is an illusion that covers up the true nature expressed at night.

10. See Wilt for a discussion of the links between women's comedy and anger.

11. The term is the last of the "Basic Victim Positions" Margaret Atwood—who created an exemplary female trickster in Joan, the narrator of the novel *Lady Oracle* (1976)—delineates in her book on Canadian literature, *Survival*. Atwood's Four Basic Victim Positions are

1. To deny the fact that you are a victim.
2. To acknowledge the fact that you are a victim, but to explain this as an act of Fate, the Will of God, the dictates of biology (in the case of women, for instance), the necessity decreed by History, or Economics, or the Unconscious, or any other large generally powerful ideas.
3. To acknowledge the fact that you are a victim but to refuse to accept the assumption that the role is inevitable.
4. To be a creative non-victim. (2)

Selected Bibliography

Primary Sources

Books

Austen, Jane. *Love and Freindship: A Novel in a Series of Letters*. 1790. In *The Norton Anthology of Literature by Women: The Tradition in English*, ed. Sandra M. Gilbert and Susan Gubar, 209–32. New York: W. W. Norton, 1985.
Barnard, A. M. [Louisa May Alcott]. *Behind a Mask, or A Woman's Power*. 1866. In *Behind a Mask: The Unknown Thrillers of Louisa May Alcott*, ed. and introd. Madeline Stern, 3–104. New York: Quill, 1984.
Cohen, Hennig, and William B. Dillingham, eds. *The Humor of the Old Southwest*. 2d ed. Athens: University of Georgia Press, 1975.
Fauset, Jessie Redmon. *Plum Bun: A Novel without a Moral*. 1928. Reprint, London: Pandora Press, 1985.
Freeman, Mary Wilkins. "The Old Maid Aunt." In *The Whole Family: A Novel by Twelve Authors*, 30–59. 1907–8. Introd. Alfred Bendixen. New York: Ungar, 1986.
Friedan, Betty. *The Feminine Mystique*. 1963. Reprint, New York: Laurel, 1983.
Glyn, Elinor. *Romantic Adventure*. New York: E. P. Dutton, 1937.
Griffith, Richard, comp. *The Talkies: Articles and Illustrations from a Great Fan Magazine, 1928–1940*. New York: Dover, 1971.
Jordan, Elizabeth. *Three Rousing Cheers*. New York: D. Appleton-Century, 1938.
Larsen, Nella. *Passing*. 1929. Reprint, *Quicksand and Passing*, ed. Deborah McDowell. New Brunswick, NJ: Rutgers University Press, 1986.
Levin, Martin, ed. *Hollywood and the Great Fan Magazines*. New York: Arbor House, 1970.
Loos, Anita. *But Gentlemen Marry Brunettes*. 1927. Reprint, New York: Penguin, 1989.
———. *Cast of Thousands*. New York: Grosset and Dunlap, 1977.
———. *Fate Keeps on Happening*. Ed. Ray Pierre Corsini. London: Harrap, 1984.
———. *Gentlemen Prefer Blondes*. 1925. Reprint, New York: Penguin, 1989.
———. *A Girl Like I*. New York: Viking, 1966.
———. *Kiss Hollywood Goodbye*. New York: Viking, 1974.
Marston, William Moulton. *Wonder Woman*. A *Ms.* Book. New York: Holt, Rinehart and Winston, 1972.
Parker, Dorothy. *The Portable Dorothy Parker*. Ed. Brendan Gill. New York: Viking, 1973.

Ravitch, Diane, ed. *The American Reader: Words That Moved a Nation.* New York: Harper Perennial, 1991.

Silko, Leslie Marmon. "Yellow Woman." 1981. In *"Yellow Woman,"* ed. and introd. Melody Graulich. *Women Writers: Texts and Contexts.* New Brunswick, NJ: Rutgers University Press, 1993.

Southworth, E. D. E. N. *The Hidden Hand, or Capitola the Madcap.* 1859. Ed. Joanne Dobson. New Brunswick, NJ: Rutgers University Press, 1988.

Stettheimer, Florine. *Crystal Flowers.* New York: Privately printed, 1949.

Stowe, Harriet Beecher. *Uncle Tom's Cabin.* 1852. Reprint, Toronto: Bantam, 1981.

Tenney, Tabitha Gilman. *Female Quixotism Exhibited in the Romantic Opinions and Extravagant Adventures of Dorcasina Sheldon.* 1801. Reprint, New York: Oxford University Press, 1992.

Thackeray, William Makepeace. *Vanity Fair.* 1847–48. Reprint, New York: Signet-NAL, 1962.

Thurman, Wallace. *Infants of the Spring.* New York: Macaulay Co., 1932.

Vizenor, Gerald. *The Trickster of Liberty.* Minneapolis: University of Minnesota Press, 1988.

Warner, Susan. *The Wide, Wide World.* 1850. Reprint, New York: Feminist Press, 1987.

West, Mae. *Goodness Had Nothing to Do with It.* 1959. Reprint, New York: McFadden, 1970.

Wharton, Edith. *The Custom of the Country.* 1913. Reprint, New York: Scribner's, 1941.

Periodicals

Allerton, May. "Don't Go Platinum Yet! Read Before You Dye!" *Photoplay* November 1931. Reprinted in *The Talkies: Articles and Illustrations from a Great Fan Magazine 1928–1940.* Richard Griffith, comp. New York: Dover Publications, Inc., 1971.

"Beauty into Buffoon." *Life,* February 18, 1952, 93–97.

"Desilu Formula for Top TV: Brains, Beauty, Now a Baby." *Newsweek,* January 19, 1953, cover, 56–59.

Glyn, Elinor. "It." *Cosmopolitan* (February 1927): 44+.

———. "It." *Cosmopolitan* (March 1927): 64+.

Goldberg, Hyman. "Her Brains Didn't Get in Her Way." *Cosmopolitan* (March 1953): 25–29.

"The Many Faces of *Thelma and Louise.*" *Film Quarterly* (Winter 1991): 20–31.

McIntyre, O. O. "Little—But." *Cosmopolitan* (February 1927): 64–65.

Morehead, Albert. " 'Lucy' Ball." *Cosmopolitan* (January 1953): cover, 15–19.

Murphy, Mary, and Frank Swertlow. "The Roseanne Report." *TV Guide,* January 4, 1992, cover, 6–13, 18–22.

Oppenheimer, Jess. "Lucy's Two Babies." *Look,* April 21, 1953, 20–24.

Parker, Dorothy. "Madame Glyn Lectures on 'It,' with Illustrations." Rev. of *It,* by Elinor Glyn. *New Yorker* November 26, 1927. Reprint, in *The Portable Dorothy Parker,* ed. Brendan Gill, 464–68. New York: Viking, 1973.

"Sassafrassa, the Queen." *Time,* May 26, 1952, cover, 62–68.

Silvian, Leonore. "Laughing Lucille." *Look,* June 3, 1952, 7–8.

"There's No Accounting for TV Tastes." *TV Guide,* September 4, 1953, 20.

"Unaverage Situation." *Time*, February 18, 1952, 73.

Waterbury, Ruth. "Fashions in Passions." *Photoplay* July 1938. Reprinted in *The Talkies: Articles and Illustrations from a Great Fan Magazine, 1928–1940*. Richard Griffith, comp. New York: Dover Publications, Inc., 1971.

"Why Is a Movie Star?" *Look*, February 10, 1953, 54–56.

Wilde, Hagar. "Bringing Up Baby." *Collier's*, April 10, 1937. Reprint, in *Bringing Up Baby*, ed. Gerald Mast, 235–48. New Brunswick, NJ: Rutgers University Press, 1988.

Films, Plays, and Other Media

The Awful Truth. Dir./prod. Leo McCarey. With Irene Dunne, Cary Grant, Ralph Bellamy, and Alexander D'Arcy. Columbia, 1937.

Ball of Fire. Dir. Howard Hawks. With Gary Cooper and Barbara Stanwyck. RKO, 1941.

Batman Returns. Dir. Tim Burton. Based upon Batman characters created by Bob Kane and published by DC Comics. With Michael Keaton, Michelle Pfeiffer, Danny DeVito, and Christopher Walken. Warner Brothers, 1992.

Bringing Up Baby. Dir./prod. Howard Hawks. Screenplay by Dudley Nichols and Hagar Wilde, from a Hagar Wilde story. With Katharine Hepburn and Cary Grant. RKO Radio, 1938.

Capitola, or The Masked Mother and the Hidden Hand: A Drama in Three Acts. By C. H. Hazelwood. Based on E. D. E. N. Southworth's novel *The Hidden Hand, or Capitola the Madcap*. London: T. H. Lang, 186?. Reprint, New York: Readex Microprint, 1967.

Desperately Seeking Susan. Dir. Susan Seidelman. With Rosanna Arquette and Madonna. Orion, 1985.

Gentlemen Prefer Blondes. Dir. Howard Hawks. With Marilyn Monroe, Jane Russell, and Charles Coburn. Twentieth Century Fox, 1953.

The Hidden Hand: A Drama in Five Acts. By Robert Jones. Based on E. D. E. N. Southworth's novel *The Hidden Hand, or Capitola the Madcap*. Boston: W. H. Baker, c. 1889. Reprint, New York: Readex Microprint, 1967.

House of Games. Dir. David Mamet. With Lindsay Crouse and Joe Mantegna. Orion, 1987.

I'm No Angel. Dir. Wesley Ruggles. With Mae West and Cary Grant. Paramount, 1933.

It. Dir. Clarence Badger. Prod. Ben Schulberg and Elinor Glyn. Screenplay by Elinor Glyn, Buddy Leighton, and Hope Loring Leighton from an Elinor Glyn story. With Clara Bow, Antonio Moreno, and Elinor Glyn. Paramount, 1927.

The Lady Eve. Dir./screenplay Preston Sturges. With Barbara Stanwyck, Henry Fonda, Charles Coburn, and William Demarest. Paramount, 1941.

The Last Seduction. Dir. John Dahl. With Linda Fiorentino, Peter Berg, and Bill Pullman. HBO, 1994.

My Little Chickadee. Dir. Edward Cline. With Mae West and W. C. Fields. Universal, 1940.

Nichols, Dudley, and Hagar Wilde. *Bringing Up Baby*. 1938. Reprint, *Bringing Up Baby*, ed. Gerald Mast, 29–206. Script variations 207–33. New Brunswick, NJ: Rutgers University Press, 1988.

Oboler, Arch. "Adam and Eve Sketch." *Chase and Sanborn Hour.* Audiotape. With Mae West, Don Ameche, and Edgar Bergen. Rec. December 12, 1937. National Recording Company, 1981.

Pin Up Girl. Dir. Bruce Humberstone. With Betty Grable and John Harvey. Twentieth Century Fox, 1944.

She Done Him Wrong. Dir. Lowell Sherman. With Mae West and Cary Grant. Paramount, 1933.

Sister Act. Dir. Emile Ardolino. With Whoopi Goldberg, Maggie Smith, and Harvey Keitel. Touchstone, 1992.

Thelma and Louise. Dir. Ridley Scott. Screenplay by Callie Khouri. With Geena Davis, Susan Sarandon, and Harvey Keitel. MGM/Pathe, 1991.

Theodora Goes Wild. Dir. Richard Boleslanski. Prod. Everett Riskin. Screenplay by Sidney Buchman from a Mary McCarthy story. With Irene Dunne and Melvyn Douglas. Columbia, 1936.

Working Girl. Dir. Mike Nichols. With Melanie Griffith, Harrison Ford, and Sigourney Weaver. Twentieth Century Fox, 1988.

Secondary Sources

Affron, Charles. "Performing Performing: Irony and Affect." *Cinema Journal* 20 (Fall 1980): 42–52.

Allen, Robert C., ed. *Channels of Discourse, Reassembled: Television and Contemporary Criticism.* 2d ed. Chapel Hill and London: University of North Carolina Press, 1992.

———. *Horrible Prettiness: Burlesque and American Culture.* Chapel Hill: University of North Carolina Press, 1991.

Althusser, Louis. "Ideology and Ideological State Apparatuses (Notes Towards an Investigation)." In *Lenin and Philosophy,* trans. Ben Brewster, 127–86. London: Monthly Review Press, 1971.

Anderson, Christopher. "Jesse James, the Bourgeois Bandit: The Transformation of a Popular Hero." *Cinema Journal* 26 (1986): 43–64.

Andrews, Bart. *The "I Love Lucy" Book.* New York: Doubleday, 1985.

Andrews, William L. *To Tell a Free Story: The First Century of Afro-American Autobiography, 1760–1865.* Urbana: University of Illinois Press, 1986.

Arbuthnot, Lucie, and Gail Seneca. "Pre-text and Text in *Gentlemen Prefer Blondes.*" *Issues in Feminist Film Criticism,* ed. Patricia Erens, 112–25. Bloomington: Indiana University Press, 1990.

Ardener, Shirley, ed. *Women and Space: Ground Rules and Social Maps.* New York: St. Martin's Press, 1981.

Atwood, Margaret. *Survival: A Thematic Guide to Canadian Literature.* Toronto: Anansi, 1972.

Babington, Bruce, and Peter William Evans. *Affairs to Remember: The Hollywood Comedy of the Sexes.* Manchester: Manchester University Press, 1989.

Babcock, Barbara, and Jay Cox. "The Native American Trickster." In *Dictionary of Native American Literature,* ed. Andrew Wiget, 99–105. New York: Garland Publishing, Inc., 1994.

Babcock-Abrahams, Barbara. " 'A Tolerated Margin of Mess': The Trickster and His Tales Reconsidered." *Journal of the Folklore Institute* 9 (1975): 147–86.

Bailey, Beth L. *From Front Porch to Back Seat: Courtship in Twentieth-Century America.* Baltimore: Johns Hopkins University Press, 1988.

Ballinger, Franchot. "Living Sideways: Social Themes and Social Relationships in Native American Trickster Tales." *American Indian Quarterly* 13 (Winter 1989): 15–30.

Banner, Lois W. *American Beauty.* New York: Knopf, 1983.

Barnes, Kim. "Leslie Marmon Silko Interview." 1986. Reprint, in *"Yellow Woman,"* ed. Melody Graulich, 47–65. *Women Writers: Texts and Contexts.* New Brunswick, NJ: U Rutgers P, 1993.

Barreca, Regina, ed. *Last Laughs: Perspectives on Women and Comedy.* Studies in Gender and Culture 2. Philadelphia: Gordon and Breach, 1988.

———, ed. *New Perspectives on Women and Comedy.* Studies in Gender and Culture 5. Philadelphia: Gordon and Breach, 1992.

Bartky, Sandra Lee. *Femininity and Domination: Studies in the Phenomenology of Oppression.* New York: Routledge, 1990.

Basso, Ellen B. *In Favor of Deceit: A Study of Tricksters in an Amazonian Society.* Tuscon: University of Arizona Press, 1987.

Bauer, Dale M. "The Politics of Collaboration." In *Old Maids to Radical Spinsters: Unmarried Women in the Twentieth-Century Novel,* ed. Laura L. Doan, 107–22. Urbana: University of Illinois Press, 1990.

Baym, Nina. *Woman's Fiction: A Guide to Novels by and about Women in America, 1820–1870.* Ithaca, NY: Cornell University Press, 1978.

Bell, Linda A. *Rethinking Ethics in the Midst of Violence: A Feminist Approach to Freedom.* Lanham, MD: Rowman and Littlefield Publishers, 1993.

Belton, John. *American Cinema/American Culture.* New York: McGraw-Hill, 1994.

Bendixen, Alfred. Introduction. *The Whole Family: A Novel by Twelve Authors,* by William Dean Howells, Mary Wilkins Freeman, et al., xi–li. New York: Ungar, 1986.

Berger, John et al. *Ways of Seeing.* London: Penguin, 1972.

Bergson, Henri. "Laughter." 1900. In *Comedy,* ed. Wylie Sypher, 61–190. Baltimore: Johns Hopkins University Press, 1984.

Blair, Juliet. "Private Parts in Public Places: The Case of Actresses." In *Women and Space: Ground Rules and Social Maps,* ed. Shirley Ardener, 205–28. New York: St. Martin's Press, 1981.

Blair, Walter. *Native American Humor (1800–1900).* New York: American Book Co., 1937.

Bloch, Ruth H. "American Feminine Ideals in Transition: The Rise of the Moral Mother, 1785–1815." *Feminist Studies* 4 (1978): 101–26.

Boddy, William. *Fifties Television: The Industry and Its Critics.* Urbana and Chicago: University of Illinois Press, 1990.

Brady, Kathleen. *Lucille: The Life of Lucille Ball.* New York: Hyperion, 1994.

Brodhead, Richard H. "Veiled Ladies: Toward a History of Antebellum Entertainment." *American Literary History* (Summer 1989): 273–94.

Bronner, Stephen Eric, and Douglas MacKay Kellner, eds. *Critical Theory and Society: A Reader.* New York: Routledge, 1989.

Brown, Dorothy M. *Setting a Course: American Women in the 1920s.* Boston: Twayne, 1987.

Butler, Judith. *Bodies That Matter: On the Discursive Limits of "Sex."* New York: Routledge, 1993.

Butler, Judith P. *Gender Trouble: Feminism and the Subversion of Identity.* New York: Routledge, 1990.

Camp, Claudia V. "Wise and Strange: An Interpretation of the Female Imagery in Proverbs in Light of Trickster Mythology." In *Reasoning with the Foxes: Female*

Wit in a World of Male Power, ed. J. Cheryl Exum and Johanna W. H. Bos, 14–36. *Semeia: An Experimental Journal for Biblical Criticism* 42 (1988).

Campbell, D'Ann. *Women at War with America: Private Lives in a Patriotic Era.* Cambridge: Harvard University Press, 1984.

Carey, Gary. *Anita Loos.* London: Bloomsbury, 1988.

Cavell, Stanley. *Pursuits of Happiness: The Hollywood Comedy of Remarriage.* Cambridge: Harvard University Press, 1981.

Certeau, Michel de. *The Practice of Everyday Life.* Trans. Steven Randall. Berkeley: University of California Press, 1984.

Chafe, William H. *The Paradox of Change: American Women in the Twentieth Century.* New York: Oxford University Press, 1991.

Combs, Allan, and Mark Hollander. *Synchronicity: Science, Myth, and the Trickster.* New York: Paragon House, 1990.

Coontz, Stephanie. *The Social Origins of Private Life: A History of American Families 1600–1900.* London: Verso, 1988.

Corrigan, Robert W., ed. *Comedy: Meaning and Form.* San Francisco: Chandler Publishing Company, 1965.

Costello, John. *Virtue Under Fire: How World War II Changed Our Social and Sexual Attitudes.* New York: Fromm International, 1987.

Cott, Nancy F. *The Bonds of Womanhood: "Woman's Sphere" in New England, 1780–1835.* New Haven, CT: Yale University Press, 1977.

———. *The Grounding of Modern Feminism.* New Haven, CT: Yale University Press, 1987.

———. "Passionlessness: An Interpretation of Victorian Sexual Ideology, 1790–1850." In *A Heritage of Her Own: Toward a New Social History of American Women,* ed. Nancy F. Cott and Elizabeth H. Pleck, 162–81. New York: Simon and Schuster, 1979.

Cott, Nancy F., and Elizabeth H. Pleck, eds. *A Heritage of Her Own: Toward a New Social History of American Women.* New York: Simon and Schuster, 1979.

Cowan, Ruth Schwartz. "Two Washes in the Morning and a Bridge Party at Night: The American Housewife Between the Wars." In *Decades of Discontent: The Women's Movement, 1920–1940,* ed. Lois Scharf and Joan M. Jensen, 177–96. Boston: Northeastern University Press, 1987.

Coward, Rosalind. *Female Desires.* New York: Grove Atlantic, 1985.

Cox, Jay. "Dangerous Definitions: Female Tricksters in Contemporary Native American Literature." *Wicazosa Review* 89: 17–21.

Crowley, John D. "The Whole Famdamnily." *New England Quarterly* 60 (1987): 106–13.

Curry, Ramona. *Too Much of a Good Thing: Mae West as Cultural Icon.* Minneapolis: University of Minnesota Press, 1996.

Davidson, Cathy N., ed. *Reading in America: Literature and Social History.* Baltimore: Johns Hopkins University Press, 1989.

Davis, Murray A. *What's So Funny? The Comic Conception of Culture and Society.* Chicago and London: University of Chicago Press, 1993.

D'Emilio, John, and Estelle B. Freedman. *Intimate Matters: A History of Sexuality in America.* New York: Harper and Row, 1988.

Diggins, John Patrick. *The Promise of Pragmatism: Modernism and the Crisis of Knowledge and Authority.* Chicago: University of Chicago Press, 1994.

Doane, Mary Ann. "Information, Crisis, Catastrophe." In *Logics of Television: Essays in Cultural Criticism,* ed. Patricia Mellencamp, 222–39. Volume 11, Theories of Contemporary Culture. Bloomington: Indiana University Press, 1990.

Dobson, Joanne. "The Hidden Hand: Subversion of Cultural Ideology in Three Mid-Nineteenth-Century American Women's Novels." *American Quarterly* 38 (1986): 223–42.

———. Introduction. *The Hidden Hand, or Capitola the Madcap*, by E. D. E. N. Southworth, xi–xlv. 1859. Reprint, New Brunswick, NJ: Rutgers University Press, 1988.

Doty, Alexander. "The Cabinet of Lucy Ricardo: Lucille Ball's Star Image." *Cinema Journal* 29 (1990): 3–22.

Douglas, Ann. *Terrible Honesty: Mongrel Manhattan in the 1920s*. New York: Farrar, Straus and Giroux, 1995.

Douglas, George H. *Women of the Twenties*. Dallas: Saybrook, 1986.

Douglas, Mary. *Purity and Danger: An Analysis of the Concepts of Pollution and Taboo*. 1966. Reprint, New York: Routledge, 1984.

Douglas, Susan J. *Where the Girls Are: Growing Up Female with the Mass Media*. New York: Times Books, 1994.

DuBois, W. E. B. *The Souls of Black Folk*. 1903, Reprint, New York: Viking-Penguin, 1989.

Dyer, Richard. *Stars*. London: BFI, 1979.

Eco, Umberto. "The Frames of Comic 'Freedom.'" In *Carnival!* ed. Thomas A. Sebok, 1–9. Berlin: Mouton, 1984.

Eells, George, and Stanley Musgrove. *Mae West: A Biography*. New York: William Morrow, 1982.

Elbert, Sarah. *A Hunger for Home: Louisa May Alcott and Little Women*. Philadelphia: Temple University Press, 1984.

Elshtain, Jean Bethke. *Public Man, Private Woman*. Princeton, NJ: Princeton University Press, 1981.

Etherington-Smith, Meredith, and Jeremy Pilcher. *The "IT" Girls: Elinor Glyn, Novelist and Her Sister Lucile, Couturière*. San Diego: Harcourt Brace Jovanovich, 1986.

Evans, Sara M. *Born for Liberty: A History of Women in America*. New York: Free Press, 1989.

Ewen, Stuart. *All Consuming Images: The Politics of Style in Contemporary Culture*. New York: Basic Books, 1988.

———. *Captains of Consciousness: Advertising and the Social Roots of the Consumer Culture*. New York: McGraw-Hill, 1976.

Ewen, Stuart, and Elizabeth Ewen. *Channels of Desire: Mass Images and the Shaping of American Culture*. Minneapolis: University of Minnesota Press, 1992.

Exum, J. Cheryl, and Johanna W. H. Bos, eds. *Reasoning with the Foxes: Female Wit in a World of Male Power. Semeia: An Experimental Journal for Biblical Criticism* 42 (1988).

Fetterley, Judith. "Impersonating 'Little Women': The Radicalism of Alcott's *Behind a Mask*." *Women's Studies* 10 (1983): 1–14.

Filene, Peter G. *Him/Her/Self: Sex Roles in Modern America*. 2d ed. Baltimore: Johns Hopkins University Press, 1986.

Fiske, John. *Television Culture*. London: Methuen, 1987.

Fleischer, Michael L. *Wonder Woman*. Encyclopedia of Comic Book Heroes 2. New York: Collier, 1976.

Fontaine, Carole. "The Deceptive Goddess in Ancient Near Eastern Myth: Inanna and Inaras." In *Reasoning with the Foxes: Female Wit in a World of Male Power*, ed. J. Cheryl Exum and Johanna W. H. Bos, 84–102. *Semeia: An Experimental Journal for Biblical Criticism* 42 (1988).

Fowles, Jib. *Advertising and Popular Culture.* Foundations of Popular Culture 5. Thousand Oaks: Sage Publications, 1996.

Fox, Richard Wightman, and T. J. Jackson Lears, eds. *The Culture of Consumption: Critical Essays in American History, 1880–1980.* New York: Pantheon, 1983.

———, eds. *The Power of Culture: Critical Essays in American History.* Chicago: University of Chicago Press, 1993.

Fox, Stephen. *The Mirror Makers: A History of American Advertising and Its Creators.* New York: William Morrow and Co., 1984.

Franco, Jean. "The Incorporation of Women: A Comparison of North American and Mexican Popular Narrative." In *Studies in Entertainment: Critical Approaches to Mass Culture,* ed. Tania Modleski, 119–38. Bloomington: Indiana University Press, 1986.

Freedman, Rita. *Beauty Bound.* Lexington, MA: Lexington Books, 1986.

Freibert, Lucy M. "The Artist as Picaro: The Revelation of Margaret Atwood's 'Lady Oracle'." *Canadian Literature* 92 (1982): 23–33.

Frye, Northrop. "The Argument of Comedy." 1948. In *Theories of Comedy,* ed. Paul Lauter. Garden City, NY: Doubleday-Anchor, 1964.

———. "The Mythos of Spring: Comedy" from *The Anatomy of Criticism.* 1957. In *Comedy: Meaning and Form,* ed. Robert W. Corrigan. San Francisco: Chandler Publishing Co., 1965.

Fryer, Judith. *The Faces of Eve: Women in the Nineteenth-Century American Novel.* Oxford: Oxford University Press, 1976.

Gaines, Jane. "The Showgirl and the Wolf." *Cinema Journal* 20 (Fall 1980): 53–67.

Galligan, Edward L. *The Comic Vision in Literature.* Athens: University of Georgia Press, 1984.

Gates, Henry Louis, Jr. *The Signifying Monkey: A Theory of Afro-American Literary Criticism.* New York: Oxford University Press, 1988.

Gehring, Wes D. *Screwball Comedy: A Genre of Madcap Romance.* Contributions to the Study of Popular Culture 13. New York: Greenwood, 1986.

Gilbert, Sandra M., and Susan Gubar. *The Madwoman in the Attic: The Woman Writer and the Nineteenth-Century Literary Imagination.* New Haven, CT: Yale University Press, 1979.

———. *No Man's Land: The Place of the Woman Writer in the Twentieth Century.* 3 vols. New Haven, CT: Yale University Press, 1988–94.

Ginsberg, Elaine K. "Introduction: The Politics of Passing." In *Passing and Fictions of Identity,* ed. Elaine K. Ginsberg, 1–18. Durham, NC: Duke University Press, 1996.

Glyn, Anthony. *Elinor Glyn.* 1955. London: Hutchinson and Co., 1968.

Goffman, Erving. *Frame Analysis: An Essay on the Organization of Experience.* New York: Harper and Row, 1974.

———. *The Presentation of Self in Everyday Life.* Garden City, NY: Doubleday Anchor, 1959.

Good, Edwin M. "Deception and Women: A Response." In *Reasoning with the Foxes: Female Wit in a World of Male Power,* ed. J. Cheryl Exum and Joanna W. H. Bos, 117–32. *Semeia: An Experimental Journal for Biblical Criticism* 42 (1988).

Grossman, Barbara W. *Funny Woman: The Life and Times of Fanny Brice.* Bloomington: Indiana University Press, 1992.

Grottanelli, Cristiano. "Tricksters, Scapegoats, Champions, Saviors." *History of Religions* (1983): 115–39.

Habegger, Alfred. *Gender, Fantasy, and Realism in American Literature.* New York: Columbia University Press, 1982.

Habermas, Jürgen. "The Public Sphere: An Encyclopedia Article." In *Critical Theory and Society: A Reader*, ed. Stephen Eric Bronner and Douglas MacKay, 136–42. New York: Routledge, 1989.

———. *The Structural Transformation of the Public Sphere: An Inquiry into a Category of Bourgeois Society*. Trans. Thomas Burger with Frederick Lawrence. Cambridge, MA: MIT Press, 1989.

Hall, Jacqueline Dowd. "Disorderly Women: Gender and Labor Militancy in the Appalachian South." *Journal of American History* 73 (1986): 354–82.

Hall, Stuart. "Encoding/Decoding." In *Culture, Media, Language*, ed. Stuart Hall, et al., 128–38. London: Hutchinson, 1980.

———. "Notes on Deconstructing 'the Popular'." In *People's History and Socialist Theory*, ed. Ralph Samuel, 227–40. London: Routledge and Kegan Paul, 1981.

Halttunen, Karen. *Confidence Men and Painted Women: A Study of Middle-Class Culture in America, 1830–1870*. New Haven, CT: Yale University Press, 1982.

Harstock, Nancy C. M. *Money, Sex, and Power: Toward a Feminist Historical Materialism*. Boston: Northeastern University Press, 1985.

Haskell, Molly. *From Reverence to Rape: The Treatment of Women in the Movies*. Baltimore: Penguin, 1974.

Hole, Judith, and Ellen Levine. *Rebirth of Feminism*. New York: Quadrangle/New York Times Book Co., 1971.

Holmes, Kristine. " 'This Woman Can Cross Any Line': Feminist Tricksters in the Works of Nora Naranjo-Morse and Joy Harjo." *SAIL* 7.1 (Spring 1995): 45–63.

Horkheimer, Max, and Theodor W. Adorno. *Dialectic of Enlightenment*. 1944. Reprint (John Cumming, trans.), New York: Continuum, 1995.

Huggins, Nathan Irvin. *Harlem Renaissance*. New York: Oxford University Press, 1971.

Huizinga, Johan. *Homo Ludens: A Study of the Play Element in Culture*. Trans. R. F. C. Hull. Boston: Beacon, 1949.

Hynes, William J., and William G. Doty, eds. *Mythical Trickster Figures: Contours, Contexts, and Criticisms*. Tuscaloosa: University of Alabama Press, 1993.

Jackson, Michael. *Allegories of the Wilderness: Ethics and Ambiguity in Kuranko Narratives*. Bloomington: Indiana University Press, 1982.

———. *Paths to a Clearing: Radical Empiricism and Ethnographic Inquiry*. Bloomington: Indiana University Press, 1989.

Janeway, Elizabeth. *Man's World, Woman's Place: A Study in Social Mythology*. New York: Delta, 1971.

Jenkins, Henry, and Kristine Brunovska Karnick. "Introduction: Acting Funny." In *Classical Hollywood Comedy*, ed. Kristine Brunovska Karnick and Henry Jenkins, 149–67. New York: Routledge, 1995.

Johnston, Carolyn. *Sexual Power: Feminism and the Family in America*. Tuscaloosa: University of Alabama Press, 1992.

Jung, Carl G. *The Archetypes and the Collective Unconscious*. In *Collected Works of C. G. Jung*, vol. 9, part 1. Translated by R. F. C. Hull. New York: Pantheon Books, 1959.

Jurich, Marilyn. "She Shall Overcome: Overtures to the Trickster Heroine." *Women's Studies International Forum* (1986): 273–79.

Justus, James H. Introduction. *The Flush Times of Alabama and Mississippi: A Series of Sketches*, by Joseph G. Baldwin. Baton Rouge: Louisiana State University Press, 1987.

Kaplan, Amy. *The Social Construction of American Realism*. Chicago: University of Chicago Press, 1988.

Keim, Karen Ruth King. "Trickery and Social Values in the Oral and Written Literature of Cameroon." Diss., Indiana University, 1986.

Kelley, Mary. *Private Woman, Public Stage: Literary Democracy in Nineteenth-Century America.* New York: Oxford University Press, 1984.

Kendall, Elizabeth. *The Runaway Bride: Hollywood Romantic Comedy of the 1930s.* New York: Knopf, 1990.

Koestler, Arthur. *The Act of Creation.* New York: Macmillan, 1964.

———. "Humor and Wit." In *Encyclopaedia Britannica,* 15th ed., 1974, 5–11.

———. *Insight and Outlook: An Inquiry into the Common Foundations of Science, Art, and Social Ethics.* London: Macmillan, 1949.

Landay, Lori. " 'Betwixt and Between': The Trickster and Multiculturalism." Review of Elizabeth Ammons and Annette White-Parks, eds., *Tricksterism in Turn-of-the-Century American Literature. American Quarterly* 48 (September 1996): 542–49.

Lears, T. J. Jackson. *Fables of Abundance: A Cultural History of Advertising in America.* New York: Basic Books, 1994.

———. *No Place of Grace: Antimodernism and the Transformation of American Culture.* New York: Pantheon, 1981.

Leff, Leonard J., and Jerold L. Simmons. *The Dame in the Kimono: Hollywood, Censorship and the Production Code from the 1920s to the 1960s.* New York: Grove Weidenfeld, 1990.

Lenz, William E. *Fast Talk and Flush Times: The Confidence Man as a Literary Convention.* Columbia: University of Missouri Press, 1985.

Levin, Harry. *Playboys and Killjoys: An Essay on the Theory and Practice of Comedy.* New York: Oxford University Press, 1987.

Levine, Lawrence W. *Black Culture and Black Consciousness: Afro-American Folk Thought from Slavery to Freedom.* Oxford: Oxford University Press, 1977.

Lindberg, Gary. *The Confidence Man in American Literature.* New York: Oxford University Press, 1982.

Lipsitz, George. *Time Passages: Collective Memory and American Popular Culture.* Minneapolis: University of Minnesota Press, 1990.

MacDonald, J. Frederick. *Don't Touch That Dial! Radio Programming in American Life, 1920–1960.* Chicago: Nelson-Hall, 1979.

Makarius, Laura. "The Myth of the Trickster: The Necessary Breaker of Taboos." In *Mythical Trickster Figures,* ed. William J. Hynes and William G. Doty, 66–86. Tuscaloosa: University of Alabama Press, 1993.

Marc, David. *Comic Visions: Television Comedy and American Culture.* Boston: Unwin Hyman, 1989.

———. *Demographic Vistas: Television in American Culture.* Philadelphia: University of Pennsylvania Press, 1984.

Marchand, Roland. *Advertising the American Dream: Making Way for Modernity, 1920–1940.* Berkeley: University of California Press, 1985.

Mast, Gerald. "Bringing Up Baby." Reprint, in *Bringing Up Baby,* ed. Gerald Mast, 294–311. New Brunswick, NJ: Rutgers University Press, 1988.

———. *The Comic Mind: Comedy and the Movies.* Indianapolis: Bobbs-Merrill, 1973.

———, ed. *Bringing Up Baby.* New Brunswick, NJ: Rutgers University Press, 1988.

Matthaie, Julie A. *An Economic History of Women in America: Women's Work, the Sexual Division of Labor, and the Development of Capitalism.* New York: Schocken Books, 1982.

Matthews, Glenna. *"Just a Housewife": The Rise and Fall of Domesticity in America.* New York: Oxford University Press, 1987.

———. *The Rise of Public Woman: Woman's Power and Woman's Place in the United States, 1630–1970.* New York: Oxford University Press, 1992.

May, Elaine Tyler. *Homeward Bound: American Families in the Cold War Era.* New York: Basic Books, 1988.

May, Lary. *Screening Out the Past: The Birth of Mass Culture and the Motion Picture Industry.* Chicago: University of Chicago Press, 1980.

McFadden, Margaret T. " 'America's Boy Friend Who Can't Get a Date': Gender, Race, and the Cultural Work of the Jack Benny Program, 1932–1946." *Journal of American History* (1993): 113–34.

Mellencamp, Patricia. "Situation Comedy, Feminism, and Freud: Discourses of Gracie and Lucy." In *Studies in Entertainment: Critical Approaches to Mass Culture,* ed. Tania Modleski, 80–95. Bloomington: Indiana University Press, 1986.

Melosh, Barbara. *Engendering Culture: Manhood and Womanhood in New Deal Public Art and Theater.* Washington: Smithsonian Institution Press, 1991.

Meredith, George. "An Essay on Comedy." 1877. In *Comedy,* ed. Wylie Sypher, 3–57. Baltimore: Johns Hopkins University Press, 1984.

Mile, Sian. "Roseanne Barr: Canned Laughter—Containing the Subject." *New Perspectives on Women and Comedy,* ed. Regina Barreca, 39–46. Studies in Gender and Culture 5. Philadelphia: Gordon and Breach, 1992.

Miller, Dallas. "Mythic Rage and Laughter: An Interview with Gerald Vizenor." *SAIL* 7.1 (Spring 1995): 77–96.

Miller, Douglas T., and Marion Nowak. *The Fifties: The Way We Really Were.* Garden City, NY: Doubleday, 1977.

Modleski, Tania. *Loving with a Vengeance: Mass-Produced Fantasies for Women.* New York: Routledge, 1982.

Morella, Joe, and Edward Z. Epstein. *The "It" Girl: The Incredible Story of Clara Bow.* New York: Delacorte, 1976.

Morley, David. *Television Audiences and Cultural Studies.* New York: Routledge, 1992.

Morris, Linda A. *Women's Humor in the Age of Gentility: The Life and Works of Frances Whitcher.* Syracuse, NY: Syracuse University Press, 1992.

———. *Women Vernacular Humorists in Nineteenth-Century America: Ann Stephens, Frances Whitcher, and Marietta Holley.* New York: Garland, 1988.

———, ed. *American Women Humorists: Critical Essays.* New York: Garland Publishing, 1994.

Nienkamp, Jean, and Andrea Collins. Introduction to *Female Quixotism,* by Tabitha Gilman Tenney, xiii–xxviii. New York: Oxford University Press, 1992.

Nochlin, Linda. *Women, Art, and Power and Other Essays.* New York: Harper and Row, 1988.

Norwood, Stephen H. *Labor's Flaming Youth: Telephone Operators and Worker Militancy, 1878–1923.* Urbana: University of Illinois Press, 1990.

Okin, Susan Moller. *Women in Western Political Thought.* Princeton, NJ: Princeton University Press, 1979.

Omi, Michael, and Howard Winant. *Racial Formation in the United States: From the 1960s to the 1990s.* New York: Routledge, 1994.

Otnes, Per, ed. *The Sociology of Consumption: An Anthology.* Atlantic Highlands, NJ: Humanities Press International, 1988.

Palmer, Jerry. *The Logic of the Absurd: On Film and Television Comedy.* London: BFI, 1987.

Pateman, Carole. *The Sexual Contract*. Stanford, CA: Stanford University Press, 1988.

Pearson, Carolyn, and Katherine Pope. *The Female Hero in American and British Literature*. New York: R. R. Bowker, 1981.

Pelton, Robert D. *The Trickster in West Africa: A Study of Mythic Irony and Sacred Delight*. Berkeley: University of California Press, 1980.

Polan, Dana. *Power and Paranoia: History, Narrative, and the American Cinema, 1940–1950*. New York: Columbia University Press, 1986.

Polster, Miriam F. *Eve's Daughters: The Forbidden Heroism of Women*. San Francisco: Jossey-Bass, 1992.

Radin, Paul. *The Trickster: A Study in American Indian Mythology*. New York: Philosophical Library, 1956.

Reynolds, David S. *Beneath the American Renaissance: The Subversive Imagination in the Age of Emerson and Melville*. Cambridge, MA: Harvard University Press, 1989.

Ricketts, Mac Linscott. "The North American Indian Trickster." *History of Religions* 5 (1966): 327–50.

Roberts, John W. *From Trickster to Badman: The Black Folk Hero in Slavery and Freedom*. Philadelphia: University of Pennsylvania Press, 1989.

Rosaldo, Michelle Zimbalist, and Louise Lamphere, eds. *Women, Culture, and Society*. Stanford, CA: Stanford University Press, 1974.

Rosen, Marjorie. *Popcorn Venus: Women, Movies, and the American Dream*. New York: Avon, 1973.

Rourke, Constance. *American Humor: A Study of the National Character*. New York: Harcourt, Brace, 1931.

Rowe, Kathleen. *The Unruly Woman: Gender and the Genres of Laughter*. Austin: University of Texas Press, 1995.

Santayana, George. "The Comic Mask." In *Comedy: Meaning and Form*, ed. Robert W. Corrigan, 75–80. San Francisco: Chandler, 1965.

Schatz, Thomas. *Hollywood Genres: Formulas, Filmmaking, and the Studio System*. New York: Random House, 1981.

Schechner, Richard. *Between Theatre and Anthropology*. Philadelphia: University of Pennsylvania Press, 1985.

Schmidt, Kerstin. "Subverting the Dominant Paradigm: Gerald Vizenor's Trickster Discourse." *SAIL* 7.1 (Spring 1995): 65–75.

Sennett, Ted. *Lunatics and Lovers*. New Rochelle, NY: Arlington House, 1971.

Sharistanian, Janet, ed. *Beyond the Public/Domestic Dichotomy: Contemporary Perspectives on Women's Public Lives*. Contributions in Women's Studies 78. New York: Greenwood Press, 1987.

———. *Gender, Ideology, and Action: Historical Perspectives on Women's Public Lives*. Contributions in Women's Studies 67. New York: Greenwood Press, 1986.

Sklar, Robert. *Movie-Made America: A Social History of American Movies*. New York: Random House, 1975.

Slide, Anthony, comp. and ed. *They Also Wrote for the Fan Magazines: Film Articles by Literary Giants from E. E. Cummings to Eleanor Roosevelt, 1920–1939*. Jefferson, NC: McFarland and Co., 1992.

Smith, Daniel Scott. "Family Limitation, Sexual Control, and Domestic Feminism in Victorian America." In *A Heritage of Her Own: Toward a New Social History of American Women*, ed. Nancy F. Cott and Elizabeth H. Pleck, 222–45. New York: Simon and Schuster, 1979.

Smith, Johanna M. "Feeling Right: Christianity and Women's Influence in *Uncle Tom's Cabin.*" *ESQ* 32.2 (1986): 122–34.

Smith, Patricia Clark, with Paula Gunn Allen. "Earthly Relations, Carnal Knowledge: Southwestern American Indian Women Writers and Landscape." In *"Yellow Woman,"* ed. Melody Graulich, 115–50. *Women Writers: Texts and Contexts.* New Brunswick, NJ: Rutgers University Press, 1993.

Smith, Valerie. "Reading the Intersection of Race and Gender in Narratives of Passing." *Diacritics* 24.2–3 (Summer–Fall 1994): 43–57.

Smith-Rosenberg, Carroll. *Disorderly Conduct: Visions of Gender in Victorian America.* Oxford: Oxford University Press, 1985.

Sochen, June, ed. *Women's Comic Visions.* Detroit: Wayne State University Press, 1991.

Sontag, Susan. "Notes on Camp." 1964. Reprinted in *A Susan Sontag Reader*, 105–19. New York: Farrar, Straus, Giroux, 1982.

Spigel, Lynn. "Installing the Television Set: Popular Discourses on Television and Domestic Space, 1948–1955." *Camera Obscura* 16 (1988): 11–46.

———. *Make Room for TV: Television and the Family Ideal in Postwar America.* Chicago: University of Chicago Press, 1992.

Spinks, C. W., Jr. *Semiosis, Marginal Signs and Trickster: A Dagger of the Mind.* London: Macmillan, 1991.

Stacey, Jackie. "Desperately Seeking Difference." In *The Female Gaze: Women as Viewers of Popular Culture*, ed. Lorraine Gamman and Margaret Marshment, 112–29. Seattle, WA: Real Comet, 1989.

Staiger, Janet. *Bad Women: Regulating Sexuality in Early American Cinema.* Minneapolis: University of Minnesota Press, 1995.

Stenn, David. *Clara Bow: Runnin' Wild.* New York: Doubleday, 1988.

Stern, Madeline. Introduction to *Behind a Mask: The Unknown Thrillers of Louisa May Alcott*, vii–xxxiii. New York: Quill, 1984.

Susman, Warren I. *Culture as History: The Transformation of American Society in the Twentieth Century.* New York: Pantheon, 1984.

Sypher, Wylie. "Appendix: The Meanings of Comedy." In *Comedy*, 193–255. Baltimore: Johns Hopkins University Press, 1956.

Tompkins, Jane. Afterword to *The Wide, Wide World*, by Susan Warner, 584–608. New York: Feminist Press, 1987.

———. *Sensational Designs: The Cultural Work of American Fiction, 1790–1860.* New York: Oxford University Press, 1985.

Toth, Emily. "A Laughter of Their Own: Women's Humor in the United States." In *American Women Humorists: Critical Essays*, ed. Linda A. Morris, 85–108. New York: Garland Publishing, 1994.

Turim, Maureen. "Gentlemen Consume Blondes." In *Issues in Feminist Film Criticism*, ed. Patricia Erens, 101–11. Bloomington: Indiana University Press, 1990.

Turner, Victor. *The Anthropology of Performance.* Baltimore: Johns Hopkins University Press, 1987.

———. *Dramas, Fields, and Metaphors.* Ithaca, NY: Cornell University Press, 1974.

———. *The Forest of Symbols: Aspects of Ndembu Ritual.* Ithaca, NY: Cornell University Press, 1967.

———. *From Ritual to Theatre.* New York: PAJ, 1982.

———. *The Ritual Process: Structure and Anti-Structure.* Ithaca, NY: Cornell University Press, 1967.

Tyler, Parker. *Florine Stettheimer: A Life in Art.* New York: Farrar, Straus and Company, 1963.

Vizenor, Gerald. "Trickster Discourse." *American Indian Quarterly* 14 (Summer 1990): 277–87.

Wadlington, Warwick. *The Confidence Game in American Literature.* Princeton, NJ: Princeton University Press, 1975.

Walker, Nancy. *A Very Serious Thing: Women's Humor and American Culture.* Minneapolis: University of Minnesota Press, 1988.

———. *The Tradition of Women's Humor in America.* Huntington Beach, CA: American Studies Publishing Company, 1984.

———. "Wit, Sentimentality, and the Image of Women in Nineteenth Century." In *American Women Humorists: Critical Essays,* ed. Linda A. Morris, 61–84. New York: Garland Publishing, 1994.

Walker, Nancy, and Zita Dresner, eds. *Redressing the Balance: American Women's Literary Humor from Colonial Times to the 1980s.* Jackson: University Press of Mississippi, 1988.

Walsh, Andrea S. *Women's Film and Female Experience, 1940–1950.* New York: Praeger Special Studies, 1984.

Wandersee, Winifred D. "The Economics of Middle-Income Family Life: Working Women during the Great Depression." In *Decades of Discontent: The Women's Movement, 1920–1940,* ed. Lois Scharf and Joan M. Jensen, 49–58. Boston: Northeastern University Press, 1987.

Ward, Carol. *Mae West: A Bio-bibliography.* Westport, CT: Greenwood, 1989.

Ware, Susan. *Beyond Suffrage: Women in the New Deal.* Cambridge: Harvard University Press, 1981.

———. *Holding Their Own: American Women in the 1930s.* Boston: Twayne, 1982.

Weinauer, Ellen. "'A Most Respectable Looking Gentleman': Passing, Possession, and Transgression in *Running a Thousand Miles for Freedom.*" In *Passing and Fictions of Identity,* ed. Elaine K. Ginsberg, 37–56. Durham, NC: Duke University Press, 1996.

Wertheim, Arthur Frank. *Radio Comedy.* New York: Oxford University Press, 1979.

Westbrook, Robert B. "'I Want a Girl, Just Like the Girl That Married Harry James': American Women and the Problem of Political Obligation in World War II." *American Quarterly* 42 (1990): 587–614.

Wexman, Virginia Wright. *Creating the Couple: Love, Marriage, and Hollywood Performance.* Princeton, NJ: Princeton University Press, 1993.

Wiget, Andrew. "His Life in His Tail: The Native American Trickster and the Literature of Possibility." In *The New American Literary History.* New York: MLA, 1990.

Wilson, Elizabeth. *Adorned in Dreams: Fashion and Modernity.* Berkeley: University of California Press, 1985.

Wilt, Judith. "The Laughter of Maidens, the Cackle of Matriarchs: Notes on the Collision." In *Gender and the Literary Voice,* ed. Janet Todd, 172–96. New York: Holmes and Meier, 1980.

Woll, Allen L. *The Hollywood Musical Goes to War.* Chicago: Nelson-Hall, 1983.

Young, Elizabeth. "Confederate Counterfeit: The Case of the Cross-Dressed Civil War Soldier." In *Passing and the Fictions of Identity,* ed. Elaine K. Ginsberg, 181–217. Durham, NC: Duke University Press, 1996.

Young, Iris Marion. *Throwing Like a Girl and Other Essays in Feminist Philosophy and Social Theory.* Bloomington: Indiana University Press, 1990.

Acknowledgments

Many people fostered this project and made it possible for me to write this book. Colleagues and students at Western Illinois University have been supportive; in particular, I'd like to thank Marjorie Allison, Susie El-Edrissi, Judi Hardin, Linda Hess, John Mann, Dean Phyllis Farley Rippey, English department chair Ron Walker, and my mentor, Janice Welsch. Shanee Sullivan was instrumental in helping me with the illustrations included in the book. At Indiana University, Susan Gubar and David Nordloh gave me excellent advice, much encouragement, and prompted me to do my best work by being demanding teachers and readers. Chris Anderson, Michael Jackson, and Jim Justus were inspiring professors and insightful readers. The dissertation writing group that Susan Gubar generously organized motivated me to move from writing around to producing finished work. One of its members, Beth Sutton-Ramspeck, is that rare combination of colleague, friend, and sister. I am grateful to the IU Graduate School for a fellowship in 1992–93 and to the Western Illinois University Foundation for a Faculty Summer Stipend in 1996. I thank Terry Gaskin at the Museum of Modern Art Film Stills Archive for help with the production stills. At the University of Pennsylvania Press, Mindy Brown, Carl Gross, Jennifer Shenk, and Kim Silvasy were a pleasure to work with. Andrea Press's insightful comments greatly helped the revision process. With her enthusiasm and encouragement my editor, Patricia Smith, kept me motivated and facilitated the completion of the book; I owe her special thanks.

Good friends including Demerise Bloom, Phyllis Boyd, the Breeden family, Patty Burns, Heather Craig, Jennifer Curtis, John Dehner, Jeff Farias, Gayle Margherita, Jessica Mott, Jon Nilsen, Tammy Patrick, and Max Patrick-Farias not only soothed and egged me on when appropriate, but also made the process quite enjoyable. And many thanks to John MacGibbon for joy and moonlight and helping me realize what being a partner can mean.

My family has seen me through the various stages of this project. Thanks to my brother Jonathan, Roger and Myrna Landay, and Marty Harrison. The memories and examples of my late grandparents, Sarah Harrison and Martin and Mildred Landay, have continued to provide me with the determination with which they lived their lives. Very special thanks to my grandfather, Samuel Harrison, and my parents, Sheila and Charles Landay, who have given me the emotional and material support that enabled me to pursue my dreams.

Not surprising to those familiar with the trickster, serendipity has also played a role. I found a copy of Allan Combs and Mark Hollander's *Synchronicity: Science, Myth, and the Trickster* misplaced in the wrong section of a bookstore I was procrastinating in, and that expansive feeling of how the female trickster suddenly fit into a much bigger picture has never left me. And in the final stages of revising this book, teaching Leslie Marmon Silko's "Yellow Woman" to my Women and Literature students led me back to the crucial connections between the trickster and storytelling.

Index

acting: associations with, 67, 116; in *Behind a Mask*, 41–43; in *Gentlemen Prefer Blondes*, 61, 152; impersonation likened to, 39; Lucille Ball on, 181; of performance within performance, 116–17, 135, 137–42, 169, 172, 182–86. *See also* impersonation; star personae; specific actresses and actors

Adam (biblical figure), 94–99, 117, 139, 142, 144, 145

Adams, Abigail, 218

Adams, Clifford R., 168

Adams, John, 218

Adler, Alfred, 98

The Adventures of Huckleberry Finn (Twain), 23

advertisements, 30, 31; and anxiety about appearance, 11, 67–75, 88, 92, 121, 172; co-opting of feminism by, 89–93; for eyedrops, 88–90; for gin, 113, 114; and *I Love Lucy*, 182; for jewels, 55–56; for lipstick, 66, 71, 119–22; for mascara, 51–53, 65, 68–69; for nail polish, 88, 91; for perfume, 88, 214–15; for rice flakes, 88; for shoes, 71, 72; for soap, 68–71, 74, 119; for swimsuits, 7–11, 51, 173–74, 215

Affron, Charles, 116

African-American tricksters, 3, 16–22, 194, 211

African tricksters, 2, 16, 29

agonic modes of power. *See* power

Alcott, Louisa May, 30, 33, 39, 41–43

All About Eve (film), 64, 158

Allen, Gracie, 196

Ameche, Don, 94

American Academy of Religion, 27

American Cinema/American Culture (Belton), 97

American Tobacco Company, 89, 92

animals: in screwball comedy, 106, 126–27, 131, 133, 134, 137, 215; as tricksters, 3, 17

The Anthropology of Performance (Turner), 161

appearance: advertising's exploitation of anxiety about, 11, 67–75, 88, 92, 121; beauty of, associated with whiteness, 64–66; commodification of women's, 6–11, 53, 55–64, 66–75, 83–84, 88, 156–59; in "first impression," 67–69, 71; Glyn's, 78; Mae West's, 100; as more important than talent or intelligence, 181–82; as part of construction of female identity, 113, 161, 217; women's concerns about, 197; in women's use of covert power, 6, 41, 53, 55, 197; and women's value, 21, 45–46, 56–64, 71, 75, 83, 172. *See also* blondeness; cosmetics; costume; femininity; impersonation

Arens, Egmont, 136

Arnaz, Desi, 155, 174, 177, 179, 181, 187

Arquette, Rosanna, 209, 210

The Associate (film), 213

Asta (dog), 106

"The Audition" (*I Love Lucy* episode), 182

Austen, Jane, 32

autonomy: Catwoman's, 4; female tricksters' struggle for, 29, 34, 161–66, 191–94; flappers' association with, 89, 93; Mae West's depiction of, 99–101; tricksters' association with, 2, 26; women's, in World War II, 138, 145; women's desire for, 92, 206. *See also* mobility; power

CPSIA information can be obtained
at www.ICGtesting.com
Printed in the USA
BVHW071147301020
592212BV00010B/542

9 780812 216516